Studies in the Dead Sea Scrolls and Related Literature

Martin G. Abegg, Jr. and Peter W. Flint, General Editors

The Dead Sea Scrolls have been the object of intense interest in recent years, not least because of the release of previously unpublished texts from Qumran Cave 4 since the fall of 1991. With the wealth of new documents that have come to light, the field of Qumran studies has undergone a renaissance. Scholars have begun to question the established conclusions of the last generation; some widely held beliefs have withstood scrutiny, but others have required revision or even dismissal. New proposals and competing hypotheses, many of them of an uncritical and sensational nature, vie for attention. Idiosyncratic and misleading views of the Scrolls still abound, especially in the popular press, while the results of solid scholarship have yet to make their full impact. At the same time, the scholarly task of establishing reliable critical editions of the texts is nearing completion. The opportunity is ripe, therefore, for directing renewed attention to the task of analysis and interpretation.

Studies in the Dead Sea Scrolls and Related Literature is a new series designed to address this need. In particular, the series aims to make the latest and best Dead Sea Scrolls scholarship accessible to scholars, students, and the thinking public. The volumes that are projected — both monographs and collected essays — will seek to clarify how the Scrolls revise and help shape our understanding of the formation of the Bible and the historical development of Judaism and Christianity. Various offerings in the series will explore the reciprocally illuminating relationships of several disciplines related to the Scrolls, including the canon and text of the Hebrew Bible, the richly varied forms of Second Temple Judaism, and the New Testament. While the Dead Sea Scrolls constitute the main focus, several of these studies will also include perspectives on the Old and New Testaments and other ancient writings — hence the title of the series. It is hoped that these volumes will contribute to a deeper appreciation of the world of early Judaism and Christianity and of their continuing legacy today.

Martin G. Abegg, Jr.
Peter W. Flint

Eschatology, Messianism, and the Dead Sea Scrolls

Edited by

Craig A. Evans and Peter W. Flint

William B. Eerdmans Publishing Company
Grand Rapids, Michigan / Cambridge, U.K.

255 Jefferson Ave. S.E., Grand Rapids, Michigan 49503 /
P.O. Box 163, Cambridge CB3 9PU U.K.

Printed in the United States of America

02 01 00 99 98 97 7 6 5 4 3 2 1

Library of Congress Cataloging-in-Publication Data

Eschatology, messianism, and the Dead Sea scrolls /
edited by Craig A. Evans and Peter W. Flint.
p. cm.
— (Studies in the Dead Sea scrolls and related literature; v. 1)
Includes bibliographical references and indexes.
ISBN 0-8028-4230-5 (pbk.: alk. paper)
1. Dead Sea scrolls — Criticism, interpretation, etc.
2. Messiah — Biblical teaching.
3. Eschatology, Jewish.
4. Bible. O.T. — Criticism, interpretation, etc.
5. Dead Sea scrolls — Relation to the New Testament.
I. Evans, Craig A.
II. Flint, Peter W. III. Series.
BM487.E83 1997
296.1′55 — dc21 97-14918
CIP
r97

Contents

Contributors

Martin G. Abegg, Jr.
Associate Professor of Biblical Studies and
Codirector of the Dead Sea Scrolls Institute
Trinity Western University
Langley, British Columbia

Craig C. Broyles
Associate Professor and Chair of Biblical Studies
Trinity Western University
Langley, British Columbia

John J. Collins
Professor of Hebrew Bible
University of Chicago Divinity School
Chicago, Illinois

Craig A. Evans
Professor of Biblical Studies and
Director, Graduate Program in Biblical Studies
Trinity Western University
Langley, British Columbia

Peter W. Flint
Associate Professor of Biblical Studies and
Codirector of the Dead Sea Scrolls Institute
Trinity Western University
Langley, British Columbia

CONTRIBUTORS

Paul E. Hughes
Assistant Professor of Biblical Studies
Trinity Western University
Langley, British Columbia

Dietmar Neufeld
Associate Professor of Religious Studies
University of British Columbia
Vancouver, British Columbia

James M. Scott
Associate Professor of Biblical Studies
Trinity Western University
Langley, British Columbia

Diacritical Marks, Sigla, and Abbreviations

Abbreviations of journals, reference works, and other secondary sources generally conform to the "Instructions for Contributors" in the *Membership Directory and Handbook* of the Society of Biblical Literature (1994) 223-40. For abbreviations of Qumran sigla, see J. A. Fitzmyer, *The Dead Sea Scrolls: Major Publications and Tools for Study*, rev. ed. (SBLRBS 20; Atlanta: Scholars Press, 1990) 1-8.

Diacritical Marks and Sigla

(?)	Doubt exists as to the identification of a verse or reading.
[Daniel]	The bracketed word is no longer extant but has been restored.
Da[niel]	The bracketed part of the word has been restored.
דני[אל]	As above
to (his) throne	The parenthetical word has been added to improve the English translation.
[ ] or [. . .]	There is a space between fragments or the surface of the leather is missing.
]. . .[	Letters (in this case three) with ink traces remaining cannot be identified.
א	A certain letter
א̇	A probable letter (denoted by a dot)
א̊	A possible letter (denoted by a circlet)
{א}	Legible text has been erased by the copyist.
{. . .}	Illegible text has been erased by the copyist.
דני^{א}ל	A supralinear letter has been inserted by the copyist or another scribe.
frg. 10 ii 4-5	Fragment 10, column 2, lines 4-5

4QDan[a]	The first of a series of Daniel manuscripts from Qumran Cave 4
4Q112	Document number 112 in a sequence of scrolls from Qumran Cave 4

Abbreviations

AB	Anchor Bible (Commentary Series)
ABD	*Anchor Bible Dictionary*
ABRL	Anchor Bible Reference Library
AGJU	Arbeiten zur Geschichte des antiken Judentums und Urchristentums
ANE	Ancient Near East
ANET	J. B. Pritchard, ed., *Ancient Near Eastern Texts*
ANRW	*Aufstieg und Niedergang der römischen Welt*
AOAT	Alter Orient und Altes Testament
ArBib	The Aramaic Bible
ASTI	*Annual of the Swedish Theological Institute*
BAR	*Biblical Archaeology Review*
BASOR	*Bulletin of the American Schools of Oriental Research*
BBR	*Bulletin for Biblical Research*
BETL	Bibliotheca ephemeridum theologicarum lovaniensium
BHS	*Biblia Hebraica Stuttgartensia*
Bib	*Biblica*
BibOr	Biblica et orientalia
BibSem	Biblical Seminar
BJS	Brown Judaic Studies
BK	*Bibel und Kirche*
BKAT	Biblischer Kommentar: Altes Testament
BSac	*Bibliotheca sacra*
BWANT	Beiträge zur Wissenschaft vom Alten und Neuen Testament
BZ	*Biblische Zeitschrift*
CBC	Cambridge Bible Commentary
CBQ	*Catholic Biblical Quarterly*
CBQMS	*Catholic Biblical Quarterly* Monograph Series
DJD	Discoveries in the Judaean Desert
DMMRS	Duke Monographs in Medieval and Renaissance Studies
DSD	*Dead Sea Discoveries*
EDNT	*Exegetical Dictionary of the New Testament*
EKKNT	Evangelisch-katholischer Kommentar zum Neuen Testament

FRLANT	Forschungen zur Religion und Literatur des Alten und Neuen Testaments
HAT	Handbuch zum Alten Testament
HSS	Harvard Semitic Studies
HTR	*Harvard Theological Review*
HUCA	*Hebrew Union College Annual*
ICC	International Critical Commentary
IEJ	*Israel Exploration Journal*
IM	E. Bernand, ed., *Inscriptions Métriques*
Int	*Interpretation*
JAC	*Jahrbuch für Antike und Christentum*
JBL	*Journal of Biblical Literature*
JBT	*Jahrbuch für biblische Theologie*
JJS	*Journal of Jewish Studies*
JNES	*Journal of Near Eastern Studies*
JSJ	*Journal for the Study of Judaism*
JSNT	*Journal for the Study of the New Testament*
JSNTSup	*Journal for the Study of the New Testament*, Supplements
JSOTSup	*Journal for the Study of the Old Testament*, Supplements
JSP	*Journal of the Study of the Pseudepigrapha*
JSPSup	*Journal of the Study of the Pseudepigrapha*, Supplements
JTS	*Journal of Theological Studies*
LCL	Loeb Classical Library
LS	*Louvain Studies*
MHUC	Monographs of the Hebrew Union College
NCB	New Century Bible (Commentary)
Neot	*Neotestamentica*
NIBC	New International Biblical Commentary
NIV	New International Version
NovT	*Novum Testamentum*
NovTSup	*Novum Testamentum*, Supplements
NRSV	New Revised Standard Version
NTS	*New Testament Studies*
NTTS	New Testament Tools and Studies
NumSup	*Numen*, Supplements
OBO	Orbis biblicus et orientalis
OTL	Old Testament Library
OTS	*Oudtestamentische Studiën*
PAM	Palestine Archaeological Museum
PEQ	*Palestine Exploration Quarterly*
POslo	Oslo Papyri
POxy	Oxyrhynchus Papyri

RB	*Revue biblique*
RechBib	Recherches bibliques
RevQ	*Revue de Qumran*
SB	F. Preisigke et al., eds., *Sammelbuch Griechischer Urkunden au Ägypten*
SBLDS	Society of Biblical Literature Dissertation Series
SBLEJL	Society of Biblical Literature Early Judaism and Its Literature
SBLMS	Society of Biblical Literature Monograph Series
SBLRBS	Society of Biblical Literature Resources for Biblical Studies
SBLSBS	Society of Biblical Literature Sources for Biblical Study
SBLSCS	Society of Biblical Literature Septuagint and Cognate Studies
SBLSP	Society of Biblical Literature Seminar Papers
SIG	W. Dittenberger, ed., *Sylloge Inscriptionum Graecarum*
SJLA	Studies in Judaism in Late Antiquity
SNTSMS	Society of New Testament Studies Monograph Series
SNTU	Studien zum Neuen Testament und seiner Umwelt
SPB	Studia postbiblica
SSEJC	Studies in Scripture in Early Judaism and Christianity
SSN	Studia semitica neerlandica
STDJ	Studies on the Texts of the Desert of Judah
SVTP	Studia in Veteris Testamenti pseudepigrapha
TDOT	*Theological Dictionary of the Old Testament*
TSAJ	Texte und Studien zum antiken Judentum
TU	Texte und Untersuchungen
TynBul	*Tyndale Bulletin*
VT	*Vetus Testamentum*
VTSup	*Vetus Testamentum,* Supplements
WBC	Word Biblical Commentary
WUNT	Wissenschaftliche Untersuchungen zum Neuen Testament
ZAW	*Zeitschrift für die alttestamentliche Wissenschaft*
ZNW	*Zeitschrift für die neutestamentliche Wissenschaft*

Introduction

CRAIG A. EVANS AND PETER W. FLINT

Eschatology, Messianism, and the Dead Sea Scrolls is the first volume to appear in the new series STUDIES IN THE DEAD SEA SCROLLS AND RELATED LITERATURE. The eight essays and related discussion were presented on September 30, 1995, at the first public Symposium of the Dead Sea Scrolls Institute at Trinity Western University (Langley, British Columbia). Keen public interest in these ancient documents was confirmed by the fact that nearly 400 people managed to find seats in a facility that normally accommodates 340! The keynote speaker was Professor John J. Collins whose paper, "The Expectation of the End in the Dead Sea Scrolls" (Chapter 5 in the volume), was well received by the audience and set the pace for the Symposium as a whole. The editors wish to thank the speakers, many other academic colleagues who were in attendance, the members of the audience, and the President and personnel of Trinity Western University for making the event an outstanding success. We are also grateful to Wm. B. Eerdmans Publishing Co., especially Mr. Jon Pott for supporting this new series, and Dr. Daniel C. Harlow for editing the volume and seeing it through the press. Besides offering some general observations on eschatology and messianism in the Hebrew Bible or Old Testament, this Introduction serves to introduce the essays in the volume, comment on the relationship between the Scrolls and Biblical Studies, and offer some insights on eschatology and messianism as evidenced by these ancient manuscripts.

A prominent feature of the Old Testament is the expectation of future events. In earlier times these tended to be imminent or within an historical framework: for instance, God's promise of a land and progeny to Abraham, or the hope of the exiles in Babylon to return to Judah. Over the centuries, however, it became increasingly clear that Israel (and later Judah) could not bring about the perfect kingdom of God. Even the greatest kings (David and Solomon) had serious flaws, and God's people were buffeted or ruled by a succession of foreign empires. Yet future expectation and the hope for a better world did not die;

instead, the horizon shifted to the end times and a golden age of peace, righteousness, and prosperity. This expectation is denoted by the nonbiblical term "eschatology," which refers to the "last" period of history or existence and takes two forms: prophetic and apocalyptic.[1] Although they share many traits, prophetic eschatology differs from apocalyptic eschatology in that the former understood the oppression of the Jews by other nations as punishment by God for breaking the covenant (e.g., Amos 4–8; Hosea 4–10; Jeremiah 2–8). In contrast, apocalyptic writers tended to link the oppressing nations with cosmic powers that were opposed to God (e.g., Isa 24:17-23; Dan 7:1-8). Towards the end of the Old Testament period, eschatological hope was sometimes linked with the expectation of a Messiah ("anointed one"), who would usher in the promised new age. The present volume does not deal with the development of messianic ideas in the Old Testament itself, which is a complex enterprise, but focuses rather on eschatology and messianism with particular reference to the Dead Sea Scrolls. For it is from the second century BCE to the late first century CE (when the Qumran Scrolls were written or copied) that messianic ideas in particular become most fully developed.

The Contributions to this Volume

The essays that comprise this book deal with several aspects of eschatology and messianism, especially in the late Second Temple period. Since this cannot be done without reference to the Old Testament, the first two pieces appropriately deal with aspects of messianism in the Hebrew Scriptures. In "Moses' Birth Story: A Biblical Matrix for Prophetic Messianism," Paul Hughes examines the name and figure of Moses, laying emphasis on how Israel's great lawgiver may have contributed to the messianic paradigm, both in the Dead Sea Scrolls and especially in the Gospel of Matthew. Hughes concludes that Jesus is portrayed as a second Moses, and as was the case for the earlier Moses, Jesus' name ("the Lord saves") hints at his vocation. Craig Broyles ("The Redeeming King: Psalm 72's Contribution to the Messianic Ideal") explores how Psalm 72 has played a role in the formation of messianism. He finds that this psalm has contributed to prophetic oracles that later became very significant in Jewish and Christian messianism, including the messianism that is attested in the Dead Sea Scrolls.

Some essays are devoted to the development of eschatological or messianic ideas in the intertestamental period. In "The Daniel Tradition at Qumran," Peter Flint observes that writings attributed to or associated with Daniel are remark-

1. For a useful summary, see Richard H. Hiers, "Eschatology," in *Harper's Bible Dictionary*, ed. Paul J. Achtemeier (San Francisco: Harper & Row, 1985) 275-77.

ably well attested among the Dead Sea Scrolls. Our canonical Daniel is found in eight (fragmentary) manuscripts, while four others contain apocryphal Daniel traditions. Flint concludes that members of the Qumran community apparently identified closely with Daniel's story of perseverance under the persecution of foreign rule. Martin Abegg ("Who Ascended to Heaven? 4Q491, 4Q427, and the Teacher of Righteousness") examines two scrolls in which the Teacher of Righteousness may be the implied speaker claiming to have ascended to heaven. Abegg adduces the apostle Paul's mention of his own ascent to Paradise in 2 Corinthians 12 as a New Testament parallel to the Qumran ascension texts. In "The Expectation of the End in the Dead Sea Scrolls" John Collins deals with the "end" of human history in the Scrolls. The Qumran "sectarians" apparently believed that this consummation was very close and, possibly, already unfolding. Although the end did not come as soon as was originally thought by an earlier generation of covenanters, the community continued to hold fast to its eschatological expectations. This steadfastness was made possible by the imprecise nature of some of their views, which allowed for adaptations.

The remaining three essays deal with eschatology and messianism in the New Testament, with a focus on the teachings of Jesus and Paul and how the Dead Sea Scrolls illuminate them. Craig Evans ("Jesus and the Dead Sea Scrolls from Qumran Cave 4") examines four of the recently released Scrolls from Cave 4. He finds that these fragmentary texts often clarify the context in which Jesus lived and taught, and in several instances illuminate specific aspects of his teaching. In "Throne-Chariot Mysticism in Qumran and in Paul" James Scott investigates merkabah (or throne-chariot) mysticism, aspects of which appear to be in evidence both at Qumran and in the writings of Paul. In his fresh examination of 2 Cor 2:14, Scott concludes that Paul depicted himself as God's prisoner, being led in the train following the Lord enthroned on his chariot. Like Moses before him, Paul has had an experience of God, which qualifies him now to be the Lord's ambassador and proclaimer of the new covenant. In the final essay ("'And When That One Comes': Aspects of Johannine Messianism"), Dietmar Neufeld investigates Johannine messianism, finding in 4Q521 a valuable aid for interpreting material in the Fourth Gospel. For Neufeld the concept of a divine messiah should not be viewed simply as a Christian development, but as one that has definite pre-Christian Jewish roots.

The volume is rounded out with an interchange between the Symposium presenters, accompanied by questions from the audience and the speakers' responses. A Select Bibliography of works dealing with messianism, especially as clarified by the Dead Sea Scrolls, brings the collection to a close. The editors hope that readers of this book will gain a deeper appreciation and understanding of the eschatology and messianism that was current in the days of Hillel, Jesus, and the early Church.

CRAIG A. EVANS AND PETER W. FLINT

The Dead Sea Scrolls and Biblical Studies

An introduction to the Dead Sea Scrolls is outside the scope of this volume, but some comments on these manuscripts and their relationship to Biblical Studies will be helpful to some readers (and not a few established scholars!). Between 1947 and 1956 eleven caves in the vicinity of Wadi Qumran yielded scrolls and various artifacts, with the richest finds in Caves 1, 4, and 11. Exploration and excavations elsewhere in the region led to the discovery of many more manuscripts at other locations in the vicinity of the Dead Sea, including Wadi Murabbaʿat (1951-52), Naḥal Ḥever (1951[?]-60), and Masada (1963-65).[2] Strictly speaking, the term "Dead Sea Scrolls" denotes the finds from Qumran and these other sites, but scholars sometimes ignore this distinction by equating the term with only the manuscripts from Qumran.

In recent years interest in these ancient documents has blossomed among the public and in scholarly circles. In the words of one prominent New Testament scholar, we seem to have entered a "Qumran spring."[3] This interest has been accompanied by an outpouring of editions,[4] introductions to,[5] and modern translations of[6] the Dead Sea Scrolls. Scholars have identified nearly 870 manuscripts, of which some 220 are biblical scrolls. Every book of the Old Testament is represented, with the exception of Esther (if we count Ezra-Nehemiah as a single work).[7] Since they are our oldest surviving examples of Old Testament docu-

2. For catalogues of the Dead Sea Scrolls, see J. A. Fitzmyer, *The Dead Sea Scrolls: Major Publications and Tools for Study* (SBLRBS 20; Atlanta: Scholars Press, 1990); S. A. Reed, *The Dead Sea Scrolls Catalogue: Documents, Photographs, and Museum Inventory Numbers* (SBLRBS 32; Atlanta: Scholars Press, 1994); E. Tov, with the collaboration of S. J. Pfann, *The Dead Sea Scrolls on Microfiche: A Comprehensive Facsimile Edition of the Texts from the Judaean Desert, Companion Volume* (Leiden: Brill, 1993).

3. Martin Hengel, "Aufgaben der neutestamentlichen Wissenschaft," *NTS* 40 (1994) 321-57, esp. 342-43; idem, "Tasks of New Testament Scholarship," *BBR* 6 (1996) 67-86, here p. 80.

4. The official or critical editions of the Dead Sea Scrolls are published by Oxford University Press in the series Discoveries in the Judaean Desert (DJD), of which about fourteen volumes had appeared by the end of 1995. Virtually all of the documents involved were first published as preliminary editions in books or journals.

5. One of the best introductions is J. C. VanderKam, *The Dead Sea Scrolls Today* (Grand Rapids: Eerdmans, 1994). For a more distinctly Christian emphasis, see E. Cook, *Solving the Mysteries of the Dead Sea Scrolls* (Grand Rapids: Zondervan, 1994), while a Jewish perspective is offered by L. Schiffman, *Reclaiming the Dead Sea Scrolls: The History of Judaism, the Background of Christianity, the Lost Library of Qumran* (Philadelphia and Jerusalem: Jewish Publication Society, 1994).

6. No translation of the biblical scrolls is yet available, but one is scheduled to appear in 1998. English versions of the nonbiblical scrolls are as follows: G. Vermes, *The Dead Sea Scrolls in English* (4th ed.; London: Penguin, 1995); F. García Martínez, *The Dead Sea Scrolls Translated: The Qumran Texts in English* (Leiden: Brill; Grand Rapids: Eerdmans, 1996); M. Wise, M. Abegg, and E. Cook, *The Dead Sea Scrolls: A New Translation* (San Francisco: HarperCollins, 1996).

7. There is only one manuscript of Ezra (4QEzra, containing Ezra 4:2-6, 9-11; 5:17; 6:1-5), and none containing portions of Nehemiah. However, on the assumption that Ezra-Nehemiah

ments, these biblical scrolls are of fundamental importance for understanding the canonical process and the finalization of the text of Scripture. Several books of the Apocrypha are also represented at Qumran (e.g., Tobit, Sirach, Epistle of Jeremiah). Since these documents have been accepted as Scripture by the Roman and Orthodox churches, but not by Jews and Protestants, their presence among the Scrolls is especially relevant for tracing the development of the biblical canon.

The caves also yielded several Pseudepigrapha that were previously familiar to us (e.g., *1 Enoch, Jubilees*) and many more that were completely unknown. Some scrolls contain selections of Scripture (e.g., 4QTestimonia, 4QFlorilegium, 4QTanḥumim), while others (termed *pesharim*) offer commentary on biblical texts (e.g., 4QpIsaiah^{a-e}, 4QpHosea^{a-b}, 1QpHab). Of great interest are the "sectarian" scrolls, that is, those manuscripts that relate most directly to the Qumran community and lay down their beliefs and rules. These scrolls include the *Community Rule* (1QSerek hayyaḥad and the various fragments from Cave 4), the *Thanksgiving Hymns* (1QHôdāyôt), and the *War Scroll* (1QMilḥamāh and various fragments from other caves). For Jews and Christians alike, many nonbiblical scrolls are significant because they shed light on the beliefs and practices of some or many Jews around the time of Hillel and Jesus.

The Eschatology and Messianism of the Scrolls

The eschatology evidenced by the nonbiblical scrolls does not always include a messianic dimension; many contain eschatological themes without any mention of the Messiah. Nor is there is a consistent, unified eschatology or a messianic idea in these documents; diversity of ideas is clearly evident in the Scrolls as a whole. Yet such diversity does not preclude the existence of central ideas or a common core.[8] One central theme concerns the imminent arrival of a day of judgment and restoration, at which time worship in Jerusalem will be reestablished. It is then that the "anointed of Israel" (i.e., what we usually consider as the "Messiah") will take his stand alongside the "anointed of Aaron," the true High Priest, and when the ungodly of Israel will be punished and driven from power. This will also be a time of violent conflict with the Gentile enemies of Israel, the Kittim.[9]

---

formed one book at Qumran as in Masoretic Hebrew Bibles — which is admittedly difficult or impossible to prove — it may be argued that Nehemiah was originally part of this scroll.

8. A recent book that recognizes the common elements of Jewish eschatology and messianism without the uncritical assumption that Judaism was monolithic in its ideas and practices is J. J. Collins, *The Scepter and the Star: The Messiahs of the Dead Sea Scrolls and Other Ancient Literature* (ABRL 10; New York: Doubleday, 1995).

9. The *War Scroll* (1QM) describes a final battle between the forces of good and the forces of evil. While the Cave 1 fragments of this work do not preserve any reference to the Messiah, they

A feature that has aroused much public and scholarly interest is the apparent expectation of *two* messiahs, one "of Aaron" and the other "of Israel." For example, the following passages anticipate and hope for the appearance of the "Messiah of Aaron and of Israel": CD 12:23–13:1; 14:18-19; 19:10-11; 20:1; 1QS 9:11; 4Q252 5:1-4.[10] For several years this dual messianism has stood at the center of debate. Did the people of Qumran expect two messiahs, or a single messiah who may be described as the "anointed of Aaron and Israel"? One text puts "messiah" in the plural: "until the coming of the Prophet and the Messiah*s* of Aaron and Israel" (1QS 9:11). When we also take into account the messianic feast, at which the priest and the Messiah will preside (cf. 1QSa 2:11-21), it seems best to understand Qumran's messianic expectation as diarchic (i.e., rule by two persons): a joint rule shared by a priestly Messiah, the "anointed of Aaron," and a Davidic Messiah, the "anointed of Israel."

Qumran's messianic diarchy is not without biblical basis; it has its roots in the Old Testament.[11] The *Testaments of the Twelve Patriarchs* presuppose this sort of diarchy. Many years ago, R. H. Charles concluded that the *Testaments* exhibit two competing messianisms — one priestly (of Levi), and the other Davidic (of Judah).[12] In more recent times, however, several scholars[13] have

---

were recently supplemented with several pieces from Cave 4, one of which (4Q285) describes the battle between the "Prince of the Community, the Branch of David" and the leader of the "Kittim." The original *War Scroll* seems to have envisioned a final showdown between Israel's Messiah and Belial's agent, the leader of the Kittim — most likely the Roman Emperor — ending in the death of this leader and in victory for Israel. For recent studies, see M. G. Abegg, Jr., "Messianic Hope and 4Q285: A Reassessment," *JBL* 113 (1994) 81-91; M. Bockmuehl, "A 'Slain Messiah' in 4Q Serekh Milḥamāh (4Q285)?" *TynBul* 43 (1992) 155-69; G. Vermes, T. H. Lim, and R. P. Gordon, "The Oxford Forum for Qumran Research Seminar on the Rule of War from Cave 4 (4Q285)," *JJS* 43 (1992) 85-94.

10. For two recent assessments of the messianic passages in the Scrolls, see C. A. Evans, *Jesus and His Contemporaries: Comparative Studies* (AGJU 25; Leiden: Brill, 1995) 83-154; M. G. Abegg, Jr., "The Messiah at Qumran: Are We Still Seeing Double?" *DSD* 2 (1995) 125-44.

11. 1 Sam 2:35; Jer 33:14-18; Zech 3:6-10; 6:9-15 (+ Targum); and the juxtaposition of Aaron/Israel in passages like Pss 115:9-10, 12; 118:3; 135:19. See also the following two essays in J. H. Charlesworth, ed., *The Messiah: Developments in Earliest Judaism and Christianity* (Minneapolis: Fortress, 1992): P. D. Hanson, "Messiahs and Messianic Figures in Proto-Apocalypticism," 67-75, esp. 69-71; and J. J. M. Roberts, "The Old Testament's Contribution to Messianic Expectations," 39-51, esp. 50.

12. R. H. Charles, "The Testaments of the Twelve Patriarchs," in *The Apocrypha and Pseudepigrapha of the Old Testament,* ed. R. H. Charles (2 vols.; Oxford: Clarendon, 1913) 2.294. Charles believed that the Levitical Messiah was advocated by the original author of the *Testaments* (cf. *T. Reub.* 6:7-12; *T. Levi* 8:14; 18:1-14; *T. Dan* 5:10-11). After the Hasidim (early Pharisees, as Charles understood them) broke with the Hasmoneans, a later editor championed a Judahite Messiah (cf. *T. Judah* 24:5-6; *T. Naph.* 4:5).

13. See esp. K. G. Kuhn, "The Two Messiahs of Aaron and Israel," in *The Scrolls and the New Testament,* ed. K. Stendahl (New York: Crossroad, 1992) 54-64, 256-59, esp. 57-58; G. Vermes, *The Dead Sea Scrolls: Qumran in Perspective* (Philadelphia: Fortress, 1981) 184-86, 194-97; J. A. Fitzmyer, "The Aramaic 'Elect of God' Text from Qumran Cave 4," *CBQ* 27 (1965) 348-72; reprinted

understood the *Testaments* to reflect the diarchic understanding that arose in the intertestamental period: a royal descendant of David and a Zadokite high priest would rule side by side over restored Israel.[14] It has also been plausibly suggested that the emphasis on two messiahs may have originated as a corrective of the merger of the high priestly and royal offices during the Hasmonean period.[15]

Yet difficulties attend any attempt to neatly summarize or synthesize the messianism of Qumran. Lawrence Schiffman has reminded us of an important caveat concerning the "definition of the corpus to be studied."[16] Not everything found in the Judean caves necessarily reflects the views of the Qumran community. Some ideas may reflect "minority opinions," while others may have been widely held at different periods in the history of the community. For example, while 1QS 9:9-11 speaks of "Messiahs" in the plural, it appears that this passage was not present in the oldest copy of the *Community Rule.* Here Schiffman effectively illustrates the diversity (and relative paucity) of messianic views at Qumran. We simply cannot expect a coherent, unified doctrine. Nevertheless, the corpus of materials should play a restraining role. While there may be a diversity of opinions, options that are widely out of step with the corpus as a whole should be viewed with suspicion, especially if poorly attested. Because the evidence at our disposal is incomplete, we must accept that it may not be possible to tie together all the loose ends.[17]

---

in Fitzmyer, *Essays on the Semitic Background of the New Testament* (London: Chapman, 1971) 127-60, esp. 129-40; S. Talmon, "Waiting for the Messiah: The Spiritual Universe of the Qumran Covenanters," in *Judaisms and Their Messiahs at the Turn of the Christian Era,* ed. J. Neusner et al. (Cambridge and New York: Cambridge University Press, 1987) 111-37, esp. 122-31; idem, "The Concept of *Māšîaḥ* and Messianism in Early Judaism," in *The Messiah,* ed. Charlesworth, 101-3; L. H. Schiffman, "Messianic Figures and Ideas in the Qumran Scrolls," in *The Messiah,* ed. Charlesworth, 118-29. See now R. Kugler, *From Patriarch to Priest: The Levi-Priestly Tradition from Aramaic Levi to Testament of Levi* (SBLEJL 9; Atlanta: Scholars Press, 1996).

14. The appearance of a phrase from Zech 4:14 ("the two sons of oil") in the context of an apparent interpretation of Gen 49:8-12 (Jacob's blessing of Judah) may point to the scriptural point of origin of Qumran's diarchic messianism (cf. 4Q254 frg. 4, line 2). For a preliminary study, see C. A. Evans, " 'The Two Sons of Oil': Early Evidence of Messianic Interpretation of Zechariah 4:14 in 4Q254 4 2," forthcoming. It is also possible that the quotation of Zech 4:14 was related to the blessing of Levi, the patriarch of the priestly line, in which case the diarchic implications remain.

15. For this view, see A. Hultgård, *L'Eschatologie des Testaments des Douze Patriarches* (2 vols.; Stockholm: Almquist & Wiksell, 1977) 1.60-69.

16. Schiffman, "Messianic Figures," 116-17.

17. One such loose end in Qumran research concerns the mysterious Teacher of Righteousness. Both the identity of this person and his possible role in the founding of the Community continue to be debated. In 1982 Philip Davies proposed that the "teacher of righteousness" was a messianic title (*The Damascus Covenant: An Interpretation of the "Damascus Document"* [JSOTSup 25; Sheffield: JSOT Press, 1983] 119-25). Although the suggestion has its attractions, it does not carry conviction; cf. M. A. Knibb, "The Teacher of Righteousness — A Messianic Title?" in *A Tribute to Geza Vermes: Essays on Jewish and Christian Literature and History,* ed. P. R. Davies and

Christians have understandably been interested in this debate. Many have wondered if Qumran's expectation of two messiahs was at variance with early Christianity's understanding of the messiahship of Jesus. In a sense the answer to this question is both negative and affirmative. Jesus' own understanding of messiahship may not have differed greatly from the ideas of his contemporaries, and it could be argued that he offered himself as messiah to the Jewish authorities of Jerusalem.[18] But it is clear that the crucifixion and resurrection of Jesus significantly influenced the messianism of the early Church. For early Christians, the roles of the two anointed ones became fused in the risen and exalted Christ, seated at God's right hand. The risen Christ was now *both* the anointed of David *and* the anointed High Priest (note the importance of Ps 110:1-4 for early christology). The latter christological theme is also found in Paul, where Jesus "intercedes" for believers (cf. Rom 8:34), and in greatly enhanced fashion in Hebrews, where Jesus is both the perfect sacrifice that need never be repeated and the High Priest who intercedes perfectly and continually for the people of God (cf. Heb 9:11-28).[19] In this sense at least, Christianity's understanding of Jesus' messiahship is profoundly at variance with the messianic ideas of the Dead Sea Scrolls.

Not only does the New Testament collapse the diarchic messianism into one Messiah, but Christianity's messianic idea also includes the idea of suffering. The Qumran Scrolls describe a period of struggle (a forty-year war, according to the *War Scroll*) and persecution (of the Teacher of Righteousness and of the community as a whole), but the Scrolls expect the advent of the Messiah to

---

R. T. White (JSOTSup 100; Sheffield: JSOT Press, 1990) 51-65. Earlier A. S. van der Woude had concluded that the historical Teacher of Righteousness is not "a messianic figure . . . rather he is the priest-prophet 'to whom God made known all the mysteries of the words of His servants the prophets' (1QpHab 7:4-5), the second Moses, the preparer of the way of the two Messiahs, but he is not himself a Messiah" (*Die messianischen Vorstellungen der Gemeinde von Qumrân* [Assen: Van Gorcum, 1957] 165).

18. A scenario that must await fuller treatment elsewhere by Craig Evans is that the "triumphal entry" (Mark 11:1-11 and parallels), which ended in the Temple precincts in an anticlimactic manner, may have been Jesus' offer to the Jerusalem priesthood to serve as the anointed of David (i.e., the "Messiah of Israel") alongside the anointed High Priest (i.e., the "Messiah of Aaron"). The High Priest Caiaphas and his fellow priests, however, would have none of it, and so Jesus was ignored. In response to this snub, Jesus took action in the Temple precincts and criticized Temple polity (Mark 11:15-18), at which time he evidently spoke of the Temple's doom (Mark 13:2; 14:58), warning that the priestly administration would be taken from Caiaphas and his colleagues and given to others who were more worthy (Mark 12:1-12). Jesus may have held to a form of diarchic messianism somewhat like that found in several of the Scrolls. If so, we could surmise that the anointed Jesus (cf. Matt 11:5 = Luke 7:22; 4:18-19, where Jesus alludes to and quotes Isa 61:1-2) and the anointed High Priest were expected to serve together in the kingdom of God.

19. Cf. Y. Yadin, "The Dead Sea Scrolls and the Epistle of Hebrews," in *Scripta Hierosolymitana IV: Aspects of the Dead Sea Scrolls*, ed. C. Rabin and Y. Yadin (Jerusalem: Magnes, 1958) 36-55.

precipitate a great victory over wicked Rome and the wicked of Israel. The suffering and death of Jesus led early Christians to sift through the prophetic Scriptures. The Song of the Suffering Servant (Isa 52:13–53:12) and Zechariah's pierced one (Zech 12:10), along with several of the psalms of lament (e.g., Psalms 22 and 69), clarified for the early Church the meaning of Jesus' death. Early Christians understood God's purposes to be realized through the work of one Messiah, whose death and resurrection brought an end to the old order and the beginning of the new. The idea of a suffering Messiah is almost certainly absent from the Dead Sea Scrolls, although from time to time some scholars have tried to find it.[20]

The eschatological ideas present in the Dead Sea Scrolls shed welcome light on our understanding of eschatology around the turn of the Common Era. The messianic ideas found at Qumran are also pertinent for tracing the roots of New Testament christology, both by illumining the Jewish background behind ideas and debates to be found in the New Testament and by suggesting new ways of defining Jesus' messianic expectations.

20. Recently the claim has been advanced with respect to 4Q285 that the Romans would kill the "Prince of the congregation, the Branch of David"; cf. R. H. Eisenman and M. O. Wise, *The Dead Sea Scrolls Uncovered* (Shaftesbury: Element, 1992) 24-29; J. D. Tabor, "A Pierced or Piercing Messiah? — The Verdict Is Still Out," *BAR* 18.6 (1992) 58-59. This reading, however, flies in the face of Hebrew syntax, the context of 4Q285 — in this scroll the women of Israel celebrate by playing tambourines and dancing, which would hardly be the case if the Messiah had just been killed — and Qumranic interpretation of Isa 10:34–11:1. See Abegg, "Messianic Hope and 4Q285," 81-91; Evans, *Jesus and His Contemporaries*, 129-31.

Moses' Birth Story: A Biblical Matrix for Prophetic Messianism

PAUL E. HUGHES

Introduction

Prophecy as a vocation is commonly encountered in the Old Testament tradition. Although the great classical prophets immediately come to mind when considering this phenomenon — figures like Isaiah, Jeremiah, and Ezekiel — it is with Moses that the first prophetic call narrative in the Hebrew Bible is associated (Exodus 3–4).

An emphasis on prophecy can also be seen throughout the New Testament and at Qumran in the Dead Sea Scrolls. Both the Qumran community and the New Testament believers awaited a messianic figure, some of whose features reflected those of the Old Testament prophet in general, and of Moses in particular.

What features of Moses fostered this attraction, and do the methods that we use affect the results that we obtain? The past few decades have witnessed many methodological changes in the field of biblical studies. Informed by various academic disciplines such as sociocultural anthropology, sociology, strains within philosophy, and literary domains, an exciting return to the study of biblical texts *as texts in their own right* has served to replace the sometimes dismissive comments of critics from earlier centuries. Unfortunately, however, some advocates have pitched out the more or less established findings of traditionally minded historical critics, which is a perspective not sanctioned here. This new state of affairs has been aptly summarized as follows:

> Many centuries ago biblical exegesis generated the secular discipline of literary analysis, and today the child repays the parent, applying the in-

> sights and methods of that derived discipline to its original source, the Bible.[1]

The new narrative enterprise has received appellations like *the literary method, literary theology, literary exegesis,* and *poetics.* "Poetics" is defined as:

> The general principles of poetry or of literature in general, or the theoretical study of these principles. As a body of theory, poetics is concerned with the distinctive features of poetry (or literature as a whole), with its languages, forms, genres, and modes of composition.[2]

A small sample of relatively recent books of this genre that is interested in studying Hebrew narrative on its own terms would include volumes like Robert Alter's *The Art of Biblical Narrative,*[3] Adele Berlin's *Poetics and Interpretation of Biblical Narrative,*[4] Meir Sternberg's *The Poetics of Biblical Narrative: Ideological Literature and the Drama of Reading,*[5] Shimon Bar-Efrat's *Narrative Art in the Bible,*[6] and David Gunn and Danna Nolan Fewell's *Narrative in the Hebrew Bible,*[7] to name a few.

Another designation for this type of inquiry is *Narrative Criticism,* as seen, for example, in the recent guide by Mark Allen Powell.[8] Narrative Criticism asks about the structure and function of *plot* — voiced in the question "*What* story is being told?" Narrative Criticism also asks about the devices of the text's *narratology* — voiced in the question "*How* is this story told?" Another area about which Narrative Criticism is concerned relates to the techniques involved in the narrative's *characterization* — subsumed under the question "*Who* are the main players within this story, and how are they portrayed and developed?"

On the basis of a narrative-critical methodology, this chapter will explicate the birth story of Moses (Exod 2:1-10) in an attempt to understand later uses of Moses as a prophetic and messianic figure.

1. J. P. Rosenblatt and J. C. Sitterson, Jr., "Introduction," in *"Not in Heaven": Coherence and Complexity in Biblical Narrative,* ed. H. Marks and R. Polzin (Indiana Studies in Biblical Literature; Bloomington: Indiana University Press, 1991) 1.

2. C. Baldick, *The Concise Oxford Dictionary of Literary Terms* (Oxford: Oxford University Press, 1990) 172 (s.v. "poetics").

3. R. Alter, *The Art of Biblical Narrative* (New York: Basic Books, 1981).

4. Adele Berlin, *Poetics and Interpretation of Biblical Narrative* (Sheffield: Almond, 1983).

5. M. Sternberg, *The Poetics of Biblical Narrative: Ideological Literature and the Drama of Reading* (Bloomington: Indiana University Press, 1985).

6. S. Bar-Efrat, *Narrative Art in the Bible* (JSOTSup 70; Bible and Literature Series 17; Sheffield: Almond, 1989).

7. D. Gunn and D. N. Fewell, *Narrative in the Hebrew Bible* (Oxford Bible Series; Oxford: Oxford University Press, 1993).

8. M. A. Powell, *What Is Narrative Criticism? A New Approach to the Bible* (Guides to Biblical Scholarship, New Testament Series; Philadelphia: Fortress, 1990).

A Messianic Paradigm?

Various paradigms have been utilized with which to understand aspects of messianic expectation. For example, in the Hebrew Bible, notions about the Messiah are encapsulated in the figure of a royal Davidic king. Adjoined to this is the great eschatological Day of the LORD, which will rectify the injustices that have previously gone unpunished. Zechariah (6:9-15, esp. v. 13) refers to a high priest, along with a Davidic king.

The covenanters of Qumran employed the paradigms of a royal Davidic Messiah and also of a priestly Messiah from the line of Aaron.[9] A third paradigm within the literature of this community was that of a *prophet* who was held to be in continuity with the tradition of Moses. For example, 1QS (the *Rule of the Community* or *Manual of Discipline* from Qumran Cave 1), in the context of contrasting the property of the "men of holiness" with that belonging to the "men of falsehood," instructs the "men of holiness" to obey the Law "until there shall come the Prophet and the Messiahs of Aaron and Israel" (9:11).[10] 4Q175 (the *Testimonia*), which comprises a messianic anthology of proof texts, refers to the prophet like Moses, quoting two texts from Deuteronomy, the second of which is Deut 18:18-19 about the raising up of the prophet like Moses in a context that considers the matter of prophetic authenticity. Lines 5-8 of 4Q175 read: "*I will raise up for them a Prophet like you from among their brethren.* I will put my words into his mouth and he shall tell them all that I command him. And I will require a reckoning of whoever will not listen to the words *which the Prophet shall speak in my name.*"[11] 4Q375 *(Apocryphon of Moses B)* represents an apocryphal work purportedly written by Moses and contains material that shares similar concerns with Deuteronomy 13 and 18 regarding the question of what constitutes a false prophet (1:1-9).[12]

Most germane to the present topic are the words of the recently published 4Q377 *(Apocryphon of Moses C)*, another apocryphal work of Moses.[13] 4Q377 2:4-6 refers to the post-Exodus Sinai revelation, imprecating a curse on those who fail to keep "all the commandments of the LORD as spoken by Moses his Messiah." Lines 10-12 continue with a description of Moses' role as prophet ("He [God] would speak through his mouth as though he were an

9. Note Martin Abegg's recent caution, however, in M. G. Abegg, Jr., "The Messiah at Qumran: Are We Still Seeing Double?" *DSD* 2 (1995) 125-44.

10. Geza Vermes, *The Dead Sea Scrolls in English* (4th ed.; London: Penguin, 1995) 82.

11. Vermes, *The Dead Sea Scrolls in English,* 355.

12. F. García Martínez, *The Dead Sea Scrolls Translated: The Qumran Texts in English,* trans. W. G. E. Watson (2d ed.; Leiden: Brill; Grand Rapids: Eerdmans, 1996) 278.

13. M. O. Wise, M. G. Abegg, Jr., and E. M. Cook, *The Dead Sea Scrolls: A New English Translation* (San Francisco: HarperCollins, 1996) 337-38.

angel"; line 11) and herald ("indeed, what herald of glad tidings was ever like him? [. . .] He was a man of piety and [. . .] such as were never created before or since [. . .] "; lines 11b-12). It is debated whether or not Moses receives the technical title of "Messiah" here in this text. Michael Wise suggests that reference is being made to the properly installed high priest or king;[14] Martin Abegg thinks that the force of the word is descriptive and should be translated as an adjective rather than as a title, that is, "Moses, his [God's] anointed."[15] On this matter, John Collins has issued caution: "The eschatological prophet is a shadowy figure, not only in the Scrolls, but generally in the Judaism of the time."[16]

However this term is to be precisely translated and understood as a reflection of the messianology of the Qumran group, it is clear that the person of Moses was viewed as a model prophet. Even within the biblical tradition itself, Deuteronomy promotes this idealization and esteems his role in the closing words of the Pentateuch:

> Never since has there arisen a prophet in Israel like Moses, whom the LORD knew face to face. He was unequaled for all the signs and wonders that the LORD sent him to perform in the land of Egypt, against Pharaoh and all his servants and his entire land, and for all the mighty deeds and all the terrifying displays of power that Moses performed in the sight of all Israel. (Deut 34:10-12, NRSV)

It is also apparent that Jesus is connected with Moses in the New Testament. The Gospel of Matthew presents Jesus as a second Moses in some form of continuity with the first Moses. Scholars have noted several Matthean links between Jesus and Moses: parallels between the fivefold division of the Pentateuch (the so-called books of Moses) and the five-part structural division of Matthew's Gospel; geographic symbolism between Sinai as the sacred place where the Law was originally given and the *nova lex* or "new law" promulgated via Jesus' Sermon on the Mount; similarities between the respective birth narratives such as the descent into Egypt; and several other particulars.[17] In the following discussion, I will highlight narrative features of the birth story of Moses that might assist our understanding of Matthew's portrayal of Jesus as a prophetic figure like Moses.

14. Wise, Abegg, and Cook, *The Dead Sea Scrolls.*

15. Abegg, "The Messiah at Qumran," 140-41.

16. J. J. Collins, *The Scepter and the Star: The Messiahs of the Dead Sea Scrolls and Other Ancient Literature* (ABRL 10; New York: Doubleday, 1995) 116.

17. For a recent discussion of several of these features, see W. D. Davies, "The Jewish Sources of Matthew's Messianism," in *The Messiah: Developments in Earliest Judaism and Christianity,* ed. J. H. Charlesworth (Minneapolis: Fortress, 1992) esp. 503-6.

Reading Moses' Birth

Etiological Comments

Form Critics of the earlier part of this century, such as Hermann Gunkel in his important work *The Legends of Genesis,*[18] were interested in situating segments of the biblical tradition within its original preliterary milieu. According to Gunkel, the various units of tradition that contained etiological elements (i.e., elements seeking to explain the origin of specific phenomena, or to legitimize certain practices) functioned originally at the oral phase to provide an account of particular origins. The etymology given in Exod 2:10 serves, I believe, an integral role not only within the fabric of the contours of Exod 2:1-10 but also in the passage's broader setting of the Exodus story at large.

The story has been compared with the *Legend of Sargon of Akkad,* a Mesopotamian king from the middle of the third millennium BCE — another important leader who was preserved in a basket of rushes and subsequently drawn out of the water. The first ten lines of this text afford several interesting parallels with the biblical account of Moses' birth, highlighted here in italics:

> Sargon, the mighty king, king of Agade, am I.
> My mother was a changeling [?], my father I knew not.
> The brother[s] of my father loved the hills.
> My city is Azupiranu, which is situated on the banks of the Euphrates.
> My changeling mother conceived me, in secret she bore me.
> She set me in a *basket of rushes, with bitumen she sealed my lid.*
> *She cast me into the river which rose not [over] me.*
> The river bore me up and carried me to Akki, the drawer of water.
> Akki, the drawer of water *lifted me out* as he dipped his e[w]er.
> Akki, the drawer of water, *[took me] as his son (and) reared me.*[19]

Donald B. Redford has outlined the widespread use of the motif of the exposed hero in the ancient Near East and Graeco-Roman world, citing thirty-two accounts.[20] Brevard Childs has traced the transformation of the biblical account in wisdom literature, suggesting that this story represents an historicized wis-

18. H. Gunkel, *The Legends of Genesis: The Biblical Saga and History* (New York: Schocken, 1964).

19. J. B. Pritchard, ed., *The Ancient Near East: Supplementary Texts and Pictures Relating to the Old Testament* (Princeton: Princeton University Press, 1969) 119 (my emphasis). See also W. Beyerlin, ed., *Near Eastern Religious Texts Relating to the Old Testament* (London: SCM Press, 1978) 98-99. These similarities have been discussed since Hugo Gressmann, *Mose und seine Zeit: Ein Kommentar zu den Mose-Sagen* (FRLANT 18; Göttingen: Vandenhoeck & Ruprecht, 1913).

20. D. B. Redford, "The Literary Motif of the Exposed Child," *Numen* 14 (1967) 209-28.

dom tale.[21] G. W. Coats classifies the Moses birth story as heroic saga. The form of Exod 2:1-10 signals the reader that Moses will attain a status of heroic proportions and that critical focus must be placed upon him for the events which are to follow.[22]

At the conclusion of the birth story, the daughter of Pharaoh legally adopts the Hebrew child and names him מֹשֶׁה in accord with the standard biblical form of etymological etiologies, according to Gunkel's types. The text curiously presents the princess as speaking Hebrew, naming him מֹשֶׁה because he was "drawn out" from the water. The name is associated with the verbal root משה, "to draw/pull out," a root which is employed only two other times in the Hebrew Bible (in the Hiphil stem in Ps 18:17 and 2 Sam 22:17). Several commentators have observed that the Hebrew connection with this nomenclature remains ambiguous since the name משה is an active participle of the verb but is interpreted here as if it were the passive participle — משוי.[23]

On account of this seeming difficulty, scholars have postulated a variety of linguistic derivations. Josephus and Philo rejected the Hebrew etymology and instead explained the Greek form of the name — Μωυσῆς — as meaning "saved from water," from the two Egyptian words *mōu* ("water") and *esēs* ("saved," or "rescued").[24] Similar explanations have also been given from the Coptic form of the name.[25] J. G. Griffiths records an Egyptian etymology written in Arabic which connected the discovery of Moses in the water and among the trees with the Egyptian *mo* ("water") and *se* ("a tree").[26]

Many scholars think that the name derives from Egyptian and is the Hebrew equivalent of the Egyptian *ms*, which comes from the verb *msi'* — "to bear, give birth,"[27] corresponding to the Egyptian noun *mesu*, meaning

21. B. S. Childs, *The Book of Exodus: A Critical, Theological Commentary* (OTL; Philadelphia: Westminster, 1974) 12; idem, "The Birth of Moses," *JBL* 84 (1965) 109-22 (esp. pp. 119-21).

22. G. W. Coats understands this material as heroic saga; see his *Moses: Heroic Man, Man of God* (JSOTSup 57; Sheffield: JSOT Press, 1988) 1-42 passim, 43-48.

23. U. Cassuto, *A Commentary on the Book of Exodus*, trans. I. Abrahams (Jerusalem: Magnes Press, 1967) 20; Childs, *Book of Exodus*, 19; J. P. Hyatt, *Exodus* (NCB; London: Marshall, Morgan & Scott, 1971) 64-65; M. Noth, *Exodus: A Commentary*, trans. J. S. Bowden (OTL; Philadelphia: Westminster Press, 1962) 26.

24. Josephus, *Antiquities* 2.9.6 §228; text in H. St. J. Thackeray et al., eds., *Josephus in Nine Volumes IV. Jewish Antiquities, Books I–IV* (9 vols.; LCL; London: Heinemann; Cambridge: Harvard University Press, 1926-65) 4.262-63. Philo, *De Vita Mosis* 1.4 §17; text in F. H. Colson et al., eds., *Philo in Ten Volumes and Two Supplementary Volumes VI* (12 vols.; LCL; London: Heinemann; Cambridge: Harvard University Press, 1929-53) 6.284-85.

25. J. G. Griffiths, "The Egyptian Derivation of the Name Moses," *JNES* 12 (1953) 225-26.

26. Griffiths, "The Egyptian Derivation of the Name Moses," 226.

27. G. Beer, *Exodus* (HAT; Tübingen: Mohr-Siebeck, 1939) 20-21; Henri Cazelles, "La Figure Théologique de Moïse dans les Traditions Bibliques," in *Autour de L'Exode (Études)* (Paris: Gabalda, 1987) 360; Childs, *Book of Exodus*, 7, who describes the name as a "hypocoristic form of a theophoric name"; J. I. Durham, *Exodus* (WBC 3; Waco: Word, 1987) 17; P. Heinisch, *Das Buch Exodus:*

"child."[28] Supporting this interpretive angle, Willi-Plein highlights the *leitmotif* of birth in the introductory chapters of Exodus, noting that each subsection contains a form of the root ילד,[29] which can be used verbally as "to bear, give birth," or as a noun meaning "son."[30] Commentators connect the form *ms* with other common Egyptian theophoric names — names containing the name of a god — like Ah-mose, Amen-mose, Ptah-mose, and Thut-mose. They suggest the possibility that מֹשֶׁה has been shortened and originally may have contained the name of a deity in the first element.[31]

Parallel terms exist in the Semitic language family as well. The Hebrew noun מת ("men," "people") is quite common, occurring some twenty-one times in the Hebrew Bible.[32] J. M. Sasson discusses the related Ugaritic noun *mṯ*, which seems to indicate the offspring of the marriage of Baal with a cow.[33] The root *mut* is also attested nominally in Amorite, meaning "man,"[34] and possesses Old Akkadian,[35] Akkadian,[36] Ethiopic,[37] and perhaps Aramaic[38] cognates. H. B. Huffmon examines this Amorite term in his discussion of genitive compound names and notes from his many examples that the second or final part of the compound is normally a divine name or theophorous element.[39]

Übersetzt und Erklärt (Bonn: Hanstein, 1934) 40-41; Hyatt, *Exodus,* 65; F. Michaeli, *Le Livre de L'Exode* (Neuchâtel: Delachaux & Niestle, 1974) 36, 43; M. Noth, *Die israelitischen Personennamen im Rahmen der gemeinsemitischen Namengebung* (BWANT 3/10; Stuttgart: Kohlhammer, 1928) 63; idem, *Exodus,* 26; J. Plastaras, *The God of Exodus: The Theology of the Exodus Narratives* (Milwaukee: Bruce, 1966) 42; N. Sarna, *Exploring Exodus* (New York: Schocken, 1987) 32-33.

28. H. Marks, "Biblical Naming and Poetic Etymology," *JBL* 114 (1995) 30.

29. I. Willi-Plein, "Ort und Literarische Funktion der Geburtsgeschichte des Mose," *VT* 41 (1991) 110-18.

30. Note that the birth/life motif has already been intimated in Exodus with the use of this root for the "midwives" in Exod 1:15-21.

31. Childs, *Book of Exodus,* 7; R. E. Clements, *Exodus* (CBC; Cambridge: University Press, 1972) 15; Durham, *Exodus,* 17; Noth, *Exodus,* 26.

32. See G. Lisowsky, *Konkordanz zum Hebräischen Alten Testament* (2d ed.; Stuttgart: Deutsche Bibelgesellschaft, 1981) 884.

33. J. M. Sasson, "Bovine Symbolism in the Exodus Narrative," *VT* 18 (1968) 380-87. W. H. Schmidt accepts the possibility that this word corresponds to the Egyptian *msi'*; see W. H. Schmidt, *Exodus 1,1–6,30* (BKAT; Neukirchen-Vluyn: Neukirchener Verlag, 1988) 74.

34. H. B. Huffmon, *Amorite Personal Names in the Mari Texts: A Structural and Lexical Study* (Baltimore: Johns Hopkins University Press, 1965) 234.

35. J. D. Fowler, *Theophoric Personal Names in Ancient Hebrew: A Comparative Study* (JSOTSup 49; Sheffield: JSOT Press, 1988) 229, where she discusses the genitival use of the element *mutum,* which describes the one who bears the name as a "man of" the deity.

36. *mutu,* with the suggested meanings of: (1) "spouse," found in names of the children of widows who depicted the deity as a husband ("My spouse is god"); and (2) "man," "warrior"; cf. Fowler, *Theophoric Personal Names,* 256, 275 n. 101.

37. Huffmon, *Amorite Personal Names,* 234.

38. Fowler (*Theophoric Personal Names,* 219, 282) considers the connection between this root and the name בתואל (Gen 22:22), emended to מתואל.

39. Huffmon, *Amorite Personal Names,* 105, 119-20, 124.

Poetic Observations

The argument of the present narrative-critical reading of this story is as follows. Moses (מֹשֶׁה) is an Egyptian name from the root *msi'* ("to bear, give birth") supported by several Semitic cognates as outlined above. The author of this text has, however, deliberately thrown a hook into the narrative with which to catch the ear of the hearer by crafting a Hebrew derivation for מֹשֶׁה — using as agent the daughter of Pharaoh — instead of the expected Egyptian derivation. The Egyptian root *msi'* fits perfectly with the thrust and tenor of the narrative, but this expected derivation has been bypassed in order to promote a particular point about the character of Moses. This perspective gains support through an examination of the poetics of Exod 2:1-10.

The texture of the narrative is crisp and lively, with active interchange occurring between the anonymous characters that it depicts. Within ten relatively short verses, these unnamed characters "go," "take," "become pregnant," "give birth," "see," "hide," "waterproof," "set," "stand," "discover," "go down," "wash," "send," "open," "weep," "have compassion," "speak," "summon," "nurse," "pay," "grow," "bring," "name," and "draw out." Forty-six verbs in total are used in this brief section.

The chart on page 18 portrays the microplot of Exod 2:1-10, which distills some useful results in support of the reader's expectation of a meaning for Moses' name that has something to do with the themes of birth and life. This breakdown reveals some obvious but important details. The apex of the plot tension maintains a strict focus upon the child and the king's daughter. The tension centers on whether the child will or will not be allowed to continue to live. It is the previous narrative context of Exod 1:8-22 that defines this tension, because the Moses birth story assumes in its present shape the edict of the Egyptian king to submerge Hebrew male children. A meaning for מֹשֶׁה (Moses) that relates the themes of "life" and "birth," as the Egyptian derivation does, is ideally suited to this pervasive *leitmotif.* Denouement does not occur within this microplot until it is clear that the child will be preserved and his life will not be harmed.[40]

The device of naming — which considers how and in relation to whom a character is referred[41] — is an important feature to notice here, if only by its absence.[42] A noticeable characteristic of the story's naming is anonym-

40. The papyrus *"basket"* in which Moses is preserved is the same word used for "ark" in the Noah story (תֵּבָה). Outside its usage here in Exod 2:3, 5, the word only occurs elsewhere in the Hebrew Bible in Genesis 6–9, occurring some twenty-five times. The use of טוֹב ("good," "fine") to describe the child in Exod 2:2 also offers an interesting allusion to creation in Genesis 1–2.

41. Berlin, *Poetics,* 59.

42. Under this rubric, I refer to the specification of all the characters in the episode of Exod 2:1-10 and not merely to the etiology at the end.

The Microplot of Exodus 2:1-10

MICROPLOT STRUCTURE:	DESCRIPTION:
Introduction (Beginning/Initial Situation)	1. A man and woman get married.
	2. The woman becomes pregnant.
Complication (Middle/Central Occurrence)	3. The woman bears a son.
	4. The woman observes that the child is healthy so she hides him for a period of time.
	5. Unable to hide him any longer, she takes a basket, waterproofs it, puts the boy in it and sets it by the embankment of a river.
	6. The sister of the boy stands at a distance to see what will happen to him.
	7. The king's daughter goes down to wash by the river.
	8. Her attendants walk by the riverbank.
	9. The king's daughter sees the basket and sends her maidservant to get it, which she does.
	10. The king's daughter opens the basket and recognizes him to be a Hebrew male child.
	HIGHEST POINT OF CONFLICT
	11. The sister offers the king's daughter to fetch a Hebrew midwife to nurse the child.
	12. The king's daughter consents.
	DENOUEMENT
Conclusion (End/Final Situation)	13. The child's sister summons the child's mother.
	14. The king's daughter commands the mother of the child to nurse him for a wage, so the mother does.
	15. The child grows up.
	16. The mother of the child brings him to the king's daughter.
	17. The king's daughter adopts the child.

ity.[43] Instead of meeting specific characters with proper names like Shiphrah and Puah, the midwives of the previous section, the reader is introduced to virtual nondescripts who are indicated in relation to important reference points. A certain "man of the house of Levi" (unnamed in Exod 2:1, yet called Amram in Exod 6:20) is given Levitical ancestry, obviously a genealogical link of key importance for the narrator. This progenitor finds a wife, "the daughter of Levi" (again, unnamed in 2:1 but called Jochebed in 6:20), also of Levitical ancestry.[44] She is also referred to namelessly as "the woman" (Exod 2:2, 7, 9) and "the mother of the child" (2:8). The "daughter of Pharaoh" (Exod 2:5, 7, 8, 9, 10) lacks a specific name too and is only identified in relation to her father "Pharaoh." Although later tradition ascribed several names to her, like Tharmuth, Thermouthis, Merris, Batyah, and Bithia,[45] this is not mentioned here. Other characters are the "sister" of the child (Exod 2:4, 7), also called a "young woman" (2:8) yet named Miriam in Exod 15:20 and Num 26:59, and the "maidservants" of Pharaoh's daughter (Exod 2:5). Even the infant is referred to anonymously throughout, as "a son" (Exod 2:2, "of the daughters of Levi"; 2:10, "of the daughter of Pharaoh"), "the child" (2:3, 6, 7, 8, 9 [2x], 10), "the boy" (2:6), and "one of the Hebrew children" (2:6).

With respect to the naming, two critical reference points inform this prominent characterization feature of Exod 2:1-10. Subsequent to the Levitical link in 2:1, characters are named either in relation to: (1) Pharaoh; or (2) the child. The "daughter of Pharaoh" and "maidservants" of the daughter of Pharaoh are naming terms that point the reader to Pharaoh, while the "mother" and "sister" signal the child to the reader. Only one character is named with a proper noun — the hero, מֹשֶׁה (Moses). After Shiphrah and Puah (Exod 1:15), Moses is the next character to be given a name in the Exodus story proper, as Trevor Dennis and others have observed.[46] These two reference points enable

43. J. Cheryl Exum, "'You Shall Let Every Daughter Live': A Study of Exod 1:8–2:10," *Semeia* 28 (1988) 65, 70. Both Hyatt (*Exodus*, 62-63) and Durham (*Exodus*, 17) indicate that the episode is narrated in the biblical text without specifically religious features, with the deity absent from the account. It is clear to the reader, however, that God (אֱלֹהִים), who preserved the lives of the male children through the midwives incident, is protecting Moses in Exod 2:1-10.

44. Much discussion has surrounded this Levitical connection. Durham suggests that the double authentication of Moses' priestly descent (i.e., coming from *both* parents) in this nonpriestly layer serves the literary function of anticipating the stature and sacerdotal nature of Moses' leadership (*Exodus*, 15-16). Martin Noth observes that there is something special about this descent, even though it is questionable what the original tradition meant by "house of Levi" (v. 1); see Noth, *Exodus*, 25. Childs, in contrast, focuses on the anonymous aspect and perceives the unknown name of the Levite to place emphasis on the ordinary character of the event (*Book of Exodus*, 18).

45. Childs, *Book of Exodus*, 21; S. R. Driver, *The Book of Exodus* (Cambridge: Cambridge University Press, 1918) 10; Exum, "You Shall Let Every Daughter Live," 75 n. 26; Hyatt, *Exodus*, 64.

46. See his chapter, "Unsung Heroines: The Women of Exodus 1–4," in *Sarah Laughed: Women's Voices in the Old Testament*, ed. T. Dennis (London: SPCK, 1994) 84-114.

the reader to perceive the obvious polarity between characters. This polarity of character illustrates the conflict of the plot and reinforces its tension over whether the recently born child will live.

Characterization has been defined as "the process through which the implied author provides the implied reader with what is necessary to reconstruct a character from the narrative."[47] M. H. Abrams, in his *Glossary of Literary Terms,* highlights its narrative role: "The artistic success of a character in literature does not depend on whether or not an author incorporates an established type, but on how well the type is recreated as a convincing individual."[48] This "re-creation" process consists of the careful employment of various techniques like description of characters, portrayal of their inner life, and conveyance of their speech and action.[49] Another common characterization technique in the Hebrew Bible is that of contrast. Characters can be contrasted with another character, with an earlier action of their own, or with what is perceived to be the expected norm.[50] These techniques enable the reader to situate a particular character in the context of the story as well as to enter into their interior state and understand their ontological fabric more fully.

The following figure represents the structural balance of characters within this early part of the story. The chart highlights the tension between Pharaoh and Moses and points up the contrasts of the episode.

Structural Balance of Characters: Exodus 2:1-10

PHARAOH ← tension → MOSES

daughter **attendants**	**mother** **sister of child**
Act in child's interests Act against Pharaoh's interests Function to preserve life of child	Act in child's interests Act against Pharaoh's interests Function to preserve life of child

Pharaoh and Moses are antithetical characters

An obvious feature of this section is the prominent focus on women, who comprise several of the story's key players.[51] The "daughter of Pharaoh" and

47. Powell, *What Is Narrative Criticism?* 52.

48. S.v. "stock characters," 179.

49. Berlin, *Poetics,* 34-39.

50. Berlin, *Poetics,* 40-41.

51. Exum, "You Shall Let Every Daughter Live," 63-82; A. Brenner, "Female Social Behaviour: Two Descriptive Patterns within the 'Birth of the Hero' Paradigm," *VT* 36 (1986) 257-73; J. G. Williams, *Women Recounted: Narrative Thinking and the God of Israel* (Bible and Literature Series 6; Sheffield: Almond, 1982); Sarna, *Exploring Exodus,* 31-32.

"mother of the child" are both attended by women — "maidservants" and "daughter." Every character attempts to preserve the life of the child except for Pharaoh (implied here from Exod 1:22), and there is a dissonance of character intent between Pharaoh and Moses and also between Pharaoh and his daughter. The reader's sympathies are immediately drawn to the pathos of a helpless child — the mother's care, the daughter's watch, the fight to survive. The omniscient narrator's portrayal of the Egyptian princess's inner life reveals her sensitivity to innocence and imbues her with compassion (Exod 2:6). The daughter of Pharaoh serves as a foil to her father, and she can be contrasted with him in order to appreciate the section's characterization. The narrative portrays her as possessing complete control, even though her "words" are performed indirectly through attendant functionaries (her maidservants, paralleled in the mother and sister of the child), and she causes the flow of life to continue out of deliberate intention. In contrast, although Pharaoh is the king, his "words" are not performed (Exod 1:15-22), and though he is fully intent on preventing the flow of life from continuing, his plans remain thwarted because matters are out of his control. This results in irony and a virtually archetypal depiction of the preservation of Moses' life from the potentially threatening elements.

Conclusion

The naming of מֹשֶׁה is a technique used to develop his character. Although an appellation relating to "birth" and "life" (as with the Egyptian one) would be most fitting for the narrative and follows logically from an analysis of the episode's plot and characterization, the narrator hooks a meaning upon the root that foreshadows the life of this somewhat ambiguous child. As one who was "drawn out," he also will "draw out," in the impending contest between the forces of Pharaoh and Israel's descendants at the Exodus event.[52] Isa. 63:11 remembers מֹשֶׁה as the one who "brought them up through the sea."[53] The literary portrayal of the naming of Moses can be understood by the equation: *name equals vocation.*

In the New Testament, as discussed above, Matthew presents Jesus as a second Moses. For Jesus also, name equals vocation. In Matthew's description of how "the birth of Jesus the Messiah took place in this way" (Matt 1:18, NRSV), an angel of the Lord appears to Joseph in a dream and says, "Joseph, son of David, do not be afraid to take Mary as your wife, for the child conceived in her is from the Holy Spirit. She will bear a son, and you are to name him *Jesus,*

52. Plastaras, *Theology of the Exodus Narratives,* 41-42; Exum, "You Shall Let Every Daughter Live," 79.

53. Although a different verb is used here (the Hiphil of עלה, not משה).

for he will save his people from their sins" (Matt 1:20-21, NRSV). Jesus, as the Greek form of the Hebrew name *Joshua*, is etymologically linked to salvation and deliverance. Name equals vocation. It is hoped that the above comments have brought at least a little more clarity to the possibilities inherent in the birth story of Moses for contributing to the present discussion of messianism.

The Redeeming King: Psalm 72's Contribution to the Messianic Ideal

CRAIG C. BROYLES

Introduction

The messianism that is attested in the Dead Sea Scrolls did not arise in isolation from the Scriptures of Israel or from the larger context of Judaism in late antiquity. As John Collins has recently emphasized, the messianism witnessed by the sectarian Scrolls is largely consistent with what is found in other Jewish sources from this same period of time.[1] Messianic interpretation of Gen 49:10, Num 24:17, and Isa 10:34–11:5 is common to the Qumran corpus and to much of other early Jewish literature concerned with messianic themes.

It is now abundantly clear that the messianism of the Scrolls is deeply rooted in Israel's prophetic Scriptures.[2] However, these prophetic Scriptures are not limited to the Prophets themselves. Like the New Testament, some Qumran documents view the Psalms, as well as the Prophets, as prophetic in content. This perspective is attested, for example, in the reference to David as having uttered his psalms as "prophecy" (see 11QPs[a] 27:11) as well as in the composition of pesharim devoted to some of the Psalms and Prophets.[3]

The notion of "Messiah" or "Anointed One" is based largely, though not entirely, on the model of the anointed kings of the Davidic dynasty and the

1. See J. J. Collins, *The Scepter and the Star: The Messiahs of the Dead Sea Scrolls and Other Ancient Literature* (ABRL 10; New York: Doubleday, 1995).

2. See A. S. van der Woude, *Die messianischen Vorstellungen der Gemeinde von Qumran* (SSN 3; Assen: Van Gorcum; Neukirchen-Vluyn: Neukirchener Verlag, 1957). See also the more recent assessment in C. A. Evans, *Jesus and His Contemporaries: Comparative Studies* (AGJU 25; Leiden: Brill, 1995) 83-154.

3. See M. P. Horgan, *Pesharim: Qumran Interpretations of Biblical Books* (CBQMS 8; Washington: Catholic Biblical Association, 1979).

traditions associated with it. In the Dead Sea Scrolls and other texts of Second Temple Judaism, there are, of course, other messianic paradigms — priest, prophet, and heavenly figure.[4] If we wish to focus on the royal paradigm, however, the obvious place to begin is the so-called "royal psalms" of the Hebrew Bible. Most scholars of this century have followed H. Gunkel's analysis in assigning to this category Psalms 2, 18, 20, 21, 45, 72, 89, 101, 110, 132, and 144.[5] Most scholars also agree that these psalms were originally composed in the preexilic period and originally referred to the Davidic monarchy.

Other, often conservative scholars, however, have found it incongruous that such exalted language should be applied to humans, especially to the fallible monarchs of Judah described in 1–2 Kings. They argue, therefore, that some of these psalms, even when originally composed, promise a divine Messiah. Yet Psalm 89 speaks of the king in terms no less exalted than those found in Psalms 2 and 110. In Psalm 89 the king calls Yahweh "my father," and Yahweh calls him "my first born" (vv. 26-27). But these words are addressed specifically to "David" (vv. 3, 20, 35) and to "his sons" (v. 30). And the final third of the psalm laments the king's miserable failure in battle and closes with the question, "Where are your former mercies, O Lord, which you swore to David in your faithfulness?" (v. 49). It thus becomes apparent that this exalted language was originally applied to the historical figures of the Davidic dynasty and not to an ideal Messiah of the future. Thus, while it is undeniable that the royal psalms came to be applied messianically in the Christian tradition, to be accurate historically we must recognize their original use in reference to the preexilic Davidic dynasty.

This conclusion, however, creates a problem. The final collection and editing of the book of Psalms, or the Psalter, was done in the postexilic period when Judah had no Davidic monarchy under the Persian empire. Why then were these royal psalms retained? It is doubtful the editors kept them simply as historical artifacts in a collection of liturgical and meditative songs and prayers. The most likely explanation is that they retained value because even before the Common Era they bore the hope of a new David.[6] This transfer of referent — from the past Davidic kings to a future Davidic "Messiah" — was probably engendered by the Hebrew prophets. Prophecies contained in Isaiah (9:6-7; 11:1-5), Micah (5:2-5a), Jeremiah (23:5-6), Ezekiel (34:23-24; 37:24-28), and Zechariah (9:9-10) took up the language of the royal psalms and of the Davidic court and promised a new David, in view of the repeated failures of David's sons.

The present paper intends to contribute to the theme of eschatology, messianism, and the Dead Sea Scrolls by exploring how one psalm in particular,

4. See Collins, *The Scepter and the Star.*

5. H. Gunkel, *Einleitung in die Psalmen* (Göttingen: Vandenhoeck & Ruprecht, 1933) 140.

6. See B. S. Childs, *Introduction to the Old Testament as Scripture* (Philadelphia: Fortress, 1979) 515-17; C. Westermann, *Praise and Lament in the Psalms* (Edinburgh: Clark, 1981) 257-58.

Psalm 72, contributed to the messianic ideal in early Judaism and Christianity. The importance of this psalm has been underestimated, but comparative study reveals that it made a significant contribution. We will begin our study by briefly examining the citation of royal psalms in the New Testament. We will then highlight literary echoes of Psalm 72 in messianic contexts of the New Testament and early Jewish literature, notably the *Psalms of Solomon.* Finally, an analysis of the structure and themes of Psalm 72 will clarify aspects of the New Testament portrait of Jesus as the Messiah.

The Royal Psalms Cited in the New Testament

The royal psalms most frequently cited in the NT to support Jesus' messianic claims are Psalm 2, especially verse 7, and Psalm 110, especially verses 1 and 4.[7] What is surprising, however, is that the portrayal of the king in both of these psalms is decidedly militaristic, whereas the portrayal of Jesus in the Gospels is decidedly nonmilitaristic. In fact, of the eleven psalms generally agreed to be royal or messianic, only four lie outside an explicit military context and are not dominated by militaristic language, namely Psalms 45, 72, 101, and 132. (Psalm 101 is not, in my view, a royal psalm.) Even Psalm 45, though it is a wedding song, enjoins the king, "Strap your sword on your thigh, O warrior . . . (v. 3a). With your sharpened arrows, may peoples fall under you, (may they fall) into the hearts of the king's enemies (v. 5)." Thus, if one were to attempt to paint a portrait of the Messiah prior to Jesus' coming, the artist would most certainly have painted him in military uniform. But, again, this is precisely how the Gospels do not portray Jesus.

So why does the NT make so much of Ps 2:7 and 110:1, 4 when their portrayal of the king is so incongruous with Jesus? A satisfactory answer to this question is beyond the scope of this paper, except for one observation. These passages are clearly oracular or prophetic, that is, they have God speak in the first person. Their introductory formulas make this explicit:[8]

> I will proclaim *Yahweh's decree,*
> *he said to me,* "You are my son; I today have begotten you." (Ps 2:7)
>
> *Yahweh's oracle* to my lord, "Sit (enthroned) at my right hand,
> until I make your enemies a footstool for your feet." (Ps 110:1)

7. See the "Index of Quotations," in *The Greek New Testament,* ed. Kurt Aland et al. (2d ed.; New York: United Bibles Societies, 1968) 906, 908. Psalm 2 is quoted eighteen times and Psalm 110 twenty-five times.

8. Among the royal psalms, Ps 89:19-37 and Ps 132:11-12, 14-18 are also oracular.

Yahweh has sworn and will not recant,
"You are a priest forever after the order of Melchizedek." (Ps 110:4)

It appears that the early Church cited the strongest texts to demonstrate that Jesus fulfills prophetic claims about the Messiah in order to support their apologetic interests over against Judaism. Thus, while other psalms may inform us of the messianic ideal, the NT does not cite them because they are not direct divine speech.

One makes a citation in order to prove a claim, here Jesus' identity as Messiah. Citations are marshaled to strengthen an argument. Otherwise, the precise wording is not so important; one can simply draw on the motifs or ideas of an earlier passage. Thus, citations need not provide a comprehensive reflection of the Messiah's identity. In fact, they may not even provide an entirely accurate reflection if they happen to focus on one aspect or role to the exclusion of others. In other words, in our attempt to reconstruct the early Church's understanding of the Messiah from the Hebrew Bible, we cannot limit our study to citations.

Psalm 72 is a rather unlikely candidate for a messianic citation because it is an intercession for the king. It is, therefore, not a divine promise but a human wish. To my knowledge, only one text originally written to be a messianic text includes an intercession for the Messiah, and it exhibits some dependence on Psalm 72, namely, the *Psalms of Solomon* (discussed below). The intercessory genre of Psalm 72 does, however, confirm that it was not originally composed as a messianic psalm but as a royal psalm, sung on behalf of the preexilic Davidic kings. Nonetheless, Psalm 72 is worthy of investigation as a potential messianic text for it, along with Psalm 132, is distinctive among the royal psalms because of its nonmilitaristic portrayal of the king and because this portrayal is so close to that of Jesus in the Gospels.

Psalm 72: Translation

1 For Solomon.
O God, your justice[9] give to the king,
and your righteousness to the king's son.
2 May he judge your people with righteousness,
and your poor with justice.
3 May the mountains bear well-being for the people,
and the hills righteousness.[10]

9. This translation follows the LXX and Syriac, which render משפט in the singular, unlike the MT. The word pair "righteousness" and "justice" appear to be used as abstract nouns in the opening two verses and are then unpacked in concrete terms in the rest of the psalm.

10. See *BHS*.

4 May he administer justice for the poor of your people,
save the children of the needy,
and crush the oppressor.
5 So may he extend[11] with the sun,
and before the moon generation after generation.
6 May he descend like rain on mown grass,
like showers sprinkling the land.
7 May righteousness[12] sprout in his days,
and an abundance of well-being until the moon is no more.
8 So may he rule from sea to sea,
and from the River to the ends of the earth.
9 Before him may foes[13] kneel,
and his enemies lick dust.
10 Kings of Tarshish and islands, may they return tribute;
kings of Sheba and Seba, may they bring a gift.
11 So may all kings bow down to him;
all nations may they serve him.

12 If[14] he delivers the needy who cry for help,
and the poor and those without a helper,
13 spares the poor and needy,
and saves the lives of the needy,
14 from oppression and from violence redeems their lives,
so their blood is precious in his sight,
15 So may he live and may one give him gold of Sheba,
so may one pray for him continually;

11. In the MT verse 5 appears to address God directly and reads literally, "They will fear you (יִירָאוּךָ) with the sun, and before the moon generation after generation." Not only is this direct address of God inconsistent with the rest of vv. 3-17, which use jussives in reference to the king, but the verb seems an odd choice in the verse. We would not expect Yahwism to affirm fearing Yahweh in connection with fearing the sun. The LXX probably points us to the original. Its *Vorlage* points to the verb וְיַאֲרִיךְ, "so may he extend with the sun. . . ." In 1 Kgs 3:14 Yahweh promises Solomon, "I will extend (ארך) your days." The LXX also presupposes a *waw* opening the verse.

12. Instead of the MT's adjectival form, this translation follows a few Hebrew manuscripts, the LXX, and Syriac, which read צֶדֶק. This forms a better parallel to שָׁלוֹם.

13. Instead of the MT's problematic צִיִּים, this translation reads צָרִים.

14. Translating כי as "if" makes best sense of the series of jussives from v. 2 to v. 17. If, however, we render כי as "for," vv. 12-14 would read, "*For* he delivers the needy who cry for help, and the poor and those without a helper. May he spare the poor and needy, and the lives of the needy may he save. From oppression and from violence may he redeem their lives, so may their blood be precious in his sight." In this case, verse 12 and possibly verses 12-14 together would give the cause or explanation of verses 8-11. In other words, the king will have this empire because he cares for the poor. Thus, whether כי is translated as "if" or "for," the international influence of the king (vv. 8-11, 15) is still dependent on his protection of the poor.

the whole day may one bless him.
16 Let there be an abundance of grain in the earth,
on the mountaintops let it wave;
like Lebanon may his fruit blossom,[15]
and his cut grain like the grass of the earth.
17 May his name be forever,
before the sun may his name increase;
so may they[16] bless themselves by him,
all nations pronounce him blessed.

18 Blessed be Yahweh, God of Israel,
who alone does wonders.
19 And blessed be his glorious name forever,
so may his glory fill all the earth.
Amen. Amen.

20 The prayers of David the son of Jesse are ended.

Literary Echoes of Psalm 72 in the New Testament

There are only a few literary echoes of Psalm 72 in the New Testament.

Matthew 2:11

In Matthew the story of the "wise men from the East" appears to have been shaped so as to show its "fulfillment" of Psalm 72:

Matt 2:11	*Psalm 72 (LXX)*
"and they *fell down* (πεσόντες)"	"Before him Ethiopians shall *fall down* (προπεσοῦνται)" (72:9)
"and *worshiped* (προσεκύνησαν) him"	"And all kings shall *worship* (προσκυνήσουσιν) him" (72:11)
"they offered him *gifts* (δῶρα)"	"the kings of the Arabians and Saba shall offer *gifts* (δῶρα)" (72:10)

15. See *BHS*.

16. Instead of the simple pronoun, which has no direct antecedent in the MT, the LXX supplies the subject, "all the tribes of the earth," thus establishing a more explicit echo of Gen 12:3; 28:14.

"*gold* (χρυσὸν)"	"and *gold* (χρυσίου) of Arabia shall be given to him" (72:15)

Luke 1:68

In the Benedictus (Luke 1:67-79) Zechariah praises God over the birth of his son John the Baptist and over its significance. He does so in the language of the Hebrew Bible. The specific reason for this praise is given in the statement, "for . . . he has raised up a horn of salvation for us in the house of his servant David" (vv. 68-69). This forms a clear echo of phraseology found in three royal psalms, namely, 132:17; 18:2; 89:24. The Benedictus begins with a doxology, which appears to be a literary citation of the royal Psalm 72.

Luke 1:68	*Psalm 72*
"*Blessed be the Lord God of Israel* (Εὐλογητὸς κύριος ὁ θεὸς τοῦ Ἰσραήλ)" (Luke 1:68a)	"*Blessed be the Lord God of Israel* (Εὐλογητὸς Κύριος ὁ Θεὸς τοῦ Ἰσραήλ)" (72:18)

It is possible this doxology is simply a common formula. The doxologies closing Books I and IV of the Psalter (Pss 41:13 and 106:48, respectively) are nearly identical, except that both omit τοῦ. Moreover, the tie with Psalm 72 is strengthened in the parallel line of Luke, which refers to God's redemption of his people. Most scholars, however, take the second half of the verse as an echo of Ps 111:9.

"for he has visited and performed *redemption for his people*" (ἐποίησεν λύτρωσιν τῷ λαῷ αὐτοῦ). (Luke 1:68b)	"*Redemption* he has sent *to his people*" (Λύτρωσιν ἀπέστειλε τῷ λαῷ αὐτοῦ). (Ps 111:9)

But the verb is noticeably different. In Luke, redemption is "done" or "performed"; in the LXX of Psalm 111, it is "sent." Although there can be little doubt that Psalm 111 is echoed here, there may also be an echo of Psalm 72, especially if the doxology in the first half of this Lukan verse is a deliberate echo of Ps 72:18. Verse 14 of the psalm reads, "From usury and from injustice he (i.e., the king or Messiah) will *redeem* (λυτρώσεται) their lives." Although "redeem" here appears as a verb and not a noun, it is possible that this verse provides the link between the doxology of Psalm 72 and the celebration of God's redemption in Psalm 111.

Echoes of Psalm 72 in Prophetic Passages Cited in the New Testament

Aside from these direct echoes of Psalm 72 in the New Testament, we may be able to trace another path along which Psalm 72 made its influence felt there. Psalm 72, along with other royal psalms, appears to have been a source by which the Hebrew prophets developed their vision of a new David whom God would raise up. Portions of these oracles are then cited in the New Testament as fulfilled in Jesus.

Zechariah 9:9-10

Zech 9:9 is cited in two Gospels, both in connection with Jesus' "triumphal entry" (Matt 21:5; John 12:15): "Rejoice greatly, O Daughter of Zion . . . behold your king comes to you . . . , humble and riding on a donkey and upon a colt, the foal of a donkey." Verse 10 of the oracle, "and he will proclaim peace to the nations," is echoed in Eph 2:17: "And he came and proclaimed peace to you who were far off. . . ." The echoes of Psalm 72 in Zech 9:9-10 are several, with verse 10 being a direct citation:

Zech 9:9-10	*Psalm 72*
"your *king*" (מלכך, 9:9)	"the *king*" (מלך, 72:1)
"*righteous* and *saving*" (צדיק ומושיע[17], 9:9)	"O God . . . give . . . your *righteous*ness (צדקתך) to the king's son. May he judge your people with *righteous*ness (בצדק)." (72:1-2) "May he *save* (יושיע) the children of the needy." (72:4) "He *saves* (יושיע) the lives of the needy." (72:13)
"and he will speak *peace* to the *nations*" (ודבר שלום לגוים, 9:10)	"*peace*" (72:3, 7) "*nations*" (72:11, 17)
"and his rule will be *from sea to sea, and from the River to the ends of the earth*" (ומנהר מים עד־ים ומנהר עד־אפסי־ארץ, 9:10)	"so may he rule *from sea to sea, and from the River to the ends of the earth*" (וירד מים עד־ים ומנהר עד־אפסי־ארץ, 72:8)

17. The MT reads "saved" (נוֹשָׁע). This translation follows the LXX, the Syriac, Targum, and Vulgate, which presuppose an active participle.

Isaiah 11:4

The promise of "a branch" "from the stump of Jesse" is echoed some thirteen times in the New Testament.[18] Among the Dead Sea Scrolls, "the blessing of the Prince of the Congregation in 1QSb . . . is heavily indebted to Isaiah 11."[19] In Isa 11:4 the promise of a new David parallels the intercessions for the king in Psalm 72:

Isa. 11:4	*Psalm 72*
"And he will *administer justice in righteousness* for *the poor* (ושפט בצדק דלים, 11:4a) and will arbitrate with equity for *the poor* (ענוי) of the land. (11:4b)	"May he *administer justice* for the *poor* of your people (ישפט עניי־עם)." (72:4) "May he judge your people with *righteousness,* and your *poor* with *justice* (ידין עמך בצדק וענייך במשפט)." (72:2) "spares *the poor* (דל) and needy" (72:13) "If he delivers . . . the *poor* (עני)" (72:12)

To my knowledge, the only preexilic passages referring to Davidic kings attending to the poor are Pss 72:2, 4, 12-14; 132:15 and Jer 21:11-12; 22:1-3, 16. In Ps 132:15 the action of "satisfying" Zion's "poor" (אביון, a synonym never used in prophecies of a new David) is predicated of Yahweh, who establishes David's throne (vv. 11, 17). Moreover, the Jeremiah passages do not show very much linguistic affinity to Isa 11:4, but they do show some to Psalm 72:

Jer. 21:12; 22:3, 16	*Psalm 72*
"*Judge* each morning *with justice,* and *deliver* the robbed from the hand of the *oppressor*" (דינו לבקר משפט והצילו גזול מיד עושק, 21:12).	"May he *judge* your people with *righteousness,* and your *poor with justice*" (ידין עמך בצדק ועניך במשפט, 72:2).

18. See "Index of Quotations," in *The Greek New Testament,* 910.

19. John J. Collins, "'He Shall Not Judge by What His Eyes See': Messianic Authority in the Dead Sea Scrolls," *DSD* 2 (1995) 145-64, esp. 154.

"Do *justice* and *righteousness* (עשׂו משפט וצדקה) and *deliver* the robbed from the hand of his *oppressor*" (הצילו גזול מיד עושק, 22:3). Josiah "indeed *judged* the *poor* and *needy*" (דן דין־עני ואביון, 22:16).

"May he administer *justice* for the *poor* of your people . . . and crush the *oppressor*" (ישפט עניי־עם . . . וידכא עושק, 72:4). "he *delivers* the *needy*" (יציל אביון, 72:12)

In addition, the Jeremiah passages may well postdate Isa 11:1-5.[20] Thus, Psalm 72 contains the earliest programmatic statements that the Davidic line should attend to the poor. This, of course, increases the likelihood that Isa 11:4 stems from Psalm 72.

Isaiah 9:6-7 and Jeremiah 23:5-6

Two other key prophecies of a new David are Isa 9:6-7 (see Luke 1:32-33; John 12:34; cf. Eph 2:14) and Jer 23:5-6 (= 33:15-16; cf. John 7:42; 1 Cor 1:30), fundamental to both of which is the new David's reigning with "justice and righteousness" (משפט and צדקה). These are the two key attributes that set the direction of Psalm 72 in its opening verses (as attributes of the king, they appear only here among the royal psalms). While this word pair is certainly found throughout the Hebrew Bible, there are only a few nonprophetic passages that associate them with the Davidic king (2 Sam 8:15; 1 Kgs 10:9; and Ps 72:1-2).

Also prominent in both Isa 9:6-7 and Psalm 72 is how "peace" or *shalom* will characterize the Davidic king's government:

20. In his *Isaiah 1–39* commentary (NCB; Grand Rapids: Eerdmans, 1980) R. E. Clements observes (p. 121), "A large number of modern critical commentators have regarded the prophecy [of Isa 11:1-9, the shoot from the stump of Jesse] as authentic to Isaiah and as a genuine expression of the hope which he cherished and encouraged in connection with the Davidic monarchy." Clements himself, however, argues for a postexilic date on the basis that 11:1 presupposes the demise of the Davidic dynasty (pp 121-22).

Isa. 9:6-7	*Psalm 72*
"Prince of *Peace*" (Isa 9:6) "To the *abundance* of rule and *peace* there will be no end" (למרבה . . . ולשלום, Isa 9:7).[21] "in righteousness from now until forever" (Isa 9:7)	"May righteousness sprout in his days, and an *abundance* of *peace* until the moon is no more" (ורב שלום, 72:7). "May the mountains bear *peace* for the people, and the hills righteousness." (72:3)

Both texts associate "peace" and "righteousness," and both point to their everlasting duration. Finally, we may also note that both Isa 9:6 and Psalm 72 are introduced with attention to the "son."

Thus, some of the key Israelite prophecies of the new David (Isa 9:6-7; Jer 23:5-6; Zech 9:9-10) cited in the New Testament appear to pick up the language of Psalm 72 and are carried into the New Testament's portrait of Jesus.

Literary Echoes of Psalm 72 in Early Jewish Literature

Our chief concern here is with echoes of Psalm 72 in the *Psalms of Solomon.* It may be worth briefly noting, however, that in the Targum "the entire Psalm is taken Messianically."[22] The opening verse reads: "By the hand of Solomon, spoken through prophecy. O God, give the king Messiah the laws of Thy justice, and Thy righteousness to the son of King David." According to S. H. Levey, "The dominant rabbinic opinion is that this psalm generally, and specific verses, are messianic."

In the *Psalms of Solomon* (first century BCE), the seventeenth psalm anticipates the expected reign of "the lord Messiah" (v. 32), "the son of David" (v. 21).[23] Several verbal and thematic parallels hint that it may have been shaped, in part, by Psalm 72.

21. This translation follows the *Qere* reading of the MT. For further discussion, see J. D. W. Watts, *Isaiah 1–33* (WBC 24; Waco: Word, 1985) 131-32.

22. See S. H. Levey, *The Messiah: An Aramaic Interpretation* (Cincinnati: Hebrew Union College, 1974) 115-18.

23. The translation used here is by R. B. Wright, "Psalms of Solomon," in *The Old Testament Pseudepigrapha,* ed. J. H. Charlesworth (2 vols.; New York: Doubleday, 1983-85) 2.667-68.

Psalms of Solomon	*Psalm 72*
"He will gather a holy people whom he will lead in *righteousness;* and he will *judge* the tribes of the *people* . . ." (17:26, cf. v. 43).	"May he *judge* your *people* with *righteousness*." (72:2a)
"He will *judge* peoples and nations in the wisdom of his *righteousness.* Pause. And he will have gentile *nations serving* him under his yoke . . ." (17:29-30)	"May he *judge* your people with *righteousness*" (72:2a). "So may he rule from sea to sea . . . all *nations* may they *serve* him." (72:8a, 11b)
"He shall be compassionate to all the nations (who) reverently (stand) before him." (17:34b)	

To my knowledge, *Ps Sol* 17:21-22 is the sole messianic text containing an intercession for the Messiah, which is precisely the genre of Psalm 72.

Psalm 72: Structure and Interpretation

Although Psalm 72 was not a major source for literary citations and allusions in the New Testament, we have seen enough evidence to regard it as a source for messianic expectations. As argued above, a text may be cited simply in order to draw on its motifs or ideas. We cannot, therefore, limit our reconstruction of the early Church's understanding of the Messiah to explicit citations. (The relative lack of explicit citations in the New Testament of the "Suffering Servant" passages found in Isaiah is another case in point.)

According to the witness of the Hebrew Bible itself, Psalm 72 is every bit as much a part of the Davidic paradigm as any of the royal psalms. In fact, it contributes significantly to the messianic ideal because it is not limited in reference to the historical particulars and failures of David's sons. On the contrary, as an intercession it seeks to counter any unjust use of power by David's sons, and it thus presents an ideal.

Another impetus to read Psalm 72 in light of Jesus as Messiah and to understand Jesus in light of Psalm 72 comes from B. S. Childs's work on Scripture as canon. Even aside from historical evidence in the New Testament that the early Church drew from Psalm 72 to develop its understanding of Jesus' messiahship, the very fact that Psalm 72 and the New Testament are part of the same canon invites such comparison. The fit, we will find, is remarkable. The New Testament's notion of Messiah is based largely on the Davidic model of an "anointed one," and Psalm 72 is a constituent text for that model.

Nothing in Psalm 72 gives us reason to see its original use as different from the other royal psalms. It was not originally written as a messianic prophecy, for which its intercessory genre was ill suited. Rather, it was used on behalf of the preexilic Davidic kings of Israel/Judah. It is difficult to be more precise than this. The opening parallelism of "the king" and "the son of the king" fits the official coronation of the crown prince designate, but this may be pushing poetic parallelism too far toward prosaic literalism.

Also supporting the early origins of this psalm is the observation that its elevated court language is consistent with what we see in ancient Near Eastern texts.[24] This should not surprise us. By its own admission, the Hebrew Bible is clear that kingship was a foreign import: "Appoint for us a king to judge [or: lead] us like all the nations (have)" (1 Sam 8:5). It was an expedient quickly introduced as a rallying point to counter the military threats of Ammon and Philistia. With the ancient Near Eastern institution of monarchy came the language of the court.

Psalm 72 consists of three sections or strophes (vv. 1-3, vv. 4-11, vv. 12-17). This outline is confirmed by the symmetry revealed in the Hebrew poetic lines. The entire psalm is twenty-one lines. The first section (vv. 1-3) is three lines, and each of the remaining sections (vv. 4-11 and vv. 12-17) is nine lines. Verses 18-20 are not a constituent part of the psalm but a doxology and a colophon closing Book II of the Psalter. To each of the five "Books" of the Psalter, a doxology has been attached.[25]

The first column of the table on page 36 shows how the introductory strophe (vv. 1-3) establishes the key abstract qualities that are to characterize the king's reign. The remaining columns show the four topics treated. In all three strophes, the poor are the first of the topics mentioned. The key abstract qualities of the opening verses are predicated in the same verses with the first two topics of the poor and prosperity. These topics thus appear in all three strophes. The last two topics, the king's longevity and the nations, appear in dependent clauses (v. 17a, the final verse, is one exception), and each of these topics surfaces in the second strophe and twice in the third. Characteristic of these dependent clauses is the subordinating conjunction "so." (In Hebrew when the connective *waw* is prefixed to the imperfect in an imperatival or volitional sequence, as the jussives of the entire psalm are, it signifies a con-

24. For the ancient Near Eastern parallels, see H. J. Kraus, *Psalms 60–150: A Continental Commentary* (Minneapolis: Fortress, 1993) 78-79.

25. Since other "prayers of David" follow (Psalms 86, 101, 103, 108–110, 122, 124, 131, 133, 138–45), the colophon was probably an annotation added after Books I–II were completed but before Books III–V were attached.

	Qualities of Righteousness	Actions: Poor	Prosperity	Results: Longevity	Nations
1	Give the king your justice & righteousness				
2	With righteousness & justice	may he judge your afflicted			
3	Well-being & righteousness				
4		May he defend the afflicted & needy			
5				So may he endure like the moon	
6-7	Righteousness & well-being		may he be like rain producing . . .	as long as the moon	
8-11					So may all nations serve him
12-14		If/For he delivers the needy & afflicted			
15				So may he live	& receive tribute, prayer, & blessing
16			May grain abound on the hills		
17a				May his name be forever	
17b					So may all nations bless & be blessed in him

18-19 Doxology to Book II: Blessed be Israel's God; may his glory fill all the earth

20 Colophon: Here ends the collection of David's prayers

sequence.)[26] This structural and grammatical analysis establishes that the king's longevity and empire are contingent on his provision of fertility and prosperity and especially on his care for the poor, the first topic in each strophe. In other words, the actions to which the king is to give his attention have to do with the poor and the land's fertility; the long life of the king and his dynasty and the extent of his kingdom are results following from these actions.

The only petition in the imperative mood appears in the opening line: "Give/Grant (תֵּן) your justice to the king." In keeping with this petition, the Hebrew imperfect verbs of the psalm should probably be read as jussives: thus not as "he will . . ." but as "may he. . . ." The entire psalm, therefore, consists of petitions addressed to God, even though he is mentioned only in the first two verses.

In the opening section (vv. 1-3) the key abstract qualities that are to characterize the king's reign are presented with two word pairs. The first, "justice" and "righteousness," appears twice chiastically in the opening two verses. As a word pair, they define the social relationships under the king's reign. They are exercised on behalf of "your people," "your poor," and "the poor of your people" (in v. 4 the verb form "administer justice" [שׁפט] is used).

The second word pair, "righteousness" and "well-being" (שׁלום), appears in verses 3 and 7. As a word pair, they define primarily the ecological relationships under the king's reign, though the social dimension is not excluded. They are produced by "the mountains" and "the hills" in verse 3, and they "sprout" in verse 7 as a result of the "rain" (v. 6). Both of these key terms carry a broader range of meaning than the English terms. "Righteousness" means "right order" and "shalom" means "wholeness," and each is applied in the Hebrew Bible to both society and the cosmos (see, e.g., Ps 85:9-13). In Psalm 72 the king's righteous rule is to have direct ecological benefits. To this extent, ecology follows sociology: how the king manages the people has a direct impact on the land (cf. Hos 4:1-3).

Although these terms could be taken as abstract, and therefore meaningless (a temptation common to Israelite monarchs and all persons in power), the rest of this psalm is devoted to spelling out how these moral qualities are to be manifested. The king is to give due attention to the right order ("righteousness") and the well-being *(shalom)* of his land. And closely related, he is to give due attention to right order and justice in his society, especially to its powerless.

That the king is to care for the poor is an obvious point to be drawn from this psalm. But what is most striking is that this exercise of justice is the standard

26. See B. K. Waltke and M. O'Connor, *An Introduction to Biblical Hebrew Syntax* (Winona Lake, IN: Eisenbrauns, 1990) 563; and T. O. Lambdin, *Introduction to Biblical Hebrew* (New York: Charles Scribner's Sons, 1971) 119.

by which Israelite monarchs were to be measured — not by their military campaigns or by their building projects, as in Egypt, Assyria, and Babylonia.[27] The Israelite monarchy was to be judged by how it looked after its powerless. The powerful can take care of themselves in any society. Thus, what makes his government stand above others is how its powerless are cared for. Power is not to be exercised to attract more power. The king of Psalm 72 is to exercise it in a direction contrary to the politics of power. He acts on behalf of the powerless, not to ingratiate the nobles and the powerful. And by ignoring the politics of power, he remarkably gains a powerful empire.

This caring for the poor, in the context of this psalm, is not compassion or mercy — it is justice and righteousness. It is putting things right, the way they should be. It is what is expected, not an action taken on voluntarily. Moreover, the form of the king's justice is not merely to respond where legal counsel is called for; it is to actively "save" (vv. 4, 13). He is no mere judge; he is a savior.

Particularly noteworthy among the verses describing the king's attention to the poor is verse 14: "From oppression and violence may he *redeem* their lives." Contrary to popular usage, where the duties of redemption lie within the family, this psalm calls for the chief political figure of the land to exercise the duties of redeemer. In its original use, "to redeem" was primarily an economic term meaning "to buy back." According to Lev 25:24-25, if a man falls into poverty and must sell his property, the kinsman-redeemer is to "redeem" him from debt (cf. Jer 32:7; 1 Kings 22). According to Lev 25:47-49, if a man falls into poverty and must sell himself to a foreigner, the kinsman-redeemer is to "redeem" him from debt. For those who either have no family or no family with means, God himself becomes their redeemer (Prov 23:10-11; cf. 22:23; Jer 50:33-34). But in Psalm 72 the king is to be redeemer for his people.

The success of his reign — in terms of its longevity and international influence — is determined by his exercise of saving justice for the needy and his attention to the fertility of the land. Thus, his kingdom would extend not by military takeover but by the sheer attraction of his just society and prosperous land (on the latter, cf. Psalm 67). According to the theology of this psalm, power is to be achieved not by grasping for the most but by caring for the least.

Verse 17b echoes the Abrahamic promise of blessing to the nations (Gen 12:3, etc.), but Psalm 72 here departs from the rest of the Hebrew Bible and ties it directly to the monarchy. The structural outline above shows a progression from the moral qualities of justice and righteousness to the fulfillment of the

27. A lesson here for modern believers is to abandon efforts to impress the world by the influence we wield or by the size of our buildings or programs. Our success in attracting the world and in attracting God's blessing (in prospering our work) is contingent on the care we show for society's powerless.

Abrahamic covenant. The path to international blessing begins with Yahweh's bestowal of justice and righteousness on the king. Key to remaining on this path is the king's treatment of the poor. Thus, the fulfillment of the Abrahamic promise (17b) and the nations' offering tribute follow from the king's care for the poor and the resulting prosperity.

Although Psalm 72 does not provide a comprehensive portrait of the government of the king/Messiah, it does make clear that militarism is not the defining characteristic of his government. This runs counter to the impression one might gain from the more frequently cited royal psalms, especially Psalms 2 and 110. It becomes clear that, when faced with violent opponents, the king will exercise force. Psalm 72 itself makes brief mention of this in verse 9. But the reason his action must be decisive against enemies is not that his rule must be preserved for its own sake or even simply because it is divinely appointed (as in Psalm 2). It must be preserved because he is the agent of God's just and righteous rule, particularly on behalf of society's helpless. To this extent, Psalm 72 (and perhaps Psalm 132) comes the closest to presenting the program of the government of the king/Messiah. In the Hebrew Bible the king is both judge (cf. 2 Sam 15:1-6; 1 Kgs 3:16-28) and warrior. The latter function surfaces in times of crisis (more frequent, however, than we experience today; cf. 2 Sam 11:1), but the former defines his more day-to-day function on society's behalf.

Conclusion

The above analysis shows a remarkable conjunction of themes that are also central to the New Testament. The reign of the Davidic king or Messiah is characterized by justice, righteousness, and peace. He not only attends to the poor and outcast; he also "saves" and "redeems" them. The Abrahamic promise of blessing to the nations or Gentiles is here localized to the Davidic king or Messiah. And, finally, the natural world responds with fruitfulness to his righteous reign.

Psalm 72 may, therefore, help us to make sense of why Jesus directed so much of his attention to the marginal in society, and why so much of his Church is composed of those who are not "wise" or "powerful" or "of noble birth" (1 Cor 1:26). It helps us to make sense of why the Gentile mission is so critical to Jesus' coming and why it issues forth not from Abraham's descendants in general but from the Christ in particular. One thinks here of Gal 3:14: *"Christ redeemed* us . . . in order that in *Christ* Jesus *the blessing of Abraham* might come upon *the Gentiles."* This verse thus brings together Christ's work of "redeeming" his people and the recognition that "the blessing given to Abraham" must be channeled through the "Christ" in order to reach "the Gentiles" (i.e., the nations). It also makes clear that redemption is to result in international blessing.

And Psalm 72 helps us to make sense of a passage such as Rom 8:18-25, where following the "redemption" of God's people "creation itself will be set free from its bondage to decay." The land will finally experience "shalom." So, while Psalm 72 is only seldom cited or alluded to in the New Testament, its key themes and their unique conjunction in Psalm 72 are foundational to the New Testament and surface in some of its key passages.

The Daniel Tradition at Qumran

PETER W. FLINT

At least eleven manuscripts featuring Daniel, and a twelfth containing related material, have been found among the Dead Sea Scrolls. Since the twelve scrolls are divided by scholars into two categories (biblical and nonbiblical), I will deal with each separately here. It should be added, however, that both groups of writings raise questions that are often related. When viewed together these documents bear striking testimony to the importance with which the Qumran covenanters regarded the figure Daniel and his pronouncements.

The Book of Daniel at Qumran

A total of eight manuscripts of the book of Daniel have been discovered at Qumran; none has come to light so far at other sites in the Judean desert. This is a significant number of scrolls, and exceeds the Qumran finds for most books of the Hebrew Bible or Old Testament. Compare, for example, the far lower figures for Joshua (2 scrolls), Samuel (4), Kings (3), Proverbs (2), Job (3), Chronicles (1), and Esther (0). Not even the book of Jeremiah, of which six manuscripts were found, is as well represented as Daniel. Two of the Daniel manuscripts were discovered in Cave 1, five in Cave 4, and one (written on papyrus) in Cave 6.[1] On the basis of paleographic analysis, we

1. Details of the official or preliminary publication of the Daniel scrolls from Qumran are as follows: 1QDan[a] and 1QDan[b] appeared in D. Barthélemy and J. T. Milik, *Qumrân Cave 1* (DJD 1; Oxford: Clarendon, 1955) 150-52, with photographs in J. C. Trever, "Completion of the Publication of Some Fragments from Qumran Cave 1," *RevQ* 5 (1964-66) 323-44, esp. pl. v-vi. For pap6QDan, see M. Baillet and J. T. Milik, *Les "Petites Grottes" de Qumran. 1. Texte. 2. Planches* (DJD 3; Oxford: Clarendon, 1962) 114-16 + pl. xxiii. The Cave 4 Daniel manuscripts are being edited for the DJD series by E. C. Ulrich, who has published 4QDan[a-c] in "Daniel Manuscripts from Qumran. Part 1: A Preliminary Edition of 4QDan[a]," *BASOR* 268 (1987) 17-37; "Part 2: A

know that four were copied in the Hasmonean period (1QDan^{b}, 4QDan^{a}, 4QDan^{c}, 4QDan^{e}),[2] and four in the Herodian period (1QDan^{a}, 4QDan^{b}, 4QDan^{d}, pap6QDan).[3] Because of the ravages of time, the elements and humans, none of these finds preserves a complete copy of the book of Daniel. However, between them they preserve a substantial amount of it. These scrolls occupy a special place among the Dead Sea Scrolls, because they are nearer in time to the original composition than any other surviving manuscript of a book in the Hebrew Bible.[4]

Biblical scrolls such as these raise at least four issues for scholars, the first being the identification of their precise *contents.* Before the significance of any specific passage at Qumran can be discussed, it is crucial to determine whether or not it has been preserved in these damaged documents. The complete contents of the eight scrolls are given below in two tables: the first by manuscript, and the second in the order of the received text.[5]

Table 1: Manuscripts of the Book of Daniel

1QDan^{a}
1:10-17
2:2-6
1QDan^{b}
3:22-30
4QDan^{a}
1:16-20
2:9-11, 19-49
3:1-2
4:29-30
5:5-7, 12-14, 16-19
7:5-7, 25-28
8:1-5
10:16-20
11:13-16
plus fragments
4QDan^{b}
5:10-12, 14-16, 19-22
6:8-22, 27-29
7:1-6, 11(?), 26-28
8:1-8, 13-16
plus fragment
4QDan^{c}
10:5-9, 11-16, 21
11:1-2, 13-17, 25-29
4QDan^{d}
3:23-25
4:5(?)-9, 12-14
7:15-19, 21-23(?)
4QDan^{e}
9:12-14, 15-16(?), 17(?)
pap6QDan
8:16-17(?), 20-21(?)
10:8-16
11:33-36, 38
plus fragments

Preliminary Edition of 4QDan^{b} and 4QDan^{c}," *BASOR* 274 (1989) 3-26. The remaining manuscripts, 4QDan^{d} and 4QDan^{e}, are very fragmentary. My thanks to Prof. Ulrich for information on these two manuscripts and on the other six biblical scrolls.

2. A note on sigla: 1QDan^{a} = the first Daniel scroll from Cave 1 at Qumran; 4QDan^{b} = the second Daniel scroll from Cave 4; pap6QDan = the single Daniel scroll from Cave 6, written on papyrus.

3. Scholars date individual scrolls in the Archaic (250-150 BCE), Hasmonean (150-30 BCE), or Herodian periods (30 BCE–70 CE). The earliest Daniel manuscript is 4QDan^{c}, which Frank Moore Cross dates to the late second century BCE; see F. M. Cross, *The Ancient Library of Qumran and Modern Biblical Studies* (2d ed.; Grand Rapids: Baker, 1961) 43. For the dates of individual manuscripts, see the editions listed in n. 1 above.

4. Cf. Ulrich, "Preliminary Edition of 4QDan^{a}," 17.

5. Cf. E. Ulrich, "An Index of the Passages in the Biblical Manuscripts from the Judean Desert (Part 2: Isaiah-Chronicles)," *DSD* 2 (1995) 86-107, esp. 106.

Table 2: Contents of the Daniel Scrolls in Biblical Order

1:10-17	1QDan[a]	7:15-19, 21-23(?)	4QDan[d]
1:16-20	4QDan[a]	8:1-5	4QDan[a]
2:2-6	1QDan[a]	8:1-8, 13-16	4QDan[b]
2:9-11, 19-49	4QDan[a]	8:16-17(?), 20-21(?)	pap6QDan
3:1-2	4QDan[a]	9:12-14, 15-16(?), 17(?)	4QDan[e]
3:22-30	1QDan[b]	10:5-9, 11-16, 21	4QDan[c]
3:23-25	4QDan[d]	10:8-16	pap6QDan
4:5(?)-9, 12-14	4QDan[d]	10:16-20	4QDan[a]
4:29-30	4QDan[a]	11:1-2, 13-17, 25-29	4QDan[c]
5:5-7, 12-14, 16-19	4QDan[a]	11:13-16	4QDan[a]
5:10-12, 14-16, 19-22	4QDan[b]	11:33-36, 38	pap6QDan
6:8-22, 27-29	4QDan[b]	misc. fragments	4QDan[a]
7:1-6, 11(?), 26-28	4QDan[b]	one fragment	4QDan[b]
7:5-7, 25-28	4QDan[a]	misc. fragments	pap6QDan

Every chapter of Daniel is represented in these manuscripts, except for Daniel 12. However, this does not mean that the book lacked the final chapter at Qumran, since Dan 12:10 is quoted in the *Florilegium* (4Q174), which explicitly tells us that it is written in "the book of Daniel, the Prophet."[6]

The second issue involves the *form* of the book found in these manuscripts. Is it similar to the traditional Masoretic Text, or to the longer form found in the Greek Septuagint, or different from both of these? Despite the fragmentary state of most of the Daniel scrolls, they reveal no major disagreements against the Masoretic Text, although individual readings differ on occasion. We may conclude that seven scrolls originally contained the entire book of Daniel in a form very much like that found in the received text. However, the eighth manuscript, 4QDan[e], may have contained only part of Daniel, since it only preserves material from Daniel's prayer in chapter 9.[7] If this is the case — which is likely but impossible to prove — 4QDan[e] would not qualify as a copy of the book of Daniel.

The third issue concerns *individual readings*. Even though the Daniel scrolls are similar to the Masoretic Text, do they contain any "interesting" readings — which for biblical scholars means variants, or readings that differ from the received text? Between them the eight scrolls preserve many variants, of which some are minor and others more important. Several examples are to be found in 4QDan[a]. (a) Dan 2:24-45 describes how Daniel interpreted Nebuchadnezzar's dream of a great statue representing four kingdoms. For verse 40, which describes the fourth

6. Frgs. 1-3, col. ii, lines 3-4[a]; see J. M. Allegro, with A. A. Anderson, *Qumrân Cave 4.I [4Q158–4Q186]* (DJD 5; Oxford: Clarendon, 1968) 54-55 + pl. xix.

7. Cf. Ulrich, "Preliminary Edition of 4QDan[a]," 18.

kingdom, the received Masoretic Text reads as follows: ". . . and like iron which crushes, it will break and crush *all these.*"[8] But 4QDan^{a} has a longer text at this point: "[and like iron which c]rushes *all th[ese,* it will break and cru]sh *all the earth*" (frg. 5 ii 9). The added words ("all the earth") make better sense syntactically by allowing "all these" to be read after "which crushes." It should be noted that the longer text is also found in the Septuagint and in the Greek papyrus 967. (b) In Daniel 3, which deals with the golden statue, verse 2 opens as follows in the received text: "And *King Nebuchadnezzar* sent . . ." However, the reading found in 4QDan^{a} is substantially different: "And *Michadnezzar* sent . . ." (frg. 7, line 8).[9] One of these two variants in the scroll (the lack of "king") may reflect a different Hebrew text, but the other ("Michadnezzar") seems to be an error in textual transmission rather than an alternative ancient name for the king.[10] (c) Daniel's vision of one who looked like a man is described in chapter 10. In verse 19, after this "man" encourages Daniel, the Masoretic Text continues: "And when he spoke to me, I was strengthened and said: '*Let my lord speak,* for you have strengthened me.'" But in fragment 15 of 4QDan^{a} the following is found: "[. . .] and I said: '*Speak, my lord* (or possibly, '*My lord has spoken*'), for you have strengthened me'" (line 18).

While such variants are quite significant, minor ones cannot be ignored by anyone conducting a serious study of the book of Daniel. An example is found — once again — in Nebuchadnezzar's dream of the great statue, where for Dan 2:34 the received text literally reads: "You kept looking *until that* a stone was cut out . . ." Compare the reading found in 4QDan^{a}: "You kept looking *until* [a stone was cu]t out" (frg. 3 ii 1). Here the meaning of both texts is identical, and should be translated "until." The additional word in the Masoretic Text (*di* = "that") pertains to Aramaic style rather than a real difference in meaning.

The fourth issue: What was the *status* of the book of Daniel at Qumran? Was it regarded as Scripture, or only as an important writing alongside many others? We may conclude that Daniel was regarded as a scriptural book at Qumran for two reasons. First, the large number of preserved copies is a clear indication of Daniel's importance among the Qumran covenanters. Second, the way in which Daniel was used at Qumran is indicative of its authoritative status; for instance, the *Florilegium* (4Q174) quotes Dan 12:10 as "written in the book of Daniel, the Prophet" (frgs. 1-3 ii 3-4^{a}).[11] This reference has two implications: that Daniel was regarded by the writer as Scripture and that it may have belonged among the "Prophets." The development of the Old Testament canon is complex and need not detain us here. Yet texts such as this indicate that by

8. "All these" refers to the preceding three kingdoms.

9. In the scroll, the Aramaic text has actually been corrected from "Michnezzar" to "Michadnezzar."

10. Cf. Ulrich, "Preliminary Edition of 4QDan^{a}," 18.

11. The *Florilegium* is dated to the late first century BCE or the early first century CE.

the end of the Qumran period[12] the first two divisions of the Hebrew Bible (the Torah and Prophets) were complete, but the third division (the Writings) was still being assembled.[13] It is very possible that the Qumran covenanters viewed Daniel as the last of the Prophets, and so included his book in the second division.[14]

Other Daniel Prophecies at Qumran

Prophecies or other material related to Daniel are found in at least four more Qumran manuscripts, all of which — like Dan 2:4b to 7:28 — are written in Aramaic. Three of the scrolls are collectively known as "The *Pseudo-Daniel* Fragments," and the fourth as the *Prayer of Nabonidus.* Most commentators have assumed all three *Pseudo-Daniel* manuscripts to be part of the same document, but this is manifestly not the case since one very likely belongs to a different work.[15] Thus these four "nonbiblical" scrolls contain not two but three separate compositions. I will first discuss the two *Pseudo-Daniel* documents,[16] which recently appeared in the Oxford series Discoveries in the Judaean Desert.[17]

12. I.e., 68 CE, when the settlement was destroyed by the Romans.

13. Evidence includes the important halakhic document, 4QMMT, which shows that three groupings of Scripture were envisaged at Qumran: the "Book of Moses," the "Prophets," and "David"; cf. 4Q397 (4QMMT[d]) 14-21 C, line 10, which reads: "And we have also written to you that you should examine the book of Moses and the books of the Prophets and David. . . ."

14. Daniel is also placed among the prophetic books in the Septuagint and, in turn, Christian Bibles.

15. Cf. P. W. Flint, "4Qpseudo-Daniel ar[c] (4Q245) and the Restoration of the Priesthood," in *Hommage à Józef T. Milik,* ed. F. García Martínez and É. Puech, *RevQ* 65-68 (1996) 137-50.

16. BIBLIOGRAPHY: K. Beyer, *Die aramäischen Texte vom Toten Meer* (Göttingen: Vandenhoeck and Ruprecht, 1984) 224-25; idem, *Ergänzungsband* (1994) 105-07; J. J. Collins, "Pseudo-Daniel Revisited," in *Hommage à Józef T. Milik,* ed. García Martínez and Puech, 111-135; R. H. Eisenman and M. Wise, *The Dead Sea Scrolls Uncovered* (Shaftesbury, UK and Rockport, MA: Element, 1992) 64-68; J. A. Fitzmyer and D. J. Harrington, *A Manual of Palestinian Aramaic Texts* (Rome: Biblical Institute Press, 1978) 4-9 (text and translation) and 193 (description); P. W. Flint, "4Qpseudo-Daniel ar[c] (4Q245) and the Restoration of the Priesthood" (see n. 15 above); F. García Martínez, "Notas al margen de 4QpsDaniel Arameo," *Aula Orientalis* 1 (1983) 193-208, reprinted in *Qumran and Apocalyptic: Studies on the Aramaic Texts from Qumran,* by F. García Martínez (Leiden: Brill, 1992) 137-49; A. Mertens, *Das Buch Daniel im Lichte der Texte vom Toten Meer* (Würzburg: Echter; Stuttgart: KBW, 1971) 42-50; J. T. Milik, " 'Prière de Nabonide' et autres écrits d'un cycle de Daniel," *RB* 63 (1956) 411-15; É. Puech, *La Croyance des Esséniens en la Vie Future: Immortalité, Résurrection, Vie Éternelle* (Paris: Gabalda, 1993) 568-70.

17. J. J. Collins and P. W. Flint, "Pseudo-Daniel," in *Qumran Cave 4.XVII: Parabiblical Texts, Part 3,* ed. J. C. VanderKam (DJD 22; Oxford: Oxford University Press, 1996) 95-164.

The First Pseudo-Daniel *Document*

This work is represented by two manuscripts: 4QpsDan ar^{a} (4Q243) and 4QpsDan ar^{b} (4Q244). Analysis of the handwriting shows that both were copied in the Herodian period (probably early first century CE).[18] Although the two scrolls are fragmentary, when they are viewed together the main components of the composition can be recognized. The combined text is given below, but for purposes of clarity has been divided into sections with a brief commentary after each segment. The commentary is neither detailed nor exhaustive, but serves rather to explain difficult or obscure portions of the text. The manuscript and fragment number(s) for each passage are indicated on the right margin.

A. The Court Setting

1. . . . Daniel before . . . (243, frg. 2)
2. . . . Belshazzar . . .
3. . . . before the nobles of the king and the Assyrians (?) . . . of the king . . . (244, frgs. 1-3)
4. . . . He appointed . . .
5. . . . and how . . .
6. . . . O king, (or: the king) . . .
7. . . . before . . . (244, frg. 4)
8. . . . Daniel said . . .
9. He asked Daniel saying "On account of [what] . . . (243, frg. 1)
10. your God, and the number . . .
11. he prayed . . .
12. . . . there is . . . (243, frg. 3)
13. . . . O King (or: the king) . . .
14. . . . Daniel . . . (243, frg. 5)
15. . . . and in it was written . . . (243, frg. 6)
16. . . . Daniel, who . . .
17. . . . was found written . . .

Commentary:

Here Daniel is speaking before a king and his court, as in the book of Daniel.

Line 2. Belshazzar is described as king in Daniel 5, but was technically the vice-regent in Babylon during the absence of King Nabonidus.

Lines 15-17. Daniel seems to be explaining a writing or book, which most probably contained the overview of biblical history that follows.

18. See F. M. Cross, "The Development of the Jewish Scripts," in *The Bible and the Ancient Near East: Essays in Honor of William Foxwell Albright,* ed. G. E. Wright (Garden City: Doubleday, 1965) 170-264, esp. 176-77, fig. 2, lines 6 and 7.

B. The Primeval History

18. . . . Enoch . . . (243, frg. 9)
19. . . . after the Flood . . . (244, frg. 8)
20. . . . Noah from (Mount) Lubar
21. . . . a city . . .
22. . . . a tower, its height . . . (244, frg. 9)
23. . . . on the tower, and he sent (?) . . . (243, frg. 10)
24. . . . to inspect the building . . .
25. . . . and he scattered them . . . (244, frg. 13)

Commentary:

This passage deals with the events or material found in Genesis 5–11. It appears that the stories of creation and fall did not feature in Daniel's survey of history.

Line 18. For Enoch, see Gen 5:18-24. It has been suggested (Milik, "Prière de Nabonide," 413 n. 1) that Daniel was expounding a *Book of Enoch,* but this seems unlikely.

Line 20. In Gen 8:4 we are told that Noah's ark came to rest on the mountains (plural) of Ararat, which suggests a general location rather than a specific one. Josephus reports traditions that it settled on the mountain of the Cordaeans (*Antiquities* 1.3.6 §93) or Baris (§95) in Armenia, or alternatively on a mountain at Carrhae, southeast of Edessa (*Antiquities* 20.2.2 §24-§25; cf. Epiphanius, *Panarion* 2.1). Other traditions place Ararat in Phrygia (*Sibylline Oracles* 1.261-67) or in Parthia (Africanus, as reported by Syncellus; cf. J. J. Collins, "Sibylline Oracles," in *The Old Testament Pseudepigrapha. Volume 1: Apocalyptic Literature and Testaments,* ed. J. H. Charlesworth [Garden City, NY, 1983] 341 note u). The tradition that it grounded on Lubar, a peak of Ararat, is found in *Jubilees* (5:28; 7:1, 17; 10:15) and in the *Genesis Apocryphon* (1QapGen 12:13; cf. 10:12).

Lines 21-22. The "city" has two possible explanations. It may be one that was built after the flood, since according to *Jubilees* (7:14-17) Noah's sons built three cities in the vicinity of Mt. Lubar and named them after their wives. However, in view of reference to the tower of Babel (cf. Gen 11:1-9), the city may simply be Babylon where the tower of Babel was built (cf. v. 4, "Come, let us build ourselves a city . . .").

Line 24. Compare Gen 11:5, which says that the Lord came down to "see" the city and the tower.

C. From the Patriarchs to the Exile

26. . . . his reward . . . (243, frg. 35)
27. . . . the land . . .
28. . . . Egypt, by the hand . . . (243, frg. 11 col. ii)
29. . . . ruler in the land . . .
30. . . . fo]ur hundred [years], and from . . . (243, frg. 12)
31. . . . their [ ] and they will come out of . . .
32. . . . their crossing the river Jordan . . .
33. . . . and their children . . .
34. . . . -el and Qa[hath . . . (243, frg. 28)
35. . . . Phineha]s, Abish[ua . . .

36. . . . from the tabernacle . . .	(243, frg. 34)
37. The Israelites chose their presence rather than [the presence of God]	(243, frg. 13 + 244, frg. 2)
38. [and they were] sacrificing their children to demons of error, and their God became angry at them and said to give them	
39. into the hand of Nebuchadnezzar [king of] Babylon, and to make their land desolate of them, which . . .	
40. . . . the exiles . . .	
41. . . . After] this it shall be . . .	(243, frg. 14)
42. . . . hundred kin[gs	
43. . . . them in the midst of the p[eoples]	
44. . . . the Chaldeans . . . the children of [Israel?]	(243, frg. 7)
45. . . . the way of tr[uth]	
46. . . . [from] Israel men	(243, frg. 8)
47. . . . unchangeable	

Commentary:

The events referred to in this section are relatively straightforward, beginning with Abraham and concluding with the Babylonian exile.

Line 30. Although Exod 12:40-41 specifies 430 years, 400 years is found in Gen 15:13 and *Jubilees* 14:13. The two may be reconciled if the latter is regarded as a round number.

Line 31. The future tense ("and they will come out") is unexpected in this survey of past events. Perhaps an actual speech is being reported in this passage, including a reference to the future (cf. God's promises to Abram in Genesis 15; see Mertens, *Buch Daniel,* 46). It has also been suggested (Milik, "Prière," 413 n. 1) that Daniel is here reading to his audience the revelations of a figure from the distant past, such as Enoch.

Line 34. "Qahath" is the Aramaic form of Qohath, who was the second of Levi's three sons (Gen 46:11), the grandfather of Moses and Aaron (Exod 6:16-20), and an ancestor of Samuel (1 Chron 6:22-28). See also frg. 1, line 5 of the second *Pseudo-Daniel* document.

Line 35. The first word seems to be "Phinehas," since Abishua is listed as the son of Phinehas in 1 Chron 6:4 (Hebrew 5:30).

Line 36. This fragment possibly deals with the transfer of the ark from the Tabernacle to the Temple by David.

Lines 37-39. The two manuscripts overlap in this passage, which provides strong evidence that they belong to the same document.

Line 37. The expression "chose their presence" seems to be unique. The Israelites chose the presence of idols rather than the presence of God.

Lines 38-39. See especially Ps 106:37, "they sacrificed their sons and daughters to the demons," and verses 40-41, "Then the anger of the Lord was kindled against his people, . . . he gave them into the hand of the nations." The specific phrase "demons of error" is found at *Jubilees* 10:1. For the sacrifice of humans to idols such as Moloch, cf. 2 Kgs 16:3; 21:6; 23:10; and *Targum Neophiti I* at Deut 32:17 ("They sacrificed before the idols of the demons"). In *T. Moses* 2:8 it is predicted that four of the twelve tribes will sacrifice their sons to foreign gods and set up idols in the Temple. At Qumran the term "demons" occurs in the *Songs of the Sage* (4Q510 frg. 1, line 5), and King Solomon is apparently responsible for the exorcism of demons in 11QPsAp[a] (col. I, line 3; cf. frg. 1, line 9); See also García Martínez, "Notas," 198.

Line 39. Deliverance into the hand of Nebuchadnezzar as a punishment for Israel's sin is also found in CD 1:6, "to give them into the hand of Nebuchadnezzar, king of Babylon" (cf. *T. Moses* 3:1-3). Such passages are dependent on one or more of the following biblical texts: Jer 27:6; 29:21; 32:28; Ezra 5:12.

Line 45. For the "way of truth," compare *1 Enoch* 91:14, 18; 94:1; *Aramaic Levi* 5:12; and the "Son of God" text (4Q246, col. II, line 5).

D. The Hellenistic Era

48. . . . shall rule for years (243, frg. 21)
49. . . . Balakros
50. . . . y]ears (243, frg. 19)
51. . . .]rhos son . . .
52. . . .]os . . . years
53. . . . they will speak . . .
54. . . . a son and his name . . . (243, frg. 22)
55. . . . to them two . . .
56. . . . spoke . . .
57. . . .]s son of M[. . . (243, frg. 20)
58. . . . twenty years . . .
59. . . . which . . .

Commentary:

This section is distinguished from the preceding ones by the presentation of events as yet to come and by the presence of Greek proper names.

Line 48. From this point, as Mertens observes (*Buch Daniel,* 46), the history is no longer presented as having occurred in the past, but as still to take place in the future. Having surveyed the history of the Israelites for his audience, Daniel now proceeds to describe the future destiny of his people and of all humankind.

Line 49. This apparent reference to an actual person is one of the most significant aspects of the texts under discussion. Balakros is a relatively common Hellenistic name and is of Macedonian origin (cf. W. Pape and G. E. Benseler, *Wörterbuch der griechischen Eigennamen* [Braunschweig: Friedrich Bieweg und Sohn, 1884] 194). According to Milik ("Prière," 414 n. 1), it is a nickname for [Alexander] Balas (152-145 BCE), the third of Antiochus Epiphanes' successors. In 152 BCE Balas installed the Hasmonean Jonathan as high priest, thereby eliminating the Zadokites from the Temple hierarchy (cf. 1 Maccabees 10). Pauly's *Real-Encyclopädie* (rev. G. Wissowa; Stuttgart: Metzler, 1896) lists six men by the name "Balakros" (vol. 4, p. 238). Four of these were associated with Alexander the Great: the viceroy of Cilicia, a general in Egypt, and two commanders in Alexander's army. The other two are the father and son, respectively, of Pantauchos, an associate of Perseus. Another possibility is to view "Balakros" as a generic name. The word is used by Plutarch and Herodian in derisive references to Macedonians as people who say "Balakros" instead of "Phalakros." So "Balakros" may simply have been a nickname, perhaps a pejorative one, for Macedonians (and Greeks?) in general in the first century CE and earlier. Therefore, "Balakros" may signify any Macedonian or Greek commander, such as Alexander Balas, Alexander the Great, or even Antiochus Epiphanes.

Lines 51-52. These names are obviously Hellenistic or Roman, but they have not been positively identified. Here the narrative is apparently assigning specific terms of office to various Hellenistic rulers. One possibility for *]rhos* in line 51 is "Demetrius" (so Milik, "Prière," 414 n. 2), for which two possibilities exist: Demetrius I Soter (162-150 BCE), the second successor of Antiochus Epiphanes and Balas' predecessor, or his son Demetrius II Nikator (146-139 BCE), who conquered and succeeded Alexander Balas. However, the combination *rh* in Aramaic presumably reflects double *rho* in Greek or *rh* in Latin. A more suitable name from the Hellenistic period would be Pyrrhus; however, Pyrrhus of Epirus (319-272 BCE) is not appropriate in this context, although he had dealings with Ptolemy of Egypt.

Line 58. The number "twenty years" probably refers to the term of the Hellenistic ruler indicated in line 48. However, this number could also be "five and twenty" or any figure between twenty and thirty.

E. The Eschatological Period

60. will oppress(?) [seven]ty years (243, frg. 16)
61. with his great hand and he will save them . . .
62. powerful . . . and the kingdoms of the peoples
63. This is the h[oly] kingdom.
64. . . . until . . . (243, frg. 25)
65. . . . and the land will be filled . . .
66. . . . all their decayed carcasses . . .
67. . . . those who l]eft the wa[y of truth . . . (243, frg. 33)
68. . . . the sons of] wickedness have led astray (243, frg. 24)
69. . . . after this the elect (of . . . ?) shall be gathered . . .
70. . . . the peoples, and it shall be from the day . . .
71. . . . and the kings of the peoples . . .
72. . . . they will be d]oing to the day . . .
73. . . . their numbers . . . (243, frg. 26)
74. . . . without number . . .
75. . . . Israel . . .

Commentary:
Several key terms in this section show that it refers to the destruction and restoration associated with the eschatological age.

Lines 60-62. The placement of this fragment is not completely certain, since it could refer to God's deliverance of Israel in the Exodus, or in the return from the Babylonian exile, or at the end of time. However, the "kingdoms of the peoples" seems to denote world powers in general rather than specific ones, which does not fit the context of the Exodus or that of the return. Since the other fragments do not refer to specific kingdoms, but are instead concerned with individual rulers, these lines are most likely concerned with the eschatological period. The statement "with his great hand and he will save them" thus refers to God's eschatological intervention, when he will destroy mighty forces and kingdoms of peoples.

Line 63. The kingdom cannot be the "kingdom of the holy ones" (cf. Dan 7:18, 22, 27), which would require a different Aramaic form.

Line 66. The reference is presumably to the fallen enemy; cf. Isaiah 66, Ezekiel 38–39, etc.

Line 67. The placement and restoration of this tiny fragment is not certain.

Line 69. For the "elect," compare the "[men] called by name" in the *Damascus Document* (CD 2:11; cf. 4:4).

Line 72. For "the kings of the peoples," cf. CD 8:10, where they are identified as the serpents of Deut 32:33. Note also the "kingdoms of the peoples" in line 62 above.

Lines 73-74. These lines refer to the number of the elect. Compare Rev 7:4-9, where John hears the number of the 144,000 who were sealed from the tribes of Israel, and then "a great number that no one could count, from every nation."

The Second Pseudo-Daniel *Document*[19]

This work is found in only one manuscript, 4QpsDan ar^{c} or 4Q245, which is dated to the Herodian period (probably the early first century CE).[20] There is no physical overlap between 4Q245 and what remains of the first *Pseudo-Daniel* document (4Q243-244), but previous commentators have regarded them as part of the same composition because of the occurrence of the name Daniel in all three manuscripts. However, it now seems clear that any attempt at integrating the fragments of 4Q245 into the first document is untenable.[21] The mere occurrence of "Daniel" in each constitutes no solid basis for establishing a relationship. On the contrary, the reference to Daniel and a book in fragment 1 (lines 3-4) suggests that 4Q245 is presenting a new revelation, rather than simply continuing the one found in the first document.

A. A List of Priests and Kings

Frg. 1

1. [ ]. . .
2. [ ]. . . and what
3. [ ] Daniel
4. [ ]a book/writing that was given
5. [Lev]i, Qahath
6. [ ] Bukki, Uzzi
7. [Zado]k, Abiathar

19. For bibliography, see the list for the first *Pseudo-Daniel* document in n. 16 above.

20. See Cross, "Development of the Jewish Scripts," 176-77, fig. 2, lines 6 and 7.

21. Cf. Flint, "4Qpseudo-Daniel ar^{c} (4Q245) and the Restoration of the Priesthood," 137-50.

8. [Hi[l]kiah
9. [ ]. [ ] and Onias
10. [Jona]than, Simon
11. [ ] and David, Solomon
12. [ ] Ahazia[h, Joa]sh
13. [ ].[

Commentary:

This fragment offers several challenges to scholars. It consists mostly of a list of names, which were apparently contained in a book given to Daniel, or which Daniel is reading aloud.

Lines 1-4. The biblical book of Daniel refers to two books that may be of relevance. Dan 12:1 promises that "at that time your people shall be delivered, everyone who is found written in the book." This is the "Book of Life," which contains the names of those destined for deliverance at the resurrection. Dan 10:21 mentions a second kind of book: "the Book of Truth," whose contents are disclosed to Daniel by the angel Gabriel. These contents turn out to be a survey of Hellenistic history, culminating in the death of Antiochus Epiphanes and the resurrection of the dead. This provides a more promising analogy for the book in 4Q245, insofar as the list of priests and kings in lines 5-13 also constitutes a survey of history.

Lines 5-10. The names of several priests or high priests are given, ranging from Levi (probably) and Qahath to Onias, Jonathan, and Simon in the Hellenistic period (for the form "Qahath," see line 34 of the [combined] first *Pseudo-Daniel* document). The missing text must have contained many other names, most of which are found in the priestly list in 1 Chron 6:1-15 (Hebrew 5:27-41). The priestly list in 4Q245 probably extended to Jehozadak, Judah's last high priest before the exile (cf. 1 Chron 6:15 [Hebrew 5:41]). The extant document then suggests that Onias followed in the line of Zadokite high priests. The direct sequence of Jonathan–Simon is found only in the Hasmonean line, although both names occur in Zadokite listings: for example, Jonathan in Neh 12:11, and Simon II the Just (219-196 BCE).

Lines 11-13. The royal names are even more fragmentary than the priestly ones, but David, Solomon, and Ahaziah are clearly legible, with traces of Joash and presumably one later name also visible. This is sufficient evidence to indicate that a kingly list is being presented. Since the preceding list of priests continued into the Hellenistic era, and in view of the royal list found in 1 Chronicles 10–16, we may reasonably conclude that the list of kings continued beyond line 12 down to Zedekiah, the last king of Judah.

B. The Eschatological Conclusion

Frg. 2

1. [ ]. . .[
2. [ ]to exterminate wickedness
3. [ ]these in blindness, and they have gone astray
4. [th]ese then will arise
5. [ ]the [h]oly [ ], and they will return
6. [ ]. iniquity

Commentary:

This fragment presents language that is clearly eschatological and describes two groups of people.

Line 2. The extermination of wickedness is clearly an eschatological theme. An interesting parallel appears in 1QS 4:18, "But in the mysteries of His understanding, and in His glorious wisdom, God has ordained an end for evil, and at the time of the visitation He will destroy it for ever."

Line 3. The notion of a blind man losing his way is common in the Hebrew Bible (cf. Deut 27:18; 28:29; Isa 59:10; Zeph 1:17; Lam 4:14). Other relevant material is found in the *Damascus Document.* For instance, CD 1:9 reads: "And they were like the blind and like those who grope their way," referring to the remnant of Israel. For twenty years they were like blind men groping for the way, and subsequently they sought God with a perfect heart; God then raised up for them a teacher of righteousness (CD 1:10-11). Other passages are more negative: the "Mocker" dripped over Israel the waters of his lies and caused them to wander in a pathless wilderness or chaos (CD 1:15); and "those whom [God] hates he has allowed to go astray" (CD 2:13). We are also told that the children of Noah and Jacob (CD 3:1, 4), and even all Israel (CD 3:14; 4.1) had gone astray.

Lines 3-4. Two groups ("these . . . [th]ese") seem to be contrasted here, with two explanations possible. According to Émile Puech (*La croyance des Esséniens,* 569), the opposition of the two groups must be understood in the context of final judgment. On the other hand, this contrast may simply reflect the parting of the ways when an elect group arises in the end time.[22]

Line 4. In the words "(these then) will arise" some commentators (e.g., É. Puech and F. García Martínez) have found an allusion to Daniel 12 and to the resurrection of the dead. However, in Dan 12:2 a different verb ("they will awake") is used. Moreover, in Daniel the other group will awake "to shame and everlasting contempt," whereas in this document (line 3) they are said to be in blindness and to have gone astray — scarcely a postresurrection condition. The contrast, then, is not between two groups who are resurrected, but between some who persist in error and others who rise and walk in the way of truth (cf. CD 1:11-15).

Lines 5-6. Although these lines are fragmentary, the references to the "holy [Kingdom?]" and a return have strong eschatological connotations. "Iniquity" seems to be the last word in the manuscript, which suggests that this entire document ended with the extermination of wickedness (cf. line 2).

4QpsDan ar^{c} is rather complex and raises several interesting issues. Two of these are the inclusion of Hasmonean names and the relationship between fragments 1 and 2.

The Hasmonean Names. The inclusion of Jonathan and Simon in the list of priests in fragment 1 is surprising, since the Qumran covenanters were generally opposed to the Hasmoneans. Three explanations are possible for the presence of these names. First, they may have been included simply for chronological purposes, in order to identify the time at which the eschatological events of fragment 2 would take place. Usually, however, historical reviews in apoca-

22. Collins and Flint, "Pseudo-Daniel," 95-164.

lyptic and pseudoprophetic literature include a negative judgment on the period before the rise of the elect group (cf. the negative view of Hellenistic history in Daniel 11, and of the Second Temple period in the Enochic *Apocalypse of Weeks*). A second possibility is that the priestly and royal lists are meant to show how in the author's time these institutions have failed and now include unacceptable names. This implies that the missing portion of fragment 1 may have included negative sentiments before the mention of Jonathan and Simon, since they were not descendants of Aaron. However, this seems unlikely because there is no evidence of any comment in what remains of the priestly and royal lists. Just as Abiathar's descent seems not to have been regarded as problematic, the names Onias, Jonathan, and Simon all appear to enjoy equal status in this list.

The final, and perhaps best, explanation is that Jonathan and Simon were accepted by the author of 4Q245 as legitimate high priests and that the Hasmonean line only incurred blame when it combined the offices of high priesthood and king. This solution is favored by the fact that the priestly list is followed by a separate list of kings. The Qumran covenanters appear to have insisted on the distinction between royal and priestly offices; hence the expectation of two Messiahs — of Aaron and Israel — rather than a single one.[23] This would mean that the author of 4Q245 was not specifically anti-Hasmonean but accepted a "mixed" line of priestly succession as long as the offices of priest and king remained separate. The tenure of Simon (142-135 BCE) was thus acceptable to him, but the increased proximity of priestly and kingly offices in the period that followed was not, because the boundary between priesthood and kingship had been transgressed.

The Relationship between the Fragments. The purpose of the two lists in fragment 1 must be understood in light of the eschatological conclusion of history found in fragment 2. This passage contrasts two groups, one of which is "in blindness" and has "gone astray," while the other is said to "arise" and "return." As indicated in the commentary above, any reference to resurrection here is unlikely; a better parallel is found in the *Damascus Document,* where the blindness is merely a stage in the evolution of the community of the elect (CD 1:9). Another analogy is provided by those who are led astray by the Mocker in CD 1:15. The contrast between the groups in 4Q245 strongly suggests that those who have gone astray are not the people who will later arise and return.

How are the two groups to be related to the lists in fragment 1? The fact that one group is said to return at the end suggests a reversal of the course of history. Such reversals are standard in apocalyptic and pseudoprophetic texts; we may note, for instance, the *Apocalypse of Weeks* and the *Animal Apocalypse* in *1 Enoch* and Daniel 10–12. The list of legitimate priests in 4Q245 almost definitely ended in line 10 with Simon. This document seems to suggest that

23. See J. J. Collins, *The Scepter and the Star: The Messiahs of the Dead Sea Scrolls and Other Ancient Literature* (ABRL 10; New York: Doubleday, 1995) 74-101.

subsequent priests were not acceptable because the boundary between priesthood and kingship had been transgressed. Thus fragment 2 anticipates the eschatological restoration in accordance with the divine order — which would include a return of a priesthood that was legitimate in the eyes of God.

The Prayer of Nabonidus

Our final document is the *Prayer of Nabonidus* (abbreviated 4QPrNab or 4Q242),[24] which does not mention Daniel but is clearly related to parts of the canonical book of Daniel. 4QPrNab is written in Aramaic, and analysis of the handwriting indicates that it was copied between 75-50 BCE.[25] The edition recently appeared in the Oxford series Discoveries in the Judaean Desert.[26]

Frgs. 1, 2a-b, 3

1. The words of the pray[er] which Nabonidus, king [of Baby]lon, the [great k]ing, prayed [when he was smitten]
2. with a bad disease by the decree of [Go]d in Teima. [I, Nabonidus] was smitten [with a bad disease]

24. BIBLIOGRAPHY: K. Beyer, *Die aramäischen Texte vom Toten Meer* (Göttingen: Vandenhoeck & Ruprecht, 1984) 223-24; J. Carmignac, E. Cothenet, and H. Lignée, *Les textes de Qumrân traduits et annotés* (Paris: Letouzey et Ane, 1963) 2.289-94; F. M. Cross, "Fragments of the Prayer of Nabonidus," *IEJ* 34 (1984) 260-64; W. Dommershausen, *Nabonid im Buche Daniel* (Mainz: Matthias-Grünewald, 1964) 68-76; A. Dupont-Sommer, "Remarques linguistiques sur un fragment araméen de Qoumrân (Prière de Nabonide)," *Comptes Rendus du Groupe Linguistique d'Etudes Chamito-Sémitiques* 8 (1958-60) 48-56; idem, "Exorcismes et guérisons dans les écrits de Qoumrân," in *Oxford Congress Volume*, ed. J. A. Emerton (VTSup 7; Leiden: Brill, 1960) 246-61; J. A. Fitzmyer and D. J. Harrington, *A Manual of Palestinian Aramaic Texts* (Rome: Biblical Institute, 1978) 2-4; D. N. Freedman, "The Prayer of Nabonidus," *BASOR* 145 (1957) 31-32; F. García Martínez, "4Q Or Nab. Nueva síntesis," *Sefarad* 40 (1980) 5-25, translated as "The *Prayer of Nabonidus:* A New Synthesis," in *Qumran and Apocalyptic: Studies on the Aramaic Texts from Qumran*, by F. García Martínez (Leiden: Brill, 1992) 116-36; P. Grelot, "La prière de Nabonide (4Q Or Nab). Nouvel Essai de restauration," *RevQ* 9 (1978) 483-95; B. Jongeling, C. J. Labuschagne, and A. S. van der Woude, *Aramaic Texts from Qumran, with Translations and Annotations* (Leiden: Brill, 1976) 1.121-31; R. Meyer, *Das Gebet des Nabonid. Eine in den Qumran-Handschriften wiederentdeckte Weisheitserzählung* (Berlin: Akademie Verlag, 1962); A. Mertens, *Das Buch Daniel im Lichte der Texte vom Toten Meer* (Würzburg: Echter, 1971) 34-42; J. T. Milik, " 'Prière de Nabonide' et autres écrits d'un cycle de Daniel," *RB* 63 (1956) 411-15; S. Segert, "Sprachliche Bemerkungen zu einigen aramäischen Texten von Qumran," *Archív Orientální* 33 (1965) 190-206; A. S. van der Woude, "Bemerkungen zum Gebet des Nabonid," in *Qumrân. Sa piété, sa théologie, son milieu*, ed. M. Delcor (Leuven: Leuven University, 1978) 121-29.

3. for seven years and sin[ce] I [was made like a beast. I prayed to the gods],
4. and a diviner remitted my sins. He was a Jew fr[om among the exiles, and he said]:
5. "Pro[cla]im and write to give honor and exal[tati]on to the name of G[od Most High," and I wrote as follows]:
6. "I was smitten by a b[ad] disease in Teima [by the decree of the Most High God].
7. For seven years [I was] praying [to] the gods of silver and gold [and bronze, iron],
8. wood, stone, clay, since [I thou]ght that they were gods . . .
9. . . .
10. . . . from them . . .

Commentary:
This fragment fortunately preserves the title and introductory lines of the document, which presents the prayer of a king named "Nabunay." There can be little doubt that the king is Nabonidus (Akkadian: Nabû-na'id), the last king of Babylon (556-539 BCE), especially in view of the reference to Teiman or Teima in line 2. For a period of ten years Nabonidus was absent from Babylon and took up residence at Teima in Arabia,[27] probably because of opposition from the Babylonian clergy to his devotion to the moon god Sin and his plans to rebuild the temple of Sin at Harran.[28]

Line 2. "Disease" is the same word used for the boils of the sixth plague in Egypt (Exod 9:8-11 and Deut 28:27); cf. also Deut 28:35; Job 2:7.

Line 2. Teima is the city in Arabia where Nabonidus sojourned during his ten-year absence from Babylon (cf. Gen 25:15; Isa 21:14; Jer 25:23; 1 Chron 1:30).

Line 3. While the inscriptions give the length of Nabonidus' sojourn as ten years, seven years are mentioned in Dan 4:32 (Aramaic 4:29).

Line 3. The proposal that the king was like a beast (so F. M. Cross) is attractive in the light of Dan 5:21, ". . . and his mind was like that of a beast." The apparent transformation of the king into a beast, such as is found in Daniel 4, does not take place in 4QPrNab, where the image is metaphorical.

Line 3. The proposed reconstruction "I prayed to the gods" (so Collins) is preferable to most other reconstructions, which assume that the king underwent a conversion before the appearance of the Jewish diviner in the next line (cf. Cross and García

25. Cross, "Fragments," 260; idem, "Development of the Jewish Scripts," 190, fig. 4, esp. line 4.

26. J. J. Collins, "Prayer of Nabonidus," in *Qumran Cave 4.XVII: Parabiblical Texts, Part 3*, ed. J. C. VanderKam (DJD 22; Oxford: Oxford University Press, 1996) 83-93. My thanks to Prof. Collins for making this material available to me in advance of publication.

27. This sojourn is mentioned in the *Nabonidus Chronicle;* see T. G. Pinches, "On a Cuneiform Inscription Relating to the Capture of Babylon by Cyrus and the Events Which Preceded and Led Up to It," *Transactions of the Society of Biblical Archaeology* 7 (1992) 139-76; A. K. Grayson, *Assyrian and Babylonian Chronicles* (Locust Valley, NY: Augustin, 1975) 104-11; *ANET* 305-7.

Martínez: "I prayed to the Most High"). It is only with the arrival of this diviner that the king — after initially praying to the gods represented by idols — understands the nature of his sin and the identity of the true God.

Line 4. The first four Aramaic words are difficult to translate. Milik's initial interpretation, ". . . and my faults, God granted me a diviner" ("Prière de Nabonide," 408), has been widely rejected because the verb involved is usually used for the remission of sin, and the reading involves a textual emendation ("to him" instead of "to me"). As pointed out by Collins and García Martínez, the diviner's function in the narrative is more than merely exhorting the king to order his subjects to give glory to the name of God. The connection between healing and the forgiveness of sin is familiar from the Hebrew Bible (Ps 103:3), the *Genesis Apocryphon* (1QapGen 20:28-29), the Gospels (Matt 9:2; Mark 2:5; Luke 5:20), and the Talmud (*b. Nedarim* 41b). This connection explains why the diviner is not said to heal the king of his disease. Healing is to be understood as accompanying the forgiveness or as part of the remission process.

Line 4. The term "diviner" appears in the lists of Babylonian wise men in Dan 2:27; 4:7 (Aramaic 4:4); 5:7, 11. The meaning of the Aramaic word is "cut" (cf. Dan 2:34) and forms the basis of the noun "decree" (Dan 4:14).

Line 5. "Proclaim and write." Most scholars understand the text to mean that the king must make a written proclamation and publicly acknowledge God (cf. Dan 4:34-37 [Aramaic 4:31-34]), probably as a condition for the cure of his disease.

Line 5. "Most High" is necessary here to distinguish the true God from the other gods that were known to Nabonidus and are mentioned elsewhere in the fragment (lines 3, 7, 8).

Line 6. The remaining lines of the fragment belong to the king's letter of proclamation. Milik, Meyer, and Grelot maintain that the diviner here provides an explanation to the king for his malady ("You were smitten by a bad disease"). However, this is unnecessary, since the explanation is implicit in the command to give glory to the Most High God (so Collins). See also Daniel 4, where the decree of praise and thanksgiving includes an account of the king's affliction.

Lines 7-8. For the list of metals and other substances of which the gods were made, see Dan 5:4, 23. The clay is absent from those lists but features in the great statue in Dan 2:35, 45.

Frg. 4

1. . . . ap]art from them. I was made strong again . . .
2. . . . from it he cau[sed] to pass. The peace of [my re]pose [returned to me] . . .
3. . . . *nw*] my friends. I was not able . . .
4. . . . h]ow you are like . . .

Commentary:

This piece is badly damaged, with the leather distorted and the writing curved and cramped in appearance. The four fragmentary lines are highly ambiguous and difficult to interpret.

Line 1. "Them" may refer to the pagan gods, without whose help Nabonidus was healed (so Collins, following Dupont-Sommer, "Exorcismes et guerisons," 254).

Line 1. There are two possible meanings for the verb. Milik ("Prière de Nabonide," 409, followed by Meyer, *Das Gebet des Nabonid,* 28) translates "I had a dream" and understands the following lines in the context of a dream report (cf. Daniel 4). However, the Aramaic word has another meaning, "to be well," which seems to make better sense in the present context — hence the translation above (following Dupont-Sommer, Fitzmyer–Harrington, Beyer, and Collins).

Line 2. Although the meaning is uncertain, "he caused to pass" (so Collins) seems preferable to "you are a cedar" (Beyer).

Line 2. Milik (followed by Meyer and van der Woude) read the line by analogy with Dan 4:4-5 (Aramaic 4:1-2), which says that Nebuchadnezzar was at ease until he was disturbed by a dream. However, the first preserved word indicates that something (possibly the disease) passed from *him* or *it* (his body), not from *me,* as Milik proposed.

Line 2. For the statement "The peace of my repose returned to me . . . ," cf. Dan 4:36 (Aramaic 4:33).

Line 3. The word translated "friends" (so Fitzmyer–Harrington, Beyer, Collins) can also mean "entrails" (Milik), apparently referring to the discomfort caused by a bad dream. The reading given above seems preferable, since Nabonidus' friends would have comforted him after his restoration (cf. Dan 4:36 [Aramaic 4:33]).

Line 4. The interpretation of this line is difficult. Milik assumed the king to be addressing an angel, whom he saw in his dream and who reminded him of Daniel ("Prière de Nabonide," 409-10; cf. Meyer, *Das Gebet des Nabonid,* 40-41). It is equally likely, however, that these remarks are being addressed to the king by one of his friends, perhaps in reference to his restored appearance (cf. van der Woude, "Zum Gebet des Nabonid," 126).

What is the significance of the *Prayer of Nabonidus?* As Collins observes,[29] scholars suspected long before the discovery of 4QprNab that this king's exile at Teima was related to Nebuchadnezzar's madness as described in Daniel 4.[30] The relationship between the Babylonian and biblical accounts is complex and is beyond the scope of this essay, but two points may be made. First, the *Prayer of Nabonidus* supplies a missing link between the Babylonian traditions and the biblical book. The mention of Nabonidus and Teima and the proclamation in the first person (frgs. 1-3, line 5) may be modeled on a proclamation like the one found find in the H2 inscription from Harran. Yet the *Prayer of Nabonidus* agrees with Daniel 4 in giving the length of the sojourn as seven years (not ten, as in the Babylonian accounts). It also supports the book of Daniel in giving to a Jewish exile a pivotal role in the king's recovery. We may conclude that 4QPrNab occupies an intermediate place in the tradition between the Babylonian accounts of an historical incident and the formation of the book of Daniel.

28. The career of Nabonidus is treated in P. A. Beaulieu, *The Reign of Nabonidus, King of Babylon (556-539 B.C.)* (New Haven: Yale University Press, 1989). Nabonidus' own account is found in an inscription from Harran (abbreviated H2); see C. J. Gadd, "The Harran Inscriptions of Nabonidus," *Anatolian Studies* 8 (1958) 35-92.

29. Collins, "Prayer of Nabonidus," 86. Several of the observations that follow arise from Collins' edition of 4QPrNab.

Second, the Qumran text differs significantly both from the Babylonian accounts and from Daniel 4. Unlike the Babylonian texts, the *Prayer of Nabonidus* clearly mentions a disease (frgs. 1-3, lines 2, 6) and emphasizes the role of the Jewish diviner. It seems clear that 4QPrNab represents a Jewish transformation of the Babylonian source material, with Nabonidus' absence from Babylon treated as a kind of sickness from which he must be cured; this healing then takes place through the power of the God of Israel. The relation between the Qumran text and Daniel 4 is even more difficult and is dependent on one's reconstruction of the fragmentary *Prayer of Nabonidus.* Both texts present a Babylonian king who is afflicted for seven years, his recovery due to the intervention of a Jewish exile, and a king who speaks in the first person. The *Prayer of Nabonidus* must have contained Nabonidus' confession of the true God, although the extant fragments do not preserve it. The king also seems to issue a written proclamation in praise of the true God, as in Daniel 4. However, in the biblical text the king has a different name (Nebuchadnezzar, who was better known than Nabonidus), and the anonymous Jew is specifically named as Daniel. A final theme that is common to Daniel 4 and 4QPrNab is the king becoming like a "beast" (line 3, restored). In the Qumran text the transformation of Nabonidus into a beastly state is probably only mentioned once, whereas in Dan 4:32-33 (Aramaic 4:29-30) it is much more graphically and extensively described.

Drawing Conclusions

A rich diversity of texts relating to Daniel has been found among the Dead Sea Scrolls. As we read the documents preserved in these manuscripts, their importance for biblical scholarship and for research on the Qumran community becomes clear. With respect to the *canonical book of Daniel,* the biblical Daniel scrolls from Qumran present a text that is similar to the received Masoretic Text, but they also preserve significant variant readings. The *Prayer of Nabonidus* provides helpful evidence for understanding the growth of the canonical book and for assessing its relationship to earlier Babylonian traditions. As for the *wider group of writings related to Daniel,* these texts present evidence of a Daniel cycle, or at least a rich tradition in which a faithful Jew who has received God's power or inspiration performs wonders (Daniel, *Prayer of Nabonidus*) or predicts the future course of events (Daniel, *Pseudo-Daniel*). The nonbiblical writings remind us that a richer understanding of Scripture comes about when relevent noncanonical material is taken into account, since it offers insights into the circumstances and historical forces that gave rise to a book such as Daniel.

What was the *significance* of all these writings for the Qumran covenanters? I have already pointed out that both the large number of Daniel scrolls and allusions in the Qumran corpus indicate that the book of Daniel was viewed as Scripture at Qumran. The ready acceptance of this book and related writings by the people of Qumran is not surprising, since the type of material these documents present resonated with their own situation. Both the historical events that are depicted (such as exile in Babylon and persecution) and those which had given rise to it (Syrian domination, Antiochus Epiphanes, the need for perseverance) had affinities with their own circumstances. The Qumranites, too, felt threatened by foreign rule and needed to stand firm in the face of their fellow Jews' perceived apostasy. The eschatological contents of Daniel must also have made it a very welcome book; an apocalyptic community waiting in the desert for the end of the age would find such a writing both appealing and significant. This attitude is illustrated in the passage from the *Florilegium* referred to above,[31] which quotes Dan 12:10 but transposes the two halves of the verse: ". . . for [the wicked] shall act wicked[ly . . .], but the righteous will be purified and refined." Here this document seems to regard the Qumran community as the remnant that will practice the whole Law in the last days.[32]

30. H. Winckler, *Altorientalische Forschungen II.2* (Leipzig: Pfeiffer, 1900) 200-201; 213-14; F. Hommel, "Die Abfassungszeit des Buches Daniel und der Wahnsinn Nabonids," *Theologisches Literaturblatt* 23 (1902) 145-50; W. von Soden, "Eine babylonische Volksüberlieferung von Nabonid in den Danielerzählungen," *ZAW* 53 (1935) 81-89.

31. See n. 6 above.

Who Ascended to Heaven? 4Q491, 4Q427, and the Teacher of Righteousness

MARTIN G. ABEGG, JR.

But who has stood in the council of the Lord, *that he should see and hear his word? Who has given heed to his word and listened? (Jer 23:18)*

This study will attempt to answer this ancient question of the prophet Jeremiah. I invite the reader to join in a bit of detective work in order to determine the identity of the man who dared stand and answer Jeremiah's challenge with a resounding response equivalent to "I have!":

> "[My] office is among the gods!" (4Q427 7 i 11)
> "For I have sat on a [throne]e in the heavens." (4Q491 11 i 13)

The evidence for this 2,000-year-old claim is to be found in the Dead Sea Scrolls or, more accurately, the Dead Sea fragments. It is worthwhile to review a bit of background that will help us understand more clearly the nature of our investigative task. In 1956, after the discovery of Cave 4 and its marvelous contents in the marl terrace above Wadi Qumran, a group of men convened to assemble the largest jigsaw puzzle of all time. Their task was to piece together tens of thousands of fragments into what came to be recognized as hundreds of manuscripts. To capitalize for the sake of illustration on the jigsaw puzzle itself, imagine that we had to reconstruct hundreds of 500- and 1,000-piece puzzles — the pieces having been mixed together — after someone has sneaked in and thrown away approximately 90 percent of the original material. We come armed with a few of the original boxes complete with pictures, but for the large majority we have no clue of the appearance of the original image. At the end of the initial sorting process, we review our progress and notice that though we have hundreds of piles waiting for us to study individually, few of the piles represent the product of the same puzzle manufacturer. In other words, we are dealing with hundreds of puzzles from nearly the same number of puzzle companies. We suspect that a number of the individual piles may indeed represent several puzzles whose similarly sized pieces and comparable pictures have caused us to sort amiss. Several researchers have pointed to an analogous result of the initial sorting of the Dead Sea fragments and contemplated the hundreds of piles representing a nearly identical number of scribal hands. Scholars like Devorah Dimant, who has labored over the *Pseudo-Prophets* texts (4Q383-390),[1] and Esther Eshel, who has worked with 4Q471,[2] have suggested that their particular pile of fragments represents two or more manuscripts written by the same scribe, or two scribes with very similar writing styles.

4Q491 Fragment 11 Column i

It is with this bit of background that I bring to you our first exhibit, a pile of some sixty fragments labeled 4Q491. Together these fragments have been identified as the first Cave 4 manuscript of the *War Scroll,* and they are therefore referred to collectively as 4QM[a]. The Cave 1 *War Scroll* (1QM), known since 1947, describes the events at the end of the age when the forces of good — the "Sons of Light" — engage the forces of evil — the "Sons of Darkness" — in a battle whose result will be "winner take all." In a final series of seven battles — an eschatological world series, if you will — we find the opponents tied with three victories apiece as the seventh battle begins. God comes to the aid of the Sons of Light, and the seventh and deciding engagement results in a resounding victory for the forces of righteousness. According to the original round of research, published in 1982 by Maurice Baillet,[3] 4Q491 represents a copy of the *War Scroll* that differs from its Cave 1 counterpart (1QM) at many points. For the purpose of this study, one group of fragments of 4Q491 — collectively labeled as fragment 11 — is especially important. In the supposed first column of this fragment, we find a hymn whose statements promise to aid our quest for the identity of the character who dared answer the challenge of the prophet Jeremiah. Line 18 of this hymn reads:

1. D. Dimant, "New Light from Qumran on the Jewish Pseudepigrapha — 4Q390," in *The Madrid Qumran Congress: Proceedings of the International Congress on the Dead Sea Scrolls, Madrid, 18-21 March, 1991,* ed. J. Trebolle Barrera and L. Vegas Montaner (2 vols.; STDJ 11; Leiden: Brill, 1992) 2.405-13.

2. E. Eshel and H. Eshel, "4Q471 Fragment 1 and Ma'amadot in the War Scroll," in *The Madrid Qumran Congress,* ed. Trebolle Barrera and Montaner, 2.611-20; E. Eshel and M. Kister, "A Polemical Qumran Fragment," *JJS* 43 (1992) 277-81.

3. M. Baillet, *Qumrân Grotte 4, III (4Q482–4Q520)* (DJD 7; Oxford: Clarendon, 1982) 12-68.

> [Fo]r I am reck[oned] with the gods, [and] my glory with *that of* the sons of the King.

Lines 12-14 make an even greater claim:

> . . . a mighty throne in the congregation of the gods.
> None of the ancient kings shall sit on it, and their nobles [shall]not[ ]
> [There are no]ne comparable [13][to me in] my glory,[4] no one shall be exalted besides me;
> None shall associate with me.
> For I have sat on a[thron]e in the heavens, and there is no one [14][ ]. . . .
> I am reckoned with the gods and my abode is in the holy congregation.

Who is this person, that he would dare make such a fantastic claim? In 1982 Maurice Baillet proposed the angel Michael, a figure who is mentioned in column 17 of 1QM: "God will send eternal support to the company of his redeemed by the power of the majestic angel . . . Michael" (1QM 17:6).[5] In 1985 Morton Smith rightly questioned Baillet's proposal. In a seminal study of 4Q491, Smith noted that Michael is never mentioned in the text and pointed out several instances where the contents of the speech are more suitable to a human being than an archangel. In attempting to identify the speaker of 4Q491, Smith stated, "One thinks immediately of the author of the *Hodayot*." Smith proceeded, though, to outline several points of contrast between 4Q491 and 1QH. He concluded that 4Q491 provides important pre-Christian evidence of "speculation on deification by ascent towards or into the heavens, speculation which may have gone along with some practices that produced extraordinary experiences understood as encounters with gods or angels."[6] In a conference paper delivered in 1991 John J. Collins extended and refined the observations of Smith, situating 4Q491 in the context of speculation on heavenly enthronement in pre-Christian Jewish texts. Collins suggested the Teacher of Righteousness as a possible candidate for the speaker in 4Q491 but noted problems with such an identification. He concluded, "The author of this hymn may have been, not the Teacher, but a teacher in the late first century

4. ל]וא דומי [לי ב]כבודי. It would appear that the scribe wrote a *yod* (דומי) for *heh* (דומה). On this characteristic, see E. Qimron, *The Hebrew of the Dead Sea Scrolls* (HSS 29; Atlanta: Scholars Press, 1986) §100.34.

5. Baillet, *Qumrân Grotte 4, III,* 26.

6. Morton Smith, "Ascent to the Heavens and Deification in 4QM[a]," in *Archaeology and History in the Dead Sea Scrolls: The New York University Conference in Memory of Yigael Yadin,* ed. L. H. Schiffman (JSPSup 8; JSOT/ASOR Monographs 2; Sheffield: JSOT Press, 1990) 181-88 (the quote is from pp. 187-88). A revised version of Smith's study appeared as "Two Ascended to Heaven — Jesus and the Author of 4Q491," in *Jesus and the Dead Sea Scrolls,* ed. J. H. Charlesworth (ABRL; New York: Doubleday, 1992) 290-301. Smith's argument that the claims of 4Q491 are tantamount to deification is open to question.

B.C.E."[7] In a revised version of his paper, Collins has stated that "perhaps the best candidate for identification with the exalted teacher of this hymn is the one who would 'teach righteousness at the end of days' (CD 6:11) or the eschatological 'Interpreter of the Law' of the Florilegium (4Q174)."[8]

By the end of the study, it will be clear that my proposals build on the observations of Smith and Collins. With this review of the evidence behind us, I would now like to give a brief account of my experience with 4Q491. We will then need to do a bit of "lab work" before we can come to our own conclusions. Since some of the following sections are unavoidably technical, I will conclude my discussion of 4Q491 with a less detailed synopsis of the results.

Physical Evidence

My first impression upon seeing the plates of 4Q491 suggested that, on overall appearance, the fragments should be divided into two groups: one group belonging to a manuscript that was copied elegantly, and another group belonging to a manuscript that was copied roughly. This same perception must have occurred to the initial team of researchers, since the larger fragments that reflect, respectively, these two characteristics are never photographed together on any of the fifteen photographic plates. I have assigned the siglum "I" to the group of fragments written in the rougher, less elegant hand and the siglum "II" to the group written in the refined, more elegant hand.[9]

Although the fragments of these two hypothetical manuscripts have neatly justified right margins and straight lines, in none of the photographs does there remain a trace of scribal ruling. As is customary for texts copied at Qumran, the letters appear to have been hung from this now invisible "dry" line.

Since we have no fragments straddling the margin between columns, nothing can be said about this spacing.[10] No seams have been preserved to indicate the number of sheets originally present. Nor do we possess any meaningful data about the column height.[11]

7. J. J. Collins, "A Throne in the Heavens: Apotheosis in Pre-Christian Judaism," in *Death, Ecstasy, and Other Worldly Journeys,* ed. J. J. Collins and M. Fishbane (Albany: State University of New York Press, 1995) 43-58 (quote from 55).

8. J. J. Collins, *The Scepter and the Star: The Messiahs of the Dead Sea Scrolls and Other Ancient Literature* (ABRL 10; New York: Doubleday, 1995) 136-53 (quote from 148).

9. Following the pattern of the current spate of renumbered manuscripts, manuscript I would receive the designation 4Q491, while manuscript II would be labeled 4Q491[a].

10. Baillet's join between fragment 11 columns i and ii, which he himself calls "seulement probable" (*Qumrân Grotte 4, III,* 27), is rejected in my paleographic division of the manuscript.

11. In private conversation, Esther Eshel has informed me of a discussion with Hartmut Stegemann in which he claimed that the manuscript (as published by Baillet) was not sufficiently extensive to determine the order of the material or original dimensions of the scroll.

We have a bit more information concerning line length. Baillet reconstructed fragment 1-3, which I have consigned to manuscript II, to a monstrous line length of 130 characters. This is by far the widest column width found among the Dead Sea Scrolls. The width of fragment 11 column i — which I have also assigned to manuscript II — is at least 80 characters, but it is not complete. In contrast, fragment 8-10 of manuscript I reveals a width of 75 letters. Fragment 11 column ii of manuscript I is nearly identical in width. I have assigned these two fragments to manuscript I because of their less elegant script.

Whereas manuscript I has a constant line height of 3.7 mm, the line height of manuscript II suggests an additional subdivision. A height of 4.0–4.1 mm is characteristic of most of the material, but fragment 12 and the eight fragments that Baillet joined as fragment 11 column i, the so called "Song of Michael," have a uniform height of 4.3 mm. Although it is not impossible for a single manuscript to have different line heights — the change between columns 44 and 45 of the *Temple Scroll* provides one example — this is a rare feature. For this reason, I have separated from manuscript II the fragments with the greater line height — fragment 11 column i and fragment 12 — and have assigned them to a third hypothetical manuscript, labeled manuscript III.[12]

Paleographic Evidence

Paleography is the study of early handwriting styles. It has proved invaluable for marking off manuscripts and for assigning dates to them. Recent carbon 14 tests on selected Dead Sea Scrolls have served to verify, in the main, the results of this paleographic study.[13]

Paleographically, the scripts of all three of the proposed manuscripts share many characteristics with the script of 4QSam^a (4Q51), which F. M. Cross describes as a "late Hasmonaean or early Herodian book hand."[14] He has dated 4QSam^a to ca. 50-25 BCE and proposed a date of ca. 30-1 BCE. for 1QM.

In Figure 1 (p. 66), I have reproduced actual letters from scanned images of two of the three proposed manuscripts. The left column (manuscript I) reproduces letters from Baillet's fragment 11 column ii. The right column (manuscript III) reproduces letters from 4Q491 fragment 11 column i. Manuscript II, which is not represented, was in my estimation written by the same scribe as manuscript III. As I have noted, manuscript II differs from manuscript III in line height — and, therefore, in the size of the letters themselves — as

12. Manuscript III would receive the designation 4Q491^b.

13. None of the manuscripts discussed in this paper has as yet undergone radiocarbon testing.

14. F. M. Cross, "The Development of the Jewish Scripts," in *The Bible and the Ancient Near East: Essays in Honor of William Foxwell Albright*, ed. G. E. Wright (Garden City: Doubleday, 1965) 138.

FIGURE 1. Manuscripts I and II

Manuscript I (4Q491 11 ii)   Manuscript III (4Q491 11 i)

well as in line length. A brief description of the letters reproduced in Figure 1 will aid in clarifying the differences that I have noticed between the fragments represented by these columns.

To begin with, the *aleph* is a significant and consistent indicator of the two hands. In manuscripts II and III, most examples have the appearance of a three-stroke letter. The left leg is slightly bowed and begins just shy of the top of the oblique axis. The final stroke, the right arm, begins near the middle of the axis and is generally characterized by a rudimentary *keraia* (horn-like apex of a letter). The overall effect of the letter is often that of an *X*. In manuscript I, the *aleph* shows the characteristics of a two-stroke letter. The axis and left leg take on the look of an inverted *v*, with the right arm beginning near the bottom of the oblique stroke. The overall appearance of the completed letter is often that of the letter *N*.

The medial *kaph* in manuscripts II and III is easily distinguished from the *beth*, often having the characteristic bent-back or figure-3 shape. Also distinctive is the large size and the slanting extension of the base line. In contrast, manuscript I reveals a smaller form with a truncated base line. This quality is also evident in the medial *mem* and is generally true for all letters with base lines or leftward extensions.

The final *mem* in both manuscripts shows the ticked head and extreme length characteristic of the late Hasmonean script. Apparent with this letter is the line height of the two manuscripts. The *mem* of manuscript I is noticeably smaller. The extreme length of manuscript III takes full advantage of the greater line height.

Our two hypothetical scribes produced quite pleasing but different final *nuns*. In manuscript I, the *nun* shows the familiar truncation of any leftward strokes, whereas in manuscript III the *nun* extends boldly to the left.

The *shin* is perhaps the most distinctive character in the fragments. In manuscript III it is often very nearly symmetrical or slightly open to the right. The most unique property is the middle arm, which has become a mere dot. The *shin* of manuscript I is more traditional in being inclined to the right, with the center arm projecting from the middle of the left leg.

Orthographic Evidence

Orthography is the study of spelling conventions. Unlike modern practice, spelling was often quite variable in antiquity. Orthographically, all the fragments of 4Q491 are characterized by what Emanuel Tov has called "Qumran orthography and language."[15] Indeed, in consistent use are the fuller spellings of כל, "all," as כול; of לא, "no," as לוא; and of כי, "for" or "that," as כיא.

In its use of pronominal suffixes, 4Q491 shows a decided preference for the longer forms. According to Elisha Qimron, the standard second-person-masculine-singular form כה- is found in 900 out of 1,060 instances, or 85 percent of the time, in nonbiblical Qumran texts. This same form is found 8 times in manuscript I (fragment 8-10 lines 8 [2x], 10 [3x], 12 [2x], and 14) against 3 instances of the shorter form (fragment 8-10 lines 6 [2x], 7).[16] This long form is found only once in manuscript II (fragment 5-6 line 1) with no short forms. The second-person suffix is not found at all in manuscript III. Of course, no noticeable difference can be ascribed to this data. In instances of the second-person-plural, the only case in manuscript I is attested in the short form (fragment 13 line 2). The only examples in manuscript II are long (fragment 13 line 4 [2x]), while no second-plural forms are found in manuscript III. Although the sample is small, a slight variation between long and short forms is evident in manuscript I, whereas manuscript II shows a consistent preference for the long form.

We have a larger group of examples in the third-person-plural suffixes. Qimron's count reveals that the long forms, מה- or המה-, are much less frequent

15. E. Tov, "The Orthography and Language of the Hebrew Scrolls Found at Qumran and the Origin of These Scrolls," *Textus* 13 (1986) 31.

16. Qimron, *Hebrew of the Dead Sea Scrolls*, §322.12.

in the sectarian material from Qumran; they are attested in only 250 of the 900 possibilities, or 28 percent of the time. Of these 250 instances, fully 191 cases — 76 percent — occur in the *Temple Scroll*, making the long form relatively rare elsewhere.[17] In manuscript I, we find 10 instances of the long form (fragments 8-10 line 9 [2x]; 10 ii 14; 11 ii 7, 12; 13 4, 5, 7; 15 5; 24 5) against 5 examples of the short suffix (fragments 11 ii 20, 21; 13 4, 5; 26 2). Manuscript II is consistent with 13 instances of the long form (fragments 1-3 lines 3, 6 [2x], 7 [2x], 8 [3x], 9 [2x], 10, 12, 15) with no short suffixes.[18] Manuscript III has 3 long suffixes (fragment 11 i 12, 13, 15) with no short suffixes. Again, manuscript I varies slightly in its practice, while manuscripts II and III are consistent in their preference for the longer form.

We now come to diagraphs. A diagraph is an additional letter following consonants used to indicate a vowel; the consonants that serve as diagraphs are also known as *matres lectiones*, "mothers of reading." The normal diagraph is *aleph*, usually appearing in the final position (‎-יא, ‎-וא). This is the case in the word כיא, the fuller spelling of which we have already noted. In addition to this regular example, manuscript III provides eight surprising instances of this feature. Seven of these concern the first-person-singular suffix ‎-י, often spelled with the addition of an *aleph:* ו]כ̊בודיא (fragment 11 i 18), יגו{ו}נ̊י̊א (fragment 11 i 17), ב̊יא (fragment 11 i 13, 15, 16), לי̊א (fragment 11 i 15), and the personal pronoun itself: אניא (fragment 11 i 18).[19] The eighth is the name of the mysterious book: הגי, "Hagi," or "meditation."[20] In manuscript III, the "just" are admonished to ה]ש̊מיעו בהגיא רנה, "proclaim the meditation of joy" (fragment 1 i 21). Although no first-person-singular suffixes are extant in manuscripts I and II, in manuscript II the word לפיא occurs twice (fragments 1-3 8; 20 2). This form is attested elsewhere only at 1QpHab 2:2 (מפיא) and 4Q415 11 4. Also worth noting is the medial *aleph* in the unique spelling of י]אחאו (fragment 1-3 9), where it designates the vowel *e*.

Although diagraphs with *aleph* are preferred in manuscript II, the manuscript contains a unique spelling in fragment 1-3 17 and possibly 1-3 9: והלוייים, "and the Levites." This is surely significant against the spelling והלויאים in fragment 13 6 of manuscript I. This latter spelling is found elsewhere only at 4Q285 8 1.[21]

17. Qimron does not include the whole of 4Q491 in his statistics but uses only fragments 8-10, which were published previously by Claus-Hunno Hunzinger (*Hebrew of the Dead Sea Scrolls,* §0.12).

18. The longer form is used in less than 20 percent of the cases in 1QM.

19. See fragment 11 i 12, 13, 14 [2x], 15, 16, 17; and fragment 12, where the first-singular suffix occurs without the diagraph *aleph.*

20. See further examples: CD 10:6 (4Q266 17 iii 4; 4Q270 10 iv 17), 13:2; 14:8; 1QSa 1:7; 4Q417 2 i 16, 17; 4Q491 11 i 21; and 11Q14 5 1.

21. Note that manuscript I of 4Q491 also has כתיאים (fragments 10 ii 8, 10, 12; 11 ii 8, 19; 13 5).

As with the paleographic evidence, the orthography of our texts suggests that we are right to distinguish manuscript I, with its preference for but lack of consistency in the heavy suffixes of the second and third persons, from manuscripts II and III, with their consistent use of fuller suffixes. We also see, especially in manuscript III, a preference for diagraphs with the *aleph* following the *yod.*

Literary Evidence

The most dramatic difference between the three reconstructed manuscripts of 4Q491 is to be discovered in their textual relationship to 1QM. The most difficult problem is clarifying the extremely complex relationship between manuscript II of 4Q491 and 1QM. In Baillet's reconstruction, fragment 1-3 of 4Q491 echoes passages in columns 2, 7, 16, and 17 of 1QM but contains no running parallels longer than a few words. Manuscript III of 4Q491, which Baillet labeled "Song of Michael," is not represented at all in 1QM.

In contrast to these data, manuscript I, fragment 8-10 of 4Q491 is parallel in its entirety to 1QM 14. The top of the reconstructed column that Baillet labeled fragment 10 column ii is closely parallel to 1QM 16. Thus more than 40 percent of manuscript II of 4Q491 has direct parallels in 1QM. The nonparallel portions of manuscript II appear, on the whole, to represent a more detailed description of the final seven battles described in 1QM 15:4–18:8.

Manuscript III of 4Q491 contains a number of Hebrew terms that are rare in the Dead Sea Scrolls. These words point to a definite generic connection with a select group of scrolls. The term for "fine gold" (פז) occurs at 4Q491 fragment 11 i 18 and only elsewhere at 4Q381 19 i 4; 4Q427 7 i 12; and 4Q471 6 8. Another term for "gold" (כתם) is found in 4Q491 fragment 11 i 18 and elsewhere at 2Q18 2 10; 4Q179 1 ii 11; 4Q427 7 i 12; 4Q471 6 8. The command "Proclaim!" (השמיעו), which occurs in 4Q491 manuscript III at fragment 11 i 21, is present elsewhere in 1QH 27:1; 4Q401 14 ii 7; 4Q402 9 3; 4Q431 1 6; and 4Q427 7 i 17, 7 ii 7, 22.[22]

This survey establishes the relationship of three texts, namely, 1QH (the *Hôdāyôt* or *Thanksgiving Hymns* from Cave 1), 4Q427 (or 4QH[a], the first manuscript of the *Thanksgiving Hymns* from Cave 4), and fragment 6 of 4Q471. The remainder of this study will investigate the relationship between manuscript III of 4Q491, fragment 7 of 4Q427, and the *Thanksgiving Hymns.*

22. For a more extensive list, see E. Schuller, "A Hymn from a Cave Four *Hodayot* Manuscript: 4Q427 7 i + ii," *JBL* 112 (1993) 626.

Conclusions Concerning 4Q491

Based on the overall appearance, varied line height, and paleography of the fragments of 4Q491, I have apportioned the material into three groups, designating them 4Q491 manuscripts I, II, and III.

Based on the divergent spelling of לויים, I have demonstrated that manuscripts II and III use the diagraph *aleph* and more consistently prefer the heavy pronominal suffixes כה-, כמה-, and מ(ה)ה-. Thus, distinct orthographic features distinguish the fragments of manuscript I from those of manuscripts II and III.

In my comparison of 4Q491 with 1QM, I have shown that manuscript I of 4Q491 contains material that is paralleled in 1QM as well as an expanded description of the final skirmishes in the war against the Kitians recounted in 1QM 15–18. In contrast, manuscript II of 4Q491 shares no common text with 1QM but instead echoes material that is scattered throughout 1QM. Manuscript III of 4Q491, the misnamed "Song of Michael," shows no contextual connection at all with 1QM. It is best understood as an independent hymnic work containing the bold declarations of one who claims to sit in the council of heavenly beings. As we will now see, this composition has a clear generic relationship to the *Thanksgiving Hymns.*

4Q427 Fragment 7 Column i

We now move on to our second exhibit. In 1993, Eileen Schuller published a study of 4Q427. This document from Cave 4 is a copy of a work previously known from Cave 1, the *Hôdāyôt* or *Thanksgiving Hymns.*[23] The manuscript from Cave 4 is one of six fragmentary copies of the *Thanksgiving Hymns* found in this cave. It is of special importance because it preserves a large fragment that, while containing enough overlapping material to allow its placement at the end of its Cave 1 counterpart, also contains a good bit of additional material. This additional material plays a significant role in our investigation. The pertinent section of this document reads as follows:

> [6][ ] . . . [7][ ] . . . [8][ ]among the gods [9][ ] with the tongue he will arouse (?) me [10][ ] companion to the holy ones and it shall not come [11][*to] my [glor]y no one compares. For as for me, [my] office is among the gods,* [12][and glory and majes]ty is not as gold [ ]for me. *Neither pure gold or precious metal*[13] [for me] shall [not] be reckoned to me. Sing praise, O beloved ones, sing to the King [14][of glory, rejoice in the congre]gation of God. Sing for joy in the tents of salvation, praise in the [holy] habitation. [15][E]xalt together with the eternal

23. Schuller, "Hymn," 605-28.

> hosts, ascribe greatness to our God and glory to our King. [16][Sanct]ify his name with mighty speech, and with eminent oration lift up your voice together. [17][At a]ll times *proclaim,* speak it out, exult with eternal joy. (4Q427 7 i 6-17)

The italicized portions of this text show clear verbal parallels to manuscript III of 4Q491. Our study of genre in connection with that text has already highlighted the distinctiveness of this vocabulary. What we have before us in 4Q427, then, is an additional proclamation of our bold and mysterious figure who claims to be reckoned with the gods. Again, though, this figure goes unnamed.

1QHôdāyôt *(Thanksgiving Hymns)*

We now move on to our third and final exhibit, the Cave 1 manuscript of the *Thanksgiving Hymns* (1QH), which will enable us to conclude our investigation and determine the identity of our audacious individual. 1QH has been studied for nearly half a century. The name for this collection of psalms — *Hôdāyôt* in Hebrew, *Thanksgiving Hymns* in English — reflects the repeated introductory phrase **אודך אדוני**, "I give thanks to You, O Lord." A secondary formula, **ברוך אתה אדוני**, "Blessed are You, O Lord," appears to be a variant. Due to the fragmentary nature of the manuscript, only twenty of these introductions are extant. While at least ten additional songs can be determined contextually, the original manuscript may have contained as many as fifty.

The intensely personal tone of the *Thanksgiving Hymns* stands in sharp contrast with the rest of the Dead Sea Scrolls. The author speaks of himself in the first person and recounts an amazing history of persecution from those opposed to his ministry. The work's individual presentation and its implied author's sense of divine vocation have led many researchers to conclude that the hymns were written by the founder of the Qumran community, the Teacher of Righteousness himself.

Aided by clues in the Cave 1 manuscript of the *Thanksgiving Hymns*, additional information from the six Cave 4 manuscripts of the work, and the research of others involved in the same task, I would like to propose a composite manuscript. This hypothetical manuscript would be twenty-seven columns in length and would incorporate 4Q427 at the end, as columns 26 and 27.[24]

Some researchers have attempted to isolate from the *Thanksgiving Hymns*

24. For a discussion of the problems entailed in such a reconstruction, see É. Puech, "Quelques aspects de la restauration du Rouleau des Hymnes (1QH)," *JJS* 39 (1988) 38-55.

those psalms composed by the Teacher of Righteousness himself. According to some, columns 10-16 are the true Teacher hymns; according to others, columns 13-16 are. I believe this issue should be examined anew, for my own initial review has suggested that the same dramatic themes are present throughout the *Thanksgiving Hymns:* (1) humankind is a vessel of clay and prone to sin; (2) God is the creator and determiner of all things; (3) the wicked persecute the righteous but God sustains them; (4) God has commissioned the author of the psalms as his mouthpiece.

It would appear that others are beginning to reach a similar conclusion. A pattern can be discerned within the *Thanksgiving Hymns* that includes the following review of the ancient author's understanding of his mission: God has given him an empowering spirit that allows him special insight into the divine will (1QH 4:26 [17:26]);[25] God has opened his ears to wonderful divine mysteries (1QH 9:21 [1:21]); God has used him as a channel for his works (12:8 [4:8]) and as a mouthpiece for his words (1QH 16:16 [8:16]).

If we have reconstructed the *Thanksgiving Hymns* properly, these themes continue to the end in the form of 4Q427, where the psalmist claims to have sat in the very council of God with the heavenly beings. Given the repetitive, almost cyclical nature of the *Thanksgiving Hymns,* it is also quite possible that manuscript III of 4Q491 comes from a psalm that followed the current broken end of the *Thanksgiving Hymns.*

Conclusion

Whatever we conclude about the original setting of the statements in manuscript III of 4Q491, it appears clear that the answer to our quest for the identity of the implied speaker of this text and of 4Q427 rises and falls with our judgment concerning the author of the *Thanksgiving Hymns.* Although we cannot be absolutely certain of the speaker's identity, the Teacher of Righteousness, the acknowledged founder of the Qumran community, is a strong candidate.

Such an identification of the implied speaker does not necessarily mean that the historical Teacher of Righteousness actually claimed to have ascended to heaven and taken his place among the gods. The Teacher of Righteousness might have made such a claim, but it is also possible that such a claim was made *on behalf of* the Teacher of Righteousness by the author(s) of the texts we have examined.

25. Bracketed references refer to the original transcription of the manuscript by E. L. Sukenik, *The Dead Sea Scrolls of the Hebrew University,* ed. N. Avigad and Y. Yadin (Jerusalem: Magnes, 1955).

Whatever the actual state of affairs, to identify the psalm of self-exaltation in 4Q491 as part of the *Thanksgiving Hymns* allows us to lay aside another possible identification of the implied speaker of 4Q491: God himself. This is an identification that occurred to me when I first read this text, but the writer of the *Thanksgiving Hymns* clearly distinguishes himself from God when he writes:

> Who is like you among the gods, O Lord? (1QH 15:28 [7:28])
> Behold, you are chief of the gods and king of the glorious. (1QH 18:8 [10:8])

In closing, I would like to mention a New Testament parallel to the evidence we have examined. It is tempting to associate the claims of heavenly ascension made by or on behalf of the Teacher of Righteousness with the ascension of Jesus. However, the lack of transparent messianic claims associated with the Teacher, coupled with the lack of any expectation of ascension associated with any known Qumran messianic hope, makes the association with Jesus or any other messianic figure rather doubtful. A better parallel than Jesus would be the apostle Paul, who was also acknowledged as a teacher of righteousness. In a setting considerably humbler than what we have in 4Q491 and 4Q427, Paul makes his own fantastic claim:

> I know a man in Christ who fourteen years ago — whether in the body I do not know, or out of the body I do not know; God knows — such a man was caught up to the third heaven. And I know how such a man — whether in the body or apart from the body, I do not know; God knows — was caught up into Paradise and heard inexpressible words, which a man is not permitted to speak. On behalf of such a man will I boast; but on my own behalf I will not boast, except in regard to my weaknesses. (2 Cor 12:2-5)

The Expectation of the End in the Dead Sea Scrolls

JOHN J. COLLINS

The notion that history is linear and proceeds towards a foreseeable end, or eschaton, is one of the defining trademarks of Western civilization. The origin and source of that concept is disputed. A case can be made, and has been made, for tracing it back to the Iranian prophet Zoroaster.[1] A clearer and stronger case, however, can be made for the Hebrew prophets, some of whom lived two centuries before the traditional date for Zoroaster.[2] The spread of this concept of history in the West was undoubtedly due to Jewish and Christian tradition, and while this tradition was influenced to some degree by Zoroastrianism, the influence was of secondary importance and relatively late.[3] It was above all in the apocalyptic literature, which flourished in Judaism during the Hellenistic and Roman periods, that an elaborate end-oriented view of history was developed. Apocalyptic literature was not uniform; it embraced different modalities of this view of history. One distinctive mode of eschatological expectation has been brought to light in the last half century in the Dead Sea Scrolls.[4] While the Scrolls are not necessarily a coherent or consistent body of literature, there is wide agreement that they contain a core group of documents that represent

1. So Norman Cohn, *Cosmos, Chaos and the World to Come: The Ancient Roots of Apocalyptic Faith* (New Haven: Yale University Press, 1993).

2. The date of Zoroaster is disputed. The traditional date is the sixth century BCE, but Cohn argues for a much earlier date, between 1500 and 1200 BCE

3. S. Shaked, "Iranian Influence on Judaism," in *The Cambridge History of Judaism. Volume One: Introduction; The Persian Period,* ed. W. D. Davies and L. Finkelstein (Cambridge: Cambridge University Press, 1984) 308-25.

4. J. J. Collins, "Was the Dead Sea Sect an Apocalyptic Movement?" in *Archaeology and History in the Dead Sea Scrolls: The New York University Conference in Memory of Yigael Yadin,* ed. L. H. Schiffman (JSOT/ASOR Monographs 2; JSPSup 8; Sheffield: JSOT Press, 1990) 25-51.

the worldview of a particular sect, most probably to be identified as the Essenes.[5] It is with the expectations of these sectarian texts that I am concerned here.

Biblical Motifs

It will be useful at the outset to highlight two biblical motifs that exercised considerable influence on the later tradition. The first is the "end of days," Hebrew *'aḥărît hayyāmîm.* The second is the end *(qēṣ)* as the day of judgment or the day of the Lord.

The phrase *'aḥărît hayyāmîm,* or end of days, probably originally meant "in the course of time, in future days."[6] A cognate expression is found with this sense in Akkadian. The phrase appears already in the Pentateuch in Gen 49:1 (the blessing of Jacob) and Num 24:14 (Balaam's oracle). Both of these passages contain archaic prophetic texts, which originally referred to the future, in an unspecified but limited sense, but they were reinterpreted and given an eschatological sense in the postexilic period, so that they were now understood to refer to a final, definitive phase of history. The phrase "end of days" is part of the prose introduction to the poetry in both passages, and may have been added relatively late, with the eschatological sense already implied. The phrase occurs in Deuteronomy with reference to future turning points in Israel's history, in relation to the observance of the covenant (Deut 4:30; 31:29). In the prophets, the "end of days" implies a definitive transformation of Israel in the distant future. Usually, the reference is to the time of salvation. A famous oracle that appears both in Isaiah 2 and Micah 4 says that in the end of days the mountain of the Lord's house will be exalted above all mountains and all the peoples will stream to it. In Ezekiel 38, in contrast, the end of days is the time when Gog invades Israel, and so it is a time of distress, but one that culminates in the destruction of the invader. In Daniel Chapter 2 the Aramaic equivalent of the phrase is used with reference to Nebuchadnezzar's dream of the four kingdoms and the final, everlasting kingdom of the God of heaven.[7] In Ezekiel and Daniel, then, the concept was broadened to include not only the age of salvation but also the drama that leads up to it. We will find this broader usage continued in the Dead Sea Scrolls.

5. C. A. Newsom, "'Sectually Explicit' Literature from Qumran," in *The Hebrew Bible and Its Interpreters,* ed. W. H. Propp, B. Halpern, and D. N. Freedman (Winona Lake, IN: Eisenbrauns, 1990) 167-87; H. Stegemann, *Die Essener, Qumran, Johannes der Täufer und Jesus: Ein Sachbuch* (Freiburg: Herder, 1993) 148-93.

6. H. Seebass, "אחרית/'ach^{a}rîth," *TDOT* 1 (1974) 207-12. See the summary of the discussion by A. Steudel, "אחרית הימים in the Texts from Qumran," *RevQ* 16 (1993) 225-46.

7. J. J. Collins, *Daniel: A Commentary on the Book of Daniel* (Hermeneia; Minneapolis: Fortress, 1993) 161.

The expectation of an end is also found in the prophets, however, with reference to a more specific, decisive event: the day of judgment. When the prophet Amos proclaimed that "the end has come upon my people Israel" (Amos 8:2) he spoke of the end of Israel as an independent kingdom, not of the end of the world. He also spoke of this event as "the day of the Lord," which would be darkness and not light (Amos 5:18-20). Other prophets expanded this occasion into a day of cosmic judgment. So we read in Isaiah 13:

> The day of the Lord comes, cruel, with wrath and fierce anger, to make the earth a desolation and to destroy its sinners from it. For the stars of heaven and their constellations will not give their light; the sun will be dark at its rising and the moon will not shed its light. . . . Therefore I will make the heavens tremble and the earth will be shaken out of its place at the wrath of the Lord of hosts, in the day of his fierce anger. (Isa 13:9, 10, 13)[8]

The motif of the day of the Lord usually places the emphasis on destruction, but it is understood that "the Lord alone is exalted on that day" (Isa 2:11), and the exaltation of the Lord brings with it the deliverance for the faithful. The double aspect of the day of the judgment is clear in the book of Daniel:

> At that time Michael, the great prince, the protector of your people shall arise. There shall be a time of anguish, such as has never occurred since nations first came into existence. But at that time your people shall be delivered, everyone who is found written in the book." (Dan 12:1)

Deliverance in Daniel entails resurrection of the dead.

The Calculation of the End

There was another development in the book of Daniel of momentous importance for later tradition. Here for the first time we find an attempt to calculate the time of the end. The calculation is not arbitrary, but grounded in an elaborate schema that spans the whole postexilic period. The schema is spelled out in Daniel 9. Jeremiah had prophesied that Jerusalem would lie desolate for 70 years.[9] The angel Gabriel now informs Daniel that the 70 years are really 70 weeks of years, or 490 years. This period could also be interpreted as ten jubilees. According to Lev 25:1-55, a jubilee, or 7 weeks of years (49 years), was the longest period that land could be alienated from its ancestral owners or that a person could be kept in indentured slavery. The apocalyptic

8. Cf. Isa 2:10-22; Zeph 1:14-16. See R. H. Hiers, "Day of the Lord," *ABD*, 2.82-83.
9. Jer 25:11-12; 29:10. See Collins, *Daniel*, 349.

literature often divides history, or a segment thereof, into a specific number of periods, frequently choosing the number 10.[10] (The choice may be influenced by the prominence of the millennium in Persian cosmology and eschatology.)[11] Daniel puts these two motifs together to come up with the 70 weeks of years or 10 jubilees. There is no attempt to fill in a full chronology of events for this period, but we are given a few points of reference. The starting point is "the time that the word went forth to restore and rebuild Jerusalem." The reference here is to the divine word, rather than to the decree of the Persian king, and so the starting point is at some time during the exile. Daniel's vision is dated to the first year of Darius the Mede, which cannot be correlated with any actual historical date.[12] The first 7 weeks end with the coming of an anointed prince, who is usually identified as either Zerubbabel or the high priest Joshua, about the year 520 BCE. The next marker comes after 62 further weeks, when "an anointed one shall be cut off," a reference to the murder of the high priest Onias III, about 171 BCE. For the seventieth week, "the prince who is to come" (Antiochus IV Epiphanes) will make a strong covenant with many, and for half a week the Temple cult will be disrupted by "the abomination that makes desolate."

As a calculation of the period from the Babylonian exile to Antiochus IV Epiphanes, Daniel's 490 years is impossibly long, by any known chronology, ancient or modern.[13] (By modern calculations, it is about 70 years too long.) But Daniel was not interested in the chronology of the whole period, only in its conclusion. The last week of years, or 7-year period, was initiated by the murder of the high priest Onias, and the midpoint in the last week was marked by the installation that makes desolate in the Temple, an event that is usually dated to December 167 BCE.[14] The conclusion to be drawn from Daniel's prophecy, then, is that the "end" would come 3½ years after the profanation of the Temple, sometime in the summer of 163 BCE. The same chronology is implied in Dan 7:25, which gives the length of the persecution as "a time, times and half a time."

Daniel also makes three more specific attempts to calculate the precise

10. A. Yarbro Collins, "Numerical Symbolism in the Book of Revelation," *ANRW* 2.21.2 (1984) 1221-87.

11. D. Flusser, "The Four Empires in the Fourth Sibyl and in the Book of Daniel," *Israel Oriental Studies* 2 (1972) 148-75.

12. On this and various problems of interpretation in Daniel's prophecy, see Collins, *Daniel,* 354-57.

13. For discussions of Daniel's chronology, see B. Z. Wacholder, "Chronomessianism: The Timing of Messianic Movements and the Calendar of Sabbatical Cycles," *HUCA* 46 (1975) 201-18; A. Laato, "The Seventy Yearweeks in the Book of Daniel," *ZAW* 102 (1990) 212-25. Laato argues that the calculation of 490 years was taken over from a pre-Maccabean source.

14. Some scholars argue for December 168. See L. L. Grabbe, "Maccabean Chronology: 167-164 or 168-165 BCE?" *JBL* 110 (1991) 59-74.

number of days until the "end." According to Dan 8:14 the time that the Temple cult would be disrupted is given as 2,300 evenings and mornings, or 1,150 days. At the end of the book two further figures are given: "From the time that the regular burnt offering is taken away and the abomination that makes desolate is set up, there shall be one thousand two hundred ninety days. Happy are those who persevere and attain the thousand three hundred thirty-five days" (Dan 12:11-12). Two things about this passage are remarkable. First, we are given two different numbers side by side. Both may be regarded as approximations of three and a half years, but the fact that two different figures are given strongly suggests that the second calculation was added after the first number of days had passed.[15] The phenomenon of recalculation is well known in later apocalyptic movements such as the Millerite movement in nineteenth-century America.[16] Second, Daniel is not specific as to what will happen when the specified number of days has passed. Since the days are calculated from the time that the Temple cult was disrupted, we might expect that the expected "end" is simply the restoration of that cult, and this would seem to be the implication in Dan 8:14 and 9:24. But, according to 1 Macc 1:54; 4:52-54, Judas purified the Temple three years to the day after it had been polluted, so both numbers point to a date after that restoration. At least the last date must have been added after the purification had taken place. Presumably, the author of Daniel did not think that the restoration under Judas was satisfactory. But there is probably more at stake here. The numbers in Daniel 12 follow the prophecy of the victory of Michael and the resurrection of the dead. In Dan 12:13 Daniel is told that he will rise from his rest "at the end of the days." The end, then, is the time when the archangel Michael intervenes and the resurrection takes place, roughly what later tradition would call the end of the world.[17]

One other development in apocalyptic eschatology should be noted before we turn to the Dead Sea Scrolls. The *Apocalypse of Weeks* (*1 Enoch* 93:1-10 + 91:11-17) is a revelation in the name of Enoch, written about the time of the Maccabean revolt. Here, as in Daniel, history is divided into "weeks," presumably weeks of years. At the end of the seventh week, "the chosen righteous from the eternal plant of righteousness will be chosen," but history does not come to an end. In the eighth week a sword is given to the righteous, to execute judgment. In the ninth, "the righteous judgment will be revealed to the whole world . . .

15. Collins, *Daniel,* 400-401.

16. L. Festinger et al., *When Prophecy Fails: A Social and Psychological Study of a Modern Group That Predicted the Destruction of the World* (New York: Harper & Row, 1956) 12-23; P. Boyer, *When Time Shall Be No More: Prophecy Belief in Modern American Culture* (Cambridge, MA: Harvard University Press, 1992) 81-82.

17. J. J. Collins, "The Meaning of 'The End' in the Book of Daniel," in *Of Scribes and Scrolls: Studies on the Hebrew Bible, Intertestamental Judaism, and Christian Origins in Honor of John Strugnell,* ed. H. W. Attridge et al. (Lanham, MD: University Press of America, 1990) 91-98.

and the world will be written down for destruction." Finally in the tenth week there will be a great judgment, the old heaven will be taken away and a new heaven revealed. Thereafter there will be many weeks without number." Even though this apocalypse envisages an end of this world, the "end" is not exactly a fixed point. Rather, we have an eschatological scenario in which there is a series of "ends" as the old order passes away and is replaced by the new.

The End of Days in the Dead Sea Scrolls

Each of the traditions we have considered so far plays an important part in the eschatology of the Dead Sea sect. The expression *ʾaḥărît hayyāmîm* occurs more than thirty times in the Dead Sea Scrolls.[18] The so-called *Halakhic Letter,* 4QMMT, declares that "this is the end of days," and 1QSa, one of the supplements to the *Community Rule,* is introduced as "the rule for all the congregation of Israel in the end of days." There are two references in the *Damascus Document.* The great majority of the occurrences, however, are found in exegetical literature, in the pesharim, and in midrashic texts such as the *Melchizedek Scroll* and especially the so-called *Eschatological Midrash* (4Q174, the *Florilegium,* + 4Q177, the *Catena*), which contains approximately one-third of the references. Surprisingly, the phrase does not occur in the *Community Rule,* the *Thanksgiving Hymns,* or the *War Rule.*

The end of days in the Scrolls has two aspects. It is a time of testing, and it is a time of at least incipient salvation. The time of testing is explicit in the *Florilegium* (4Q174), which explains Psalm 2: "Why do the nations conspire and the peoples plot in vain against the Lord and against his anointed one," by saying that the nations conspire against the elect of Israel at the end of days. The next column continues: "It is a time of refining which co[mes . . .] . . . as is written in the book of Daniel, the prophet: 'The wicked [act wickedly . . .] and the just [. . . shall be whi]tened and refined and a people knowing God will remain strong.'" The passage weaves together two passages from Daniel, 12:10 and 11:35. In the context of Daniel, the time of refining is the period immediately before Michael rises in victory, although it may arguably continue into the time of distress that follows Michael's rise in Dan 12:1. Several other passages corroborate the view of the end of days as a time of testing. 4Q177 (the *Catena*), which may be part of the same document,[19] speaks of testing and refining the men of the community at the end of days. The *Pesher on Habakkuk* refers to traitors and ruthless ones at the end of days (1QpHab 2:5-6; cf. 4QpNah 3-4 ii

18. See Steudel, "אחרית הימים," 225-46.

19. So A. Steudel, *Der Midrasch zur Eschatologie aus der Qumran-Gemeinde (4QMidrEschat$^{a.b}$)* (STDJ 13; Leiden: Brill, 1994) 127-51.

2). But the *Florilegium* also refers to the Temple which the Lord will establish with his hands at the end of days, in contrast to the "Temple of men" (which serves in the interim)[20] and to the Branch of David who will arise with the Interpreter of the Law at the end of days.

The positive aspects of the end of days are clearly still in the future from the perspective of the authors of the Scrolls. There is no suggestion anywhere that the Messiah has already come. Many scholars hold, however, that the time of testing was already being experienced in the history of the sect.[21] This is certainly possible, but the language of the Scrolls is often ambiguous. So, for example, the phrase "a time of refining which co[mes . . .]" can mean, grammatically, either that the time has come or that it is coming. Annette Steudel has argued that it must mean that the time has already come.[22] The *Pesher on Psalms* speaks of attempts to lay hands on the Teacher of Righteousness at the time of refining, and she assumes that the Teacher was already dead when the pesher was written. This is very likely, although there is nothing explicit in the text to that effect. If Steudel is right, we must assume that the end of days entailed two phases, the time of testing and the coming of the Messiahs, and that the first phase was thought to have already begun.[23]

Only one text in the Qumran corpus says explicitly that the end of days has already begun. This is the so-called *Halakhic Letter,* 4QMMT, but its presentation of the end of days is exceptional in a number of respects. 4QMMT C 13-15 cites Deut 30:1-3: "And it is written 'and it shall come to pass, when all these things [be]fall you,' at the end of days, the blessings and the curses, ['then you will take] it to hea[rt] and you will return unto Him with all your heart and with all your soul,' at the end. . . ."[24] The text goes on to say that "we know that some of the blessings and the curses have (already) been fulfilled as it is written in the book of Moses," but the reference is apparently to the "blessings" experienced under David and Solomon and the "curses" experienced from the time of Jeroboam to the Babylonian exile. The fulfillment of these curses and blessings, then, is not itself part of the end of days and is hardly proof that the end of days is at hand. Nonetheless, 4QMMT continues: "And this is the end of days when they will return to Isra[el]." The point is

20. The interpretation of the temples of the *Florilegium* is much debated. See J. J. Collins, "Teacher and Messiah?" in *The Community of the Renewed Covenant: The Notre Dame Symposium on the Dead Sea Scrolls,* ed. E. Ulrich and J. VanderKam (Notre Dame: University of Notre Dame Press, 1994) 195-98. Compare also the two temples in 11QTemple 29.

21. E.g., G. Brooke, *Exegesis at Qumran: 4QFlorilegium in Its Jewish Context* (JSOTSup 29; Sheffield: JSOT, 1985) 206-9; Steudel, "אחרית הימים," 226-31.

22. Steudel, "אחרית הימים," 228-29.

23. This conclusion entails a modification of the position taken in Collins, "Teacher and Messiah?" 199.

24. E. Qimron and J. Strugnell, *Qumran Cave 4. V. Miqṣat Maʿaśe ha-Torah* (DJD 10; Oxford: Clarendon, 1994) 59-61.

not that signs of the eschaton have already begun to appear, as is sometimes implied in apocalyptic texts, but that the time of decision is now. It is time to usher in the end of days by returning to the covenant. 4QMMT is exceptional among the Dead Sea Scrolls insofar as it is addressed to someone outside the sectarian community. Consequently, it makes no attempt to argue from the experience of the sect that prophecy is being fulfilled, since the recipient of the letter could not be expected to accept such an argument. Instead, 4QMMT is framed in terms that might in principle be persuasive to any Jew, appealing primarily to the Law of Moses.

The precise limits of the end of days are never clearly defined in the Scrolls. The ambiguity of the situation may be illustrated with reference to the opening column of the *Damascus Document.* There we are told that at the time of the Babylonian exile God saved a remnant from Israel. Then "in the age of wrath, 390 years after having delivered them up into the hands of Nebuchadnezzar, king of Babylon, he visited them, and caused a plant root to spring from Israel and from Aaron."[25] It is not clear, however, whether the whole 390 years qualify as "the age of wrath" or whether that age only begins after 390 years. The phrase "age of wrath" (Hebrew קץ חרון) involves a wordplay on "the last age" (קץ האחרון), a phrase that we meet in the pesharim, and which can scarcely be distinguished from the end of days, and must also be related to "the last generation" (דור האחרון) of CD 1:12.[26] It is hardly possible that the end of days was thought to begin as early as the Babylonian exile,[27] but its beginning could well coincide with the emergence of the sect. As we have noted already, the period extends to the coming of the Messiahs, which clearly remains in the future in all the Dead Sea Scrolls. The so-called *Messianic Rule,* 1QSa, assumes that the conditions of human existence are not greatly altered by the coming of the Messiahs.[28] Provision must still be made for the education of children, and for community meals and regulations. One of the tasks of the princely Messiah, however, was to wage war on the Kittim, the Gentile enemies of Israel.[29] This war is included in the end of days in the *Pesher on Isaiah* (4QpIsa^{a}). The phrase is never applied, however, to the conditions that ensue after the eschatological war. We should perhaps allow for some variation in

25. On the problems of interpretation presented by this passage, see P. R. Davies, *The Damascus Covenant* (JSOTSup 25; Sheffield: JSOT, 1983) 61-69.

26. For the references to these and other related terms, see Steudel, "אחרית הימים," 239. Steudel warns against the assumption that they are all equivalent.

27. 4QDibHam (4Q504) is exceptional in seeming to include the exile in the "end of days," but this text is probably not a product of the Dead Sea sect but part of its wider literary heritage. See E. Chazon, "Is Divrei Ha-Me'orot a Sectarian Prayer?" in *The Dead Sea Scrolls: Forty Years of Research,* ed. D. Dimant and U. Rappaport (STDJ 10; Leiden: Brill, 1992) 3-17.

28. L. H. Schiffman, *The Eschatological Community of the Dead Sea Scrolls* (SBLMS 38; Atlanta: Scholars Press, 1989).

29. See J. J. Collins, *The Scepter and the Star: The Messiahs of the Dead Sea Scrolls and Other Ancient Literature* (ABRL 10; New York: Doubleday, 1995) 49-73.

the way the motif is used, but in general we may agree with Steudel that the end of days is "the last period of time, directly before the time of salvation."[30]

A Specific Ending

There are also indications in the Scrolls, however, that the Dead Sea sect envisaged a more specific endpoint. In the words of the *Community Rule,* "God, in the mysteries of his knowledge and in the wisdom of his glory, has determined an end to the existence of injustice and on the occasion of his visitation he will obliterate it forever" (1QS 4:18-19). This "end" was not in the vague and distant future but was expected at a particular time in the sect's history. There are primarily two pieces of evidence that point to such a specific expectation, one passage in the *Pesher on Habakkuk* and another at the end of the *Damascus Document.*

The *Pesher on Habakkuk* comments on Hab 2:3 as follows:

> *For there is yet a vision concerning the appointed time. It testifies to the end time* (קץ), *and it will not deceive.* The interpretation of it is that the last end time (קץ האחרון) will be prolonged, and it will be greater than anything of which the prophets spoke, for the mysteries of God are awesome. *If it tarries, wait for it, for it will surely come, and it will not be late.* The interpretation of it concerns the men of truth, those who observe the Law, whose hands do not grow slack in the service of the truth, when the last end time is drawn out for them, for all of God's end times will come according to their fixed order. (1QpHab 7:6-13)[31]

This passage from Habakkuk was cited several times in Daniel, to make the point that the vision will only be fulfilled at its appointed time (Dan 8:17; 10:14b; 11:27, 35). Habakkuk was concerned with the fulfillment of the vision: "the vision is still for the appointed time." Daniel is concerned with the sureness of the "end": "there is still an end at the appointed time" (11:27, cf. 35). A further allusion to Habakkuk can be seen in Dan 12:12, where the final prediction of the number of days is introduced: "blessed is he who waits and comes to 1,335 days" (cf. Hab 3:2b: "if it tarries wait for it"). In the latter case, it is clear that the "end" is delayed, and Daniel finds in Habakkuk a prophetic text that envisages such an eventuality.

The situation is similar in the *Pesher on Habakkuk.* The prolongation of the end time is not merely a theoretical possibility. It is the experience of the commu-

30. Steudel, "אחרית הימים," 231.

31. Trans. by M. P. Horgan, *Pesharim: Qumran Interpretations of Biblical Books* (CBQMS 8; Washington: Catholic Biblical Association, 1979) 16.

nity, for which the author seeks an explanation in the prophetic text. It is reasonable to infer, then, that the "end" was expected shortly before the pesher was written. While we do not know the exact date of the pesher, all indicators point to the middle of the first century BCE. The manuscript is dated on paleographic grounds to the Herodian period,[32] but it is not an autograph, as it contains copyist errors.[33] The Kittim in this document are clearly the Romans, who "sacrifice to their standards" (1QpHab 6:3-4). The prediction that the wealth and booty of the "last priests of Jerusalem will be given into the hand of the army of the Kittim" (1QpHab 9:6-7) suggests that the conquest of Jerusalem by the Romans (63 BCE) either was imminent or had already taken place. The *Pesher on Nahum* refers to events in the early first century, down to the time of Hyrcanus II and Aristobolus II (67-63 BCE). If we may assume that these pesharim were written about the same time, a date around the middle of the century is plausible.[34]

Our other witness to the expectation of an end at a specific time, the *Damascus Document,* also points to a date towards the middle of the first century BCE. In CD 20:14 we are told that "from the day of the gathering in of the unique teacher until the destruction of all the men of war who turned back with the man of lies there shall be about forty years." This calculation is evidently related to the figures found in column 1 of the same document. The time from the Babylonian exile to the emergence of the sect is 390 years. Then the first members wander in blindness for 20 years until the arrival of the Teacher of Righteousness. If we allow the stereotypical figure of 40 years for the Teacher's career, this brings us to 450 years. Forty years after his death would then bring us to 490 years, the time stipulated in the book of Daniel.[35] That this figure was important for the eschatology of the sect is clear from the *Melchizedek Scroll:* "Now the d[ay of expia]tion i[s the en]d of the tenth [ju]bilee, when expiation (will be made) for all the sons of [light and] for the m[e]n of the lot of Mel[chi]zedek."[36] The end of the tenth jubilee is, of course, the culmination of seventy weeks of years or 490 years.[37]

32. F. M. Cross, *The Ancient Library of Qumran and Modern Biblical Studies* (Garden City: Doubleday, 1961) 120 n. 20: "The Habakkuk Commentary (1QpHab) features an early (transitional) Herodian script."

33. Horgan, *Pesharim,* 3; Stegemann, *Die Essener, 175.*

34. Stegemann, *Die Essener,* puts the date about 50 BCE. We should allow a margin of plus or minus ten years or so.

35. F. F. Bruce, "The Book of Daniel and the Qumran Community," in *Neotestamentica et Semitica,* ed. E. E. Ellis and M. Wilcox (Edinburgh: Clark, 1969) 232; G. Vermes, *The Dead Sea Scrolls: Qumran in Perspective* (Philadelphia: Fortress, 1981) 147-48. The relevance of Daniel here is disputed by B. Z. Wacholder, *The Dawn of Qumran* (Cincinnati: Hebrew Union College, 1983) 108-9, 179. See also Wacholder, "The Date of the Eschaton in the Book of Jubilees: A Commentary on Jub. 49:22–50:5, CD 1:1-10, and 16:2-3," *HUCA* 56 (1985) 87-101.

36. P. J. Kobelski, *Melchizedek and Melchireša'* (CBQMS 10; Washington: Catholic Biblical Association, 1981) 8.

37. Periods of seventy weeks or seventy years figure in several other writings, including the

It appears, then, that the Dead Sea sect expected the fulfillment of Daniel's prophecy about 40 years after the death of the Teacher. Unfortunately, we do not know when this took place. A date around the end of the second century BCE seems likely, but we must allow a generous margin of error. If the Teacher died about 100 BCE, this would point to an "end" about 60 BCE, which would be highly compatible with the evidence of the *Pesher on Habakkuk.*

Some scholars believe they can reconstruct the date at which the end was expected with even greater specificity.[38] Fundamental to any such attempt is the assumption that the figure of 390 years in CD column 1, for the period from the exile to the rise of the sect, is reliable chronological information. Two possible calculations have been proposed. Assuming the modern chronology of the exile and postexilic period, we get the year 197/196 BCE for the emergence of the plant root from Aaron and Israel, and 177/6 for the advent of the Teacher.[39] It has been pointed out, however, that some ancient Jewish authors calculated a later date for the exile and a shorter postexilic period. The Jewish chronographer Demetrius, who wrote in Egypt in the late third century BCE, calculated that there were 338 years between the exile of Judah (587/6 BCE) and Ptolemy IV (222 BCE) rather than 364/5 as modern historians reckon.[40] This chronology would bring the dates down by 26 years, so that the Teacher would have emerged about 150 BCE, shortly after the usurpation of the high priesthood by Jonathan Maccabee, which many scholars have supposed to be the occasion for the secession of the Qumran sect.[41] If we then allow 40 years for the career of the Teacher and a further interval of 40 years after his death, we arrive at the conclusion that the "end" was expected about 70 BCE.[42]

While these suggestions are intriguing, and are not impossible, in my view they are not reliable. While there is evidence for speculation on biblical chronology, such as we find in Demetrius, in such documents as *Jubilees* and the Aramaic *Levi Apocryphon*, there is no actual evidence that CD used the chronology of Demetrius. The argument is simply that this chronology would support a popular hypothesis about the origin of the Dead Sea sect. Despite its popularity,

---

so-called *Pesher on the Periods* (4Q180-181) and 4Q390, a pseudo-Moses text. See J. T. Milik, *The Books of Enoch* (Oxford: Clarendon, 1976) 248-59, and the critique of R. V. Huggins, "A Canonical 'Book of Periods' at Qumran?" *RevQ* 59 (1992) 421-36.

38. See Steudel, "אחרית הימים," 233-40.

39. Wacholder accepts 196/195 BCE as the date for the emergence of the sect, but he also puts the arrival of the Teacher at this point (*The Dawn of Qumran*, 180-81).

40. A. Laato, "The Chronology in the Damascus Document of Qumran," *RevQ* 15 (1992) 605-7.

41. É. Puech arrives at a date of 152 BCE by assuming that CD follows a chronology attested in *2 Baruch.* See É. Puech, *La Croyance des Esséniens en la Vie Future: Immortalité, Résurrection, Vie Éternelle* (Paris: Gabalda, 1993) 506 n. 29.

42. So Stegemann, *Die Essener*, 174. Steudel, "אחרית הימים," 236-39, gives the date as 72 BCE, following Puech.

however, that hypothesis is far from established fact.[43] Besides, the chronological data attributed to Demetrius are confused and contradictory. (The calculation of the period from the exile of the northern tribes to Ptolemy IV is about 70 years too long and cannot be reconciled with his calculation of the exile of Judah.)[44] The figure of 40 years for the career of the Teacher is only a round number. The same must be said for the 390 years of CD 1, which is a symbolic number for the duration of the desolation, derived from Ezek 4:5. The attempt to derive chronological information from it rests on a shaky foundation. It is no more likely to be accurate than the 490 years in Daniel 9. The same applies to the attempt to derive chronological information from the system of jubilees in the *Melchizedek Scroll*.[45]

This is not to deny that the sectarians of Qumran had a specific time in mind for the coming of the eschaton. In order to arrive at that date, however, they did not need to verify every stage of the chronology. It was sufficient that they remember how much time had passed since the death of the Teacher. Even CD did not claim that the divine intervention would come exactly forty years after that event, but an approximate number was enough to fuel a lively expectation. I see no evidence that anyone at Qumran ever counted the days, in the manner of the book of Daniel, or that their expectation ever focused on a specific day or year. Consequently, it does not appear that they ever encountered the trauma of disappointment that the Millerites experienced in nineteenth-century America, when the appointed day passed and "we wept and wept till the day dawn."[46] Nonetheless, as the years passed, they were aware that the end time was prolonged. "About forty years" could not be extended indefinitely. The lack of a specific date, however, mitigated the disappointment and made it easier for the community to adapt to the postponement of their expectations.

The Nature of the End

But what exactly was expected to happen forty years after the death of the Teacher? The *Damsacus Document* still expected the coming of the Messiahs, so this is one obvious possibility.[47] Their coming is described as "the age of

43. See my criticism of this hypothesis in "The Origin of the Qumran Community: A Review of the Evidence," in *To Touch the Text: Biblical and Related Studies in Honor of Joseph A. Fitzmyer, S.J.*, ed. M. P. Horgan and P. J. Kobelski (New York: Crossroad, 1989) 159-78. The hypothesis rests on the assumption that the schism was caused by the usurpation of the high priesthood. Yet when the sectarian documents discuss the reasons for separation, especially in 4QMMT and CD, the high priesthood is never mentioned.

44. See Laato, "The Chronology in the Damascus Document," 605-6.

45. Steudel, "אחרית הימים," 233-34.

46. Boyer, *When Time Shall Be No More*, 81.

47. Steudel, "אחרית הימים," 238.

visitation" when the unfaithful will be put to the sword (CD 19:10). CD speaks explicitly of the destruction of the men of war who turned back with the men of the lie. CD does not indicate, however, how long the judgment will take. The *Community Rule* speaks of "an end to the existence of injustice" (1QS 4:18). The *Melchizedek Scroll* says that after the tenth jubilee is the time for "Melchizedek's year of favor" when he will exact "the ven[geance] of E[l's] judgments" (11QMelch 2:13). It is also "the day [of salvation about w]hich [God] spoke [through the mouth of Isa]iah the prophet" (2:15). From these passages it is clear that the Qumran community expected a day of judgment, as foretold by the prophets. Other passages, however, indicate that a lengthier process was envisaged. The day of salvation in the *Melchizedek Scroll* is the occasion of the arrival of the herald, the "anointed of the spirit" or eschatological prophet. We might expect that he would be followed by the Messiahs of Aaron and Israel (cf. 1QS 9:11) and then by the eschatological war, which takes forty years according to the *War Scroll.*

It is not apparent, however, that all these texts were ever synthesized into a coherent system. The *Melchizedek Scroll* does not speak of Messiahs (except the anointed of the spirit), and the *Community Rule* does not mention the tenth jubilee. Different texts provided different models for the end time, or highlighted different aspects of it. What is clear is that the "end" expected forty years after the death of the Teacher was supposed to inaugurate a new phase in the eschatological drama and to mark some dramatic advance towards the extermination of evil. It also appears that both the period before this "end" and some of the events that would follow it directly could be included in "the end of days."

The Final Salvation

While the various models of eschatology found in the Scrolls do not yield a fully coherent system, some ideas may be characterized as typical of the sect. One such idea is the expectation of an eschatological war. This is described elaborately in the *War Rule,* although even the *War Scroll* found in Cave 1 combines traditions that are in some tension, if not contradictory.[48] But it is also alluded to in the pesharim, the *Thanksgiving Hymns,* the *Community Rule,* and other texts.[49] A messianic prince would play an important role in this war.[50]

48. See the analyses of the *War Scroll* from Cave 1 by P. von der Osten-Sacken, *Gott und Belial* (Göttingen: Vandenhoeck & Ruprecht, 1969) and P. R. Davies, *1QM, the War Scroll from Qumran: Its Structure and History* (BibOr 32; Rome: Biblical Institute Press, 1977). The picture is further complicated by the evidence from Cave 4.

49. E.g., 4QpIsa^{a}; 1QH 11:35 (formerly 3:35); 1QS 10:19.

50. This is apparent from 4Q285 and the *Pesher on Isaiah.* See Collins, *The Scepter and the Star,* 58-60.

There is also place for an angelic deliverer, variously identified as Michael or Melchizedek or the Prince of Light. These deliverers are accented differently in different documents. The crucial affirmation, however, is that God would put an end to wickedness.

There are surprisingly few descriptions, however, of the state that was to follow the eschatological war. The *War Scroll* mentions the rule of Michael among the angels and the kingdom of Israel on earth (1QM 17:7-8), and this is in accordance with the book of Daniel. There are frequent references to the blessed state of the elect after death, but references to resurrection are remarkably rare and the few clear texts are of uncertain provenance.

It is interesting in this regard to compare what we find in the Scrolls with the descriptions of the eschatology of the Essenes, with whom the Dead Sea sect is most frequently identified. We have, in fact, two sharply different accounts of Essene eschatology. According to Josephus, in the *Jewish War* 2.154-58: "It is a firm belief among them that although bodies are corruptible, and their matter unstable, souls are immortal and endure forever." Josephus goes on to compare the ideas of the Essenes to those of the Greeks with respect to reward and punishment after death, comparing the abode of the righteous dead with the Isles of the Blessed. He says nothing about any transformation of this world. Hippolytus of Rome, in contrast, writing more than a century later, claims that "the doctrine of the resurrection has also derived support among them, for they acknowledge both that the flesh will rise again, and that it will be immortal, in the same manner as the soul is already imperishable." He goes on to compare Essene and Greek concepts of eschatology in terms very similar to those used by Josephus, including the comparison with the Isles of the Blessed. In addition to the postmortem rewards and punishments, however, Hippolytus allows for "both a judgment and a conflagration of the universe" (*Refutation of all Heresies* 27).

There is good evidence that Josephus and Hippolytus used a common source; Hippolytus was not dependent on Josephus for his information.[51] Some of the statements that are peculiar to Hippolytus seem to be due to confusion; he says that the Essenes are also called Zealots and Sicarii (*Refutation* 26). He may preserve some information that was omitted by Josephus. The idea of a conflagration of the universe finds striking support in a passage in 1QH 11:29-32 (formerly 3:29-32), which says that

> the torrents of Belial shall reach to all sides of the world. In all their channels a consuming fire shall destroy . . . and shall consume the foundations of the earth and the expanse of dry land. The bases of the mountains shall blaze

51. M. Smith, "The Description of the Essenes in Josephus and the Philosophoumena," *HUCA* 29 (1958) 273-313.

> and the roots of the rocks shall turn to torrents of pitch. It shall consume as far as the great abyss. The torrents of Belial shall burst into Abaddon.

While this is not as similar to Stoic teaching as Hippolytus implies, it is surely a conflagration of the universe. This is, however, the only passage in the Scrolls that attests to such a belief, so it does not appear to have played any central role in the expectations of the sect.

Hippolytus' claim that the Essenes affirmed bodily resurrection receives little support from the Dead Sea Scrolls.[52] While the belief in resurrection is prominent in the apocalypses of Enoch and Daniel, copies of which were also found at Qumran, only two of the previously unknown texts clearly affirm such a belief. These are the so-called *Messianic Apocalypse* (4Q521)[53] and *Pseudo-Ezekiel* (4Q385).[54] Neither can be identified unambiguously as a product of the Dead Sea sect. Even if they are sectarian compositions, the evidence suggests that resurrection was only a minority belief at Qumran and was not typical of the eschatology of the sect. The sectarians hoped for fellowship with the angels, and for "eternal joy in life without end" (1QS 4). The resurrection of the body did not figure prominently in their hopes. Josephus' account, although admittedly cast in Hellenistic terms, corresponds more closely to the typical expectations of the Scrolls.

It must be admitted, however, that neither Josephus' nor Hippolytus' account of the Essenes corresponds completely with what we find in the Scrolls. No ancient account of the Essenes mentions the expectation of Messiahs, nor the prospect of an eschatological war. This discrepancy is not fatal to the view that the Dead Sea sect was Essene.[55] The source on which Josephus and Hippolytus drew was evidently composed for a Hellenistic audience, and the author may have judged that some aspects of Essene belief were better ignored. But if we hold, as most scholars still do, that the Scrolls contain firsthand evidence of Essene views, we must also acknowledge that the accounts of the Greek authors (Philo, Josephus, and Hippolytus) are less than fully reliable.

52. Puech argues at length that the Scrolls support the account of Hippolytus (*La Croyance des Esséniens en la Vie Future,* 703-69). His argument depends heavily, however, on claims that a belief in resurrection is implied in several major texts where it is not explicit (the *Community Rule,* the *Damascus Document,* the *War Rule*). The evidence of the *Thanksgiving Hymns* remains ambiguous.

53. É. Puech, "Une Apocalypse Messianique (4Q521)," *RevQ* 15 (1992) 475-519.

54. J. Strugnell and D. Dimant, "4Q Second Ezekiel (4Q385)," *RevQ* 13 (1988) 45-58.

55. For the correspondences between the Scrolls and the accounts of the Essenes, see J. J. Collins, "Essenes," in *ABD* 2.619-26; T. S. Beall, *Josephus' Description of the Essenes Illustrated by the Dead Sea Scrolls* (SNTSMS 58; Cambridge: Cambridge University Press, 1988).

The Persistence of Eschatological Expectation

The expected "end" forty years after the death of the Teacher came and went. The Qumran community does not seem to have suffered any major disruption, as far as we know. It is true that the site of Qumran was abandoned for some period towards the end of the first century BCE, but the abandonment is explained as the result either of the earthquake of 31 BCE or of a violent destruction and fire about 9 or 8 BCE.[56] There is no evidence that it was related to the disappointment of eschatological hope, or that the occupants had changed their views when the site was resettled. The pesharim, and indeed much of the distinctively sectarian literature, were produced in the early or middle first century BCE. Steudel has argued that there was an upsurge in the production of pesharim when the "end" failed to come, as the sectarians sought to assure themselves that it was at hand.[57] It is also possible, however, that many of the pesharim were composed before the anticipated "end," to show that prophecy was indeed in the process of being fulfilled. Only the *Pesher on Habakkuk* betrays any anxiety about the delay. The *War Scroll* continued to be copied in the Roman period, so it appears that eschatological expectation did not cease when the "end" failed to materialize. This should not surprise us. The book of Daniel had offered far more specific calculations of an "end" than anything found at Qumran. These dates also passed without event. Nonetheless, Daniel was acknowledged as Scripture within a generation, and Josephus held that Daniel surpassed the other prophets by his ability to predict the times when events would take place.[58]

We do not know whether any further attempt was made to predict divine intervention at Qumran. The fact that the Qumran site shows signs of military destruction has often led to speculation that the community may have joined in the great revolt. The *Community Rule* contains a profession of quietism: "I shall not repay anyone with an evil reward . . . for to God (belongs) the judgment of every living being. . . . I shall not be involved at all in any dispute with the men of the pit *until the day of vengeance*" (1QS 10:17-19). But it is quite possible that the members of the community decided that the day of vengeance had come when the revolt against Rome broke out.[59] If so, they would have

56. See J. Magness, "The Chronology of the Settlement at Qumran in the Herodian Period," *DSD* 2 (1995) 58-65.

57. Steudel, "אחרית הימים," 241-42.

58. Josephus, *Antiquities* 10.266; see Collins, *Daniel,* 85.

59. Some scholars think that the "ambiguous oracle" that played a part in fomenting the revolt (Josephus, *Jewish War* 6.312) was Dan 9:24-27. See F. F. Bruce, "Josephus and Daniel," *ASTI* 4 (1965) 157-58; L. L. Grabbe, "Chronography in Hellenistic Jewish Historiography," in *Society of Biblical Literature 1979 Seminar Papers,* ed. P. J. Achtemeier (SBLSP 18; 2 vols.; Missoula, MT: Scholars Press, 1979) 2.57-58. The identification is defended by A. J. Tomasino, "Daniel and the Revolutionaries" (unpublished doctoral dissertation, University of Chicago, 1995).

presumably expected the heavenly host to come to their aid, as envisaged in the *War Rule*. Needless to say, no such help materialized. The ritualistic posturing of the *War Rule* was not an effective way to oppose the Roman legions. But whether the community joined in the revolt or not, the Romans seem to have brought about the final disconfirmation of the eschatological hopes of the Qumran covenanters. For after the Roman campaign of 68 CE, the sect disappeared from history and their writings were consigned to the caves to await a chance resurrection almost two thousand years later.

More than half a century after the destruction of Qumran, eschatological fervor again swept through Judea with the revolt of Simeon Bar Kokhba. On this occasion, no less an authority than R. Akiba is reputed to have made the leap of faith and endorsed the rebel leader as the Messiah. A contemporary rabbi, Yohanan ben Torta is said to have responded: "Aqiba, grass will grow out of your cheekbones before the son of David comes."[60] Ben Torta, of course, was right. Bar Kokhba was no Messiah. Yet despite this and similar disappointments, apocalyptic and messianic movements have continued to flourish both in Judaism and in Christianity down to the present day.

The Qumran community survived for more than a century after its attempt to calculate the end in the mid-first century BCE had failed. The prolonged vitality of the sect's eschatological expectations was due in some part to their evasiveness. They were not tied to a very specific sequence of events, or to a specific date of fulfillment. They were fluid enough to allow for some adaptation. Moreover, the members of the community believed that they were already experiencing some of the blessings of the end time in their community life, where they believed they shared in the fellowship of the angels. The delay of the end was not fatal to the community, but the belief that the end had come may very well have been. The belief that God would ultimately intervene to put an end to wickedness was no doubt essential to the worldview of the community, as it was the source of their hope. But it was also essential to recognize that God had determined the time for this "in the mysteries of his knowledge and the wisdom of his glory" (1QS 4:18). The expectation of divine intervention required the tempering recognition that it is not given to human beings to know the day or the hour.

60. *y. Ta'anit* 68d. For a critical treatment of the Bar Kokhba legend, see P. Schäfer, *Der Bar Kokhba Aufstand: Studien zum zweiten jüdischen Krieg gegen Rom* (TSAJ 1; Tübingen: Mohr-Siebeck, 1981) 29-50.

Jesus and the Dead Sea Scrolls from Qumran Cave 4

CRAIG A. EVANS

The rapid progress of research on Jesus and the Dead Sea Scrolls can be quickly illustrated by reference to the summarizing essay by Jerome Murphy-O'Connor, which appeared in an authoritative survey of New Testament scholarship published in 1989.[1] Murphy-O'Connor was able to cite five areas in which the Scrolls have shed light on various aspects of Jesus' teaching and ministry. These include Jesus' eschatology (cf. 1QH), his attitude toward riches (cf. Josephus, *Jewish War* 2.8.3 §122-23, in reference to the Essenes), his practice of laying on hands (cf. 1QapGen 20:22, 29), his strict views regarding divorce and remarriage (cf. CD 4:20-21; 11QT 57:17-19), and the date and meaning of the Last Supper.[2] Murphy-O'Connor also discussed a few important instances of the use of Aramaic, the language most scholars believe to be Jesus' principal language. One of the texts that he discussed in this connection will be taken up in greater detail below.

Although most of the essays in the anthology in which Murphy-O'Connor's is found are still more or less up to date, his is not. And this is through no fault of his own. His essay appeared in 1989; two years later, the remaining unpublished and previously inaccessible scrolls of Cave 4 were released. Photographic plates, not all of good quality, were quickly made available,[3] and

1. J. Murphy-O'Connor, "Qumran and the New Testament," in *The New Testament and Its Modern Interpreters*, ed. E. J. Epp and G. W. MacRae (Atlanta: Scholars Press, 1989) 55-71, esp. 57-60. It should be noted that several of the contributions to this volume were completed almost a decade or so before its publication and that their surveys extend only to 1979 or 1980.

2. Although much defended by Annie Jaubert (for bibliography, see Murphy-O'Connor, "Qumran and the New Testament," 68), this last alleged parallel has not won widespread support. The calendar of the Essenes really does not answer questions surrounding the date of the Last Supper.

3. R. H. Eisenman and J. M. Robinson, eds., *A Facsimile Edition of the Dead Sea Scrolls* (2

transcriptions of these texts were shortly published.[4] A flurry of studies have appeared in the last five years or so. If Murphy-O'Connor were to revise his essay today, he would have a great deal more to say about Jesus and the Scrolls.[5] The purpose of the present essay is to review four of these recently published texts and show how they help us better understand aspects of Jesus' teaching and the environment in which he lived and ministered.[6]

4Q246 and the Title "Son of God"

The frequent appearance of the title "Son of God" in the biblical period, usually in reference to a monarch, has led some scholars to suspect that the New Testament's usage of it in reference to Jesus is largely due to Graeco-Roman influence. Rudolf Bultmann thought that early Christianity's confession of Jesus as "Son of God" and as begotten through the "power of the Most High" arose in the Hellenistic (i.e., Greek-speaking) churches of the Diaspora.[7] Ferdinand Hahn agrees, arguing that although the expression "Most High" is found in the Old Testament, the confession of the demoniac in Mark 5:7, who addressed Jesus as the "Son of the Most High God," reflects not Palestinian but Hellenistic Jewish Christianity.[8]

It is true that the epithet "God Most High," which is found in the Old Testament (cf. Gen 14:18-20; Ps 57:2), was popular in the pagan world. There are numerous inscriptions in honor of "Zeus Most High" and of Zeus as "God Most High."[9] One also is reminded of the experience of Paul and Silas, who in Philippi were addressed as "servants of God Most High" (Acts 16:17). Accord-

---

vols.; Washington: Biblical Archaeology Society, 1991); E. Tov, ed., *The Dead Sea Scrolls on Microfiche: A Comprehensive Facsimile Edition of the Texts from the Judaean Desert* (Leiden: Brill, 1993). The volumes edited by Eisenman and Robinson contain 1,785 photographic plates, most of which are of scroll fragments that at the time had not been published. Tov's microfiche set contains nearly 6,000 plates and is, as the title implies, comprehensive. Thanks to recent advances in technology, newer and better photographic plates are in production.

4. B. Z. Wacholder and M. G. Abegg, Jr., *A Preliminary Edition of the Unpublished Dead Sea Scrolls: The Hebrew and Aramaic Texts from Cave Four* (4 fascicles; Washington: Biblical Archaeology Society, 1991-96).

5. See the Select Bibliography at the end of this book.

6. For a survey of many more of the newly published scrolls that are potentially significant for Jesus research, see C. A. Evans, *Jesus and His Contemporaries: Comparative Studies* (AGJU 25; Leiden: Brill, 1995) 83-154.

7. R. Bultmann, *Theology of the New Testament* (2 vols.; New York: Scribner's, 1951-55) 1.130-31.

8. F. Hahn, *The Titles of Jesus in Christology* (London: Lutterworth; Cleveland: World, 1969) 291, 293.

9. For discussion and examples, see G. H. R. Horsley, *New Documents Illustrating Early Christianity,* vol. 1 (North Sydney: Macquarie University, 1981) 25-29.

ingly there can be little doubt that the prominence in the New Testament of the epithets such as "Son of God" and "Son of the Most High" probably has something to do with their usage in the Graeco-Roman world. These and closely related epithets were everywhere applied to the Roman emperors. One inscription describes Julius Caesar (ruled 48-44 BCE) as "the manifest god from Mars and Aphrodite, and universal savior of human life" (SIG 760). In many inscriptions and papyri Augustus (30 BCE–14 CE), who was emperor when Jesus was born (ca. 4-5 BCE), is frequently called "God" and "Son of God" (e.g., POxy 257; POxy 1266; POslo 26). Tiberius (14-37 CE), who ruled the Roman Empire when Jesus was crucified (ca. 30 or 33 CE), called himself the "Son of God" and the "Son of Zeus the Liberator" (SB 8317; POxy 240). Nero (54-68 CE), who ruled when the Gospel of Mark was being written, called himself "the Son of the greatest of the gods" (IM 157b) and "Lord of the whole world" (SIG 814). Similar language was used in reference to Emperor Vespasian (69-79 CE), who ruled the Roman Empire when the Synoptic Gospels were composed and began circulating among Christians.

There can be little doubt that when the Markan evangelist began his Gospel with the words, "The beginning of the good news of Jesus Christ, the Son of God" (Mark 1:1), he deliberately imitated the language used in reference to the Roman emperors. To be sure, the word "good news," or "gospel" (εὐαγγέλιον), in the proclamation of Jesus and in earliest Christianity is rooted in the Old Testament, especially Second Isaiah.[10] But its meaning in the Graeco-Roman world of late antiquity must be taken into account. For example, a calendrical inscription from Priene describes the birthday of Emperor Augustus as "the birthday of the god (and) the beginning of the good news for the world." "Beginning" and "good news" are the very words employed in Mark. Mark's opening announcement would surely have struck an imperial note in the ears of the inhabitants of the Roman Empire: The advent of the Roman Emperor is not the beginning of the good news, the evangelist asserts, the advent of Jesus Christ is!

Nevertheless, the frequent and emphatic usage by Greeks and Romans of the language of deification should not lead us to infer that its appearance in the Gospels represents an intrusion of inauthentic and anachronistic terminology into the Jewish and Palestinian setting of the life and activities of Jesus. The usage of "God Most High" or "Yahweh Most High" is found many times in the Old Testament (Gen 14:18-20; Num 24:16; Isa 14:14; Pss 9:2; 57:2; 78:35; Dan 3:26, 42; 7:18, 22, 25, 27; Tobit 4:11; Judith 13:18), in the

10. As especially seen in Isa 40:9; 52:7. That the word "good news" (מבשרת) occurs in the same passage as Isa 40:3, which all four of the canonical Gospels cite, is probably not a coincidence. For discussion of this point, see J. Marcus, *The Way of the Lord: Christological Exegesis of the Old Testament in the Gospel of Mark* (Louisville: Westminster/John Knox, 1992) 12-47.

Dead Sea Scrolls (1QapGen 12:17; 20:12; etc.; 1QH 4:31; 6:33; 1QS 4:22; 4Q525 2:4; 11QBerakot 1 i 3, 6) and in other Jewish literature (*T. Moses* 10:7; *1 Enoch* 9:3; 10:1; etc.; 2 Baruch 17:1; *b. Soṭa* 40a). It may be admitted that in many of these examples Gentiles are speaking, or the epithet is spoken by a Jew in a Gentile setting. The example of Mark 5:7 (= Luke 8:28), where the Gerasene demoniac addresses Jesus as "Son of the Most High God," follows this pattern. The Gerasene man is probably a Gentile and the Gerasene region, which was east of the Sea of Galilee, was in the time of Jesus largely a Gentile region.

A text that became known following a public lecture more than twenty years ago, but whose photograph was not made public until 1991, sheds important light on the question of usage of the epithet "Son of the Most High" in Palestine in the time of Jesus. The text is an Aramaic fragment designated 4Q246 and often referred to either as the *Aramaic Apocalypse* or the *Son of God Text.* 4Q246 1:1–2:9 tells of the advent of a king who will conquer the nations and rule with justice. The most relevant part of the text reads as follows:

> But your son] shall be great upon the earth, [8][and all peoples sh]all make [peace with him], and they all shall serve [9][him.] (For) he shall be called [Son of] the [gr]eat [God], and by his name shall he be named. [1]He shall be hailed Son of God [ברה די אל], and they shall call him Son of the Most High [בר עליון] . . . his kingdom (shall be) an everlasting kingdom, and all his ways (shall be) in truth. He shall jud[ge] [6]the land with truth, and everyone shall make peace. (4Q246 1:7b–2:1, 5-6)

The appearance of these epithets in Luke 1:32-35, Gabriel's announcement to Mary, is very significant. It suggests that the title "Son of God" not only had a Davidic application but was also understood in a messianic sense. The relevant parts of the Lukan passage read:

> He shall be great and he shall be called Son of the Most High; and the Lord God will give to him the throne of David his father. And he will reign over the house of Jacob forever; and his kingdom will have no end. . . . The power of the Most High will overshadow you; therefore that which has been conceived will be called holy, Son of God.

Thanks to 4Q246 we now see that the angel's annunciation to Mary, as well the Gerasene demoniac's address to Jesus as "Son of the Most High God," was right at home in first-century Palestine. That both epithets, "Son of God" and "Son of the Most High," occur among the Dead Sea Scrolls tells against the view that this language derives from non-Palestinian Hellenistic sources.

4Q525 2:1-7 and Jesus' "Beatitudes"

Another surprising scroll from Qumran that has been recently published and widely discussed is 4Q525. In its second column we find beatitudes that in important respects parallel those of Jesus in Matthew's well-known Sermon on the Mount (Matt 5:3-12) or Sermon on the Plain, as Luke presents it (Luke 6:20-23). The text reads as follows:

> [Blessed is he who walks] [1]with a pure heart and who does not slander with his tongue. Blessed are they who hold fast to her (Wisdom's) laws and do not hold [2]to the ways of evil. Bless[ed] are they who rejoice in her and do not overflow with the ways of folly. Blessed are they who ask for her [3]with clean hands and do not seek her with a deceitful [heart]. Blessed is the man who grasps hold of Wisdom and walks [4]in the Torah of the Most High and directs his heart to her ways and restrains himself with her disciplines and always accepts her chastisements [5]and does not cast her off in the misery of [his] affliction[s] nor forsake her in a time of trouble, nor forget her in [days of ter]ror, [6]and in the meekness of his soul does not despis[e her], but rather always meditates on her, and when in affliction occupies himself [with Torah; who al]l [7]his life [meditates] on her [and places her continually] before his eyes so he will not walk in the ways of [evil . . . [8]. . .] in unity and his heart if perfect. God. . . ."

Several parallels immediately suggest themselves:

> [Blessed is he who walks] with a pure heart. (4Q525 2:1)
> Blessed are the pure in heart. (Matt 5:8)
>
> Blessed are those who rejoice in her. (4Q525 2:2)
> Blessed are you when men revile you . . . rejoice and be glad. (Matt 5:11-12)
>
> Blessed is the man who . . . in the meekness of his soul, does not despise her. (4Q525 2:3-6)
> In the meekness of righteousness bring forth [your] words. . . . (4Q525 4:20)
> Blessed are the meek. (Matt 5:5)

These parallels tell against the proposal of some members of the Jesus Seminar that Jesus' teaching is best understood against the backdrop of Graeco-Roman philosophy, especially Cynicism. These parallels from 4Q525 offer important support to the contention that the content and style of Jesus' teaching are right at home in Jewish wisdom tradition.[11] Of course, Jesus' beatitudes are not

11. See B. Witherington III, *Jesus the Sage: The Pilgrimage of Wisdom* (Minneapolis: Fortress, 1994). Witherington, however, does not discuss 4Q425.

identical to those of 4Q525; the former are eschatological and the latter are sapiential. But they are similar in important ways. Jesus apparently took over a manner of speaking rooted in Israel's wisdom tradition and gave it his own eschatological spin.

4Q521 and Jesus' Reply to John the Baptist

4Q521 is one of the most important of the recently published scrolls. It begins with an explicit reference to God's "Messiah":

> [1][. . . the hea]vens and the earth will obey His Messiah, [2][. . . and all th]at is in them. He will not turn aside from the commandments of the holy ones. [3]Take strength in His service, (you) who seek the Lord. [4]Will you not find the Lord in this, all you who wait patiently in your hearts? [5]For the Lord will visit the pious ones, and the righteous ones He will call by name. [6]Over the meek His Spirit will hover, and the faithful He will restore by His power. [7]He will glorify the pious ones on the throne of the eternal kingdom. [8]He will release the captives, make the blind see, raise up the do[wntrodden.] [9]For[ev]er I shall cling to Him . . .], and [I shall trust] in His lovingkindness, [10]and [His] goo[dness . . .] of holiness will not delay [. . .] [11]And as for the wonders that are not the work of the Lord, when He [. . .] [12]then he will heal the slain, resurrect the dead, and announce glad tidings to the poor. [13][. . .] He will lead the [hol]y ones; he will shepherd [th]em; he will do [. . .] [14]and all of it. . . .

Shortly after the publication of this text, a remarkable parallel with a saying of Jesus was observed:

> (John) sent word by his disciples and said to him (Jesus), "Are you he who is to come, or shall we look for another?" And Jesus answered them, "Go and tell John what you hear and see: the blind receive their sight and the lame walk, lepers are cleansed and the deaf hear, and the dead are raised up, and the poor have good news preached to them." (Matt 11:2-5 = Luke 7:19-22)[12]

Jesus' reply alludes to Isa 61:1-2 and 35:5-6. But these passages say nothing about the *dead being raised up.* This element is, however, present in 4Q521. The parallel columns highlight this important point of agreement between Jesus' saying and the tradition preserved in the fragmentary Dead Sea text:

12. M. O. Wise and J. D. Tabor were the first to recognize the significance of the parallel between 4Q521 and Jesus' reply to John the Baptist; see their study "The Messiah at Qumran," *BAR* 18/6 (1992) 60-65. See also the discussion in J. D. Tabor and M. O. Wise, "4Q521 'On Resurrection' and the Synoptic Gospel Tradition: A Preliminary Study," *JSP* 10 (1994) 149-62.

Q (Matt 11:5 = Luke 7:22)	*Isaiah 35 + 61*	*4Q521*
he cured many of diseases		he will heal the slain
blind receive sight	blind receive sight	make blind see
lame walk	lame walk	
lepers are cleansed		
deaf hear	deaf hear	
dead are raised up		*resurrect the dead*
poor have good news preached	poor have good news preached	poor have good news preached

John Collins has suggested that 4Q521 describes the expected activity of a prophetic Messiah.[13] This seems likely because Isaiah 61 concerns someone anointed to "bring good news" and to "proclaim liberty" and "the year of the Lord's favor." These are the responsibilities of a prophet. Indeed, the Targum renders Isa 61:1, "The Prophet said, 'A spirit of prophecy . . . is upon me . . . to announce good news. . . ." The commission to proclaim good news is also the job of the herald of Isa 52:7. Significantly, in this passage the prophetic herald announces that "God is king" (or, "God reigns"). The Aramaic paraphrase may again be significant; it reads: "The kingdom of your God is revealed."[14]

If we bring together these two passages, especially as the Targum has paraphrased them, we have a remarkably close approximation of Jesus' message: He proclaims the kingdom of God, and through his ministry of healing and exorcism he proves that it is present; and he claims to be anointed and so qualified to proclaim the good news. 4Q521 significantly supports the traditional view that Jesus did indeed see himself as Israel's Messiah.

4Q500 and Jesus' Parable of the Wicked Tenants

Jesus' parable of the wicked tenants (Mark 12:1-11) is based on the juridical parable found in Isa 5:1-7. Isaiah's parable, apparently delivered as a song, perhaps during the celebration of the grape harvest, is directed against the population at large, "the inhabitants of Jerusalem and the men of Judah" (v. 3;

13. J. J. Collins, "The Works of the Messiah," *DSD* 1 (1994) 98-112; idem, *The Scepter and the Star: The Messiahs of the Dead Sea Scrolls and Other Ancient Literature* (ABRL 10; New York: Doubleday, 1995) 117-22, 205-6.

14. On the importance of this passage for understanding the message of Jesus, see B. Chilton, *God in Strength: Jesus' Announcement of the Kingdom* (SNTU 1; Freistadt: Plöchl, 1979; reprint, Sheffield: JSOT Press, 1987) 277-93; idem, "The Kingdom of God in Recent Discussion," in *Studying the Historical Jesus: Evaluations of the State of Current Research*, ed. B. D. Chilton and C. A. Evans (NTTS 19; Leiden: Brill, 1994) 255-80.

cf. v. 7). In contrast, Jesus' parable is directed against the ruling priests (cf. Mark 11:27; 12:12). That Jesus' parable is based on Isaiah 5 is obvious, but what is not obvious is why the ruling priests readily perceived that the parable had been told "against them" (cf. Mark 12:12).

Bruce Chilton has made a convincing case that the Targum helps clarify a saying of Jesus. He has observed that in the Aramaic paraphrase of the Isaiah passage the criticism is given a distinctly anti-Temple orientation. According to the Targum, the tower is the "sanctuary" and the wine vat is the "altar." Chilton translates (with significant departures from the Masoretic Text indicated by italics):

> And I *sanctified* them and I *glorified* them and I established them as the plant of a choice vine; and I built my *sanctuary* in their midst, and I even gave my *altar to atone for their sins;* I thought that they would do good deeds, but they made their deeds evil. (v. 2)
>
> And now I will tell you what I am about to do to my people. I will take up my *Shekhinah* from them, and they shall be for plundering; I will break down *the place of their sanctuaries,* and they will be for trampling. (v. 5)[15]

The tradition preserved in the Targum illumines Jesus' use of Isaiah 5 in his parable of the wicked tenants. As in the Targum, so in Jesus' parable we find the prophetic criticism leveled against the Temple establishment and not against the general population. The Temple and the altar will be destroyed, and God's holy presence will be removed. Such an understanding of Isaiah 5 only intensifies the antipriestly tone of Jesus' parable. Their failure will result in their loss of stewardship over the vineyard (= Israel).

But was this Aramaic interpretation, preserved in a targum that was not committed to writing until two or three centuries after the New Testament period, current in the time of Jesus? Some scholars have expressed misgivings, claiming that the Targum is too late to be used in efforts to reconstruct exegetical traditions that were current in the first century. However, the recent publication of 4Q500 suggests that Isa 5:1-7 was understood in this way at the time of Jesus. This fragmentary text appears to be part of a midrashic interpretation that views the vineyard of Isa 5:1-7 as a metaphor of Jerusalem and her Temple. Lines 2-7 read as follows:[16]

> 2 . . . your baca trees will blossom and . . .
> 3 . . . a wine vat [bu]ilt among stones . . .

15. B. D. Chilton, *The Isaiah Targum* (ArBib 11; Wilmington: Glazier, 1987) 10-11.

16. See M. Baillet, *Qumrân Grotte 4 III (4Q482–4Q520)* (DJD 7; Oxford: Clarendon, 1982) 78-79 + pl. 27; J. M. Baumgarten, "4Q500 and the Ancient Conception of the Lord's Vineyard," *JJS* 40 (1989) 1-6; Marcus, *The Way of the Lord,* 120; and especially G. J. Brooke, "4Q500 1 and the Use of Scripture in the Parable of the Vineyard," *DSD* 2 (1995) 268-94.

4 . . . to the gate of the holy height . . .
5 . . . your planting and the streams of your glory . . .
6 . . . the branches of your delights . . .
7 . . . your vine[yard . . .]

The reference in line 3 to the "wine vat built among stones" is an unmistakable allusion to Isa 5:2. This reference helps restore "your vineyard" in line 7, thereby giving us an allusion to Isa 5:1. The "gate of the holy height" refers to the Temple. "Height" (מרום) agrees with the Targum's "high" (רם) hill in verse 1. The reference in line 5 to the "streams" of God's glory agrees with one of the interpretations preserved in the Tosepta (*t. Sukk.* 3.15). The Tosepta not only understands "he dug a wine vat" as a reference to the altar, in agreement with the Targum; it also repeats the phrase, "*and* he dug a wine vat," interpreting it as a reference to the water channel that streams forth from the altar (cf. *m. Yoma* 5:6; *m. Middot* 3:3).[17] These additional points of coherence strongly suggest that the interpretation preserved in the Targum predates the New Testament.

The Semitic character of Jesus' parable is also seen in the use of the concluding citation of Ps 118:22-23, which in all probability arose from a wordplay between the words "son" and "stone."[18] Together, all of the features we have noted argue against the assertion that the parable of the wicked tenants is a creation of the Greek-speaking church. Indeed, as George Brooke has concluded, the complexity, interconnectedness, and integrity of the pericope "puts the burden of proof that it contains secondary accretions firmly on those who are looking for an 'originally' simple story with a single point."[19] We may also agree with his conclusion that Jesus' "use of scripture in the pericope as a whole is not the result of the creative work of the early church, but goes back to Jesus himself, to a Jesus who even taught in the temple."[20]

17. This observation has been made by Baumgarten, "4Q500," 2.

18. As seen in the similarity of the pronunciation of *ha-ben* ("the son") and *ha-'eben* ("the stone").

19. Brooke, "4Q500," 289. Members of the Jesus Seminar have maintained that the version of the parable of the wicked tenants preserved in the Synoptic Gospels represents a secondary, embellished form of the parable that includes allegorical features (such as Israel's history of persecuting the prophets and Jesus' own rejection and martyrdom). The Seminar believes that the form of the parable preserved in the *Gospel of Thomas,* which lacks any allusions to Isaiah 5, is closer to Jesus' original teaching.

20. Brooke, "4Q500," 294.

Conclusion

These four fragmentary texts from Cave 4 should make it evident that the Dead Sea Scrolls have much light to shed on Jesus and the world in which he lived and ministered. Continuing study will doubtless point up other interesting features that will aid the interpretive task. This is not to say that the Scrolls contain all the answers, but they do shed a great deal of light on certain aspects of Jesus' teaching and the beliefs of his contemporaries.

Throne-Chariot Mysticism in Qumran and in Paul

JAMES M. SCOTT

Introduction

For almost fifty years since the discovery of the Dead Sea Scrolls, scholars have been searching for comparisons between Paul and Qumran on every level, from individual words and phrases to whole sections.[1] In fact, 2 Cor 6:14–7:1 is deemed so much like material in the Dead Sea Scrolls — and so unlike anything else in Paul — that it has sometimes been called a "Qumran fragment."[2] Now that the Dead Sea Scrolls have been released in their entirety and the enormous task of taking stock of the new, often fragmentary material has begun, we can expect many more comparisons with Paul's letters to come to light in the future.

The purpose of the present paper is to explore a possible comparison between throne-chariot mysticism in Qumran and in Paul.[3] Although this may seem at first like a recondite and obscure subject, especially when the term

1. Cf., e.g., J. Murphy-O'Connor and J. H. Charlesworth, eds., *Paul and the Dead Sea Scrolls* (New York: Crossroad, 1990); H.-W. Kuhn, "The Impact of the Qumran Scrolls on the Understanding of Paul," in *The Dead Sea Scrolls: Forty Years of Research,* ed. D. Dimant and U. Rappaport (STDJ 10; Leiden: Brill, 1992) 327-39.

2. Cf. Joseph A. Fitzmyer, "Qumran and the Interpolated Paragraph in 2 Corinthians 6:14–7:1," in *Essays on the Semitic Background of the New Testament,* by Joseph A. Fitzmyer (London: Chapman, 1971) 205-17. See, however, my essay "The Use of Scripture in 2 Corinthians 6.16c-18 and Paul's Restoration Theology," *JSNT* 56 (1994) 73-99.

3. The present paper builds on a thesis originally suggested in my article "The Triumph of God in 2 Cor 2.14: Additional Evidence of Merkabah Mysticism in Paul," *NTS* 42 (1996) 260-81.

"mysticism" is applied,[4] I hope to show that it is actually very important to understanding Paul's conception of his own apostleship.[5] First, I would like to look briefly at what we know about early Jewish throne-chariot mysticism, and particularly that in Qumran. Then, second, I would like to see how these considerations might contribute to our understanding of the apostle Paul.

Throne-Chariot Mysticism in Jewish Tradition

Old Testament

The basic elements of Jewish throne-chariot mysticism are already found in the biblical throne visions.[6] One of the most important examples of these theophanies, Ezekiel's prophetic call vision by the river Chebar (Ezek 1:4-28), gives us an extensive but cryptic picture of what became known as the מרכבה ("throne-chariot"), apparently a kind of royal throne on wheels (cf. Dan 7:9).[7] Beginning with a stormy wind and a fiery cloud approaching from the north (v. 4), Ezekiel's vision unfolds as a description of four bizarre חיות ("living creatures" or "beasts"), each with four faces (man, lion, ox, and eagle), four wings, and four wheels (vv. 5-21). Above their heads is a platform like crystal (vv. 22-25). And above the platform sits an anthropomorphic manifestation of God on a sapphire throne described as "the appearance of the likeness of the glory of the Lord" (vv. 26-28).[8]

4. The term "mysticism" is used here not in the pejorative sense of superstitious self-delusion, but rather in the sense of the diverse forms of direct realizations of divine presence, whether on earth or in heaven. Cf. I. Gruenwald, "Major Issues in the Study and Understanding of Jewish Mysticism," in *Judaism in Late Antiquity, Part Two: Historical Syntheses,* ed. J. Neusner (Leiden: Brill, 1995) 1-49 (here 7); also L. H. Schiffman, *Reclaiming the Dead Sea Scrolls: The History of Judaism, the Background of Christianity, the Lost Library of Qumran* (Philadelphia and Jerusalem: The Jewish Publication Society, 1994) 351, 446-47.

5. See further my forthcoming commentary on *2 Corinthians* (NIBC 8; Peabody, MA: Hendrickson), which develops in more detail the importance of Paul's Merkabah mysticism in the polemical situation that he faced in Corinth.

6. Cf. Exod 24:10-11; 1 Kgs 22:19; Isaiah 6; Ezekiel 1; 3:22-24; 8:1-18; 10:9-17; 43:1-4; Dan 7:9-14.

7. The idea of a divine chariot was widespread in the ancient Near East and is quite common in the Hebrew Bible (cf. Ps 68:18; 1 Kgs 23:11). See J. W. McKay, "Further Light on the Horses and Chariot of the Sun in the Jerusalem Temple (2 Kings 23:11)," *PEQ* 105 (1973) 167-69. As John Collins points out, however, the description in Dan 7:9 derives from Ezekiel's Merkabah vision in Ezek 1:15-21; 10:2 (*Daniel: A Commentary on the Book of Daniel* [Hermeneia; Minneapolis: Fortress, 1993] 302).

8. For an extensive discussion of the throne traditions in the Hebrew Bible, replete with ancient Near Eastern parallels, see M. Metzger, *Königsthron und Gottesthron: Thronformen und Throndarstellungen in Ägypten und im Vorderen Orient im dritten und zweiten Jahrtausend vor Christus und deren Bedeutung für das Verständnis von Aussagen über den Thron im Alten Testament* (AOAT; Neukirchen-Vluyn: Neukirchener Verlag, 1985) 1.309-76.

Dead Sea Scrolls

Ezekiel was evidently important to the Qumran community,[9] and its scrolls provide some of the earliest evidence that the throne in Ezekiel's vision was actually called a *Merkabah.*[10] According to 4Q385, which scholars have dubbed *Second Ezekiel,* "the vision that Ezekiel saw" was the divine מרכבה, together with the "four living creatures" (4:5-6).[11] The Dead Sea Scrolls have much to say about the divine throne-chariot.[12] Indeed, one of the highest goals of the Qumran community seems to have been to participate in the heavenly angelic liturgy and to see the great throne-chariot of God enter the heavenly Temple.[13] A pre-Christian[14] liturgical text from Qumran Cave 4, known as the *Songs of the Sabbath Sacrifice* or *Angelic Liturgy,* is comprised of thirteen separate

9. Cf. B. Z. Wacholder, "Ezekiel and Ezekielianism as Progenitors of Essenianism," in *The Dead Sea Scrolls: Forty Years of Research,* ed. Dimant and Rappaport, 186-96; G. J. Brooke, "Ezekiel in Some Qumran and New Testament Texts," in *The Madrid Qumran Congress: Proceedings of the International Congress on the Dead Sea Scrolls, Madrid, 18-21 March 1991,* ed. J. Trebolle Barrera and L. Vegas Montaner (2 vols.; STDJ 11; Leiden: Brill; Madrid: Editorial Complutense, 1992) 1.317-37. For a list of the Ezekiel manuscripts in the Dead Sea Scrolls, see E. Ulrich, "An Index of the Passages in the Biblical Manuscripts from the Judean Desert (Part 2: Isaiah-Chronicles)," *DSD* 2 (1995) 86-107 (here 94). 4QEzek[b] contains a fragment of Ezek 1:10-13, 16-17, 19-24.

10. Cf. also Sir 49:8: "Ezekiel saw a vision, and he told the different kinds of the Merkabah (מרכבה)." Old Greek: "It was Ezekiel who saw the vision of glory, which God showed him upon the chariot of the cherubim (ἐπὶ ἅρματος χερουβιν)." Cf. J. Marböck, "Henoch-Adam-der Thronwagen. Zu frühjüdischen pseudepigraphischen Traditionen bei *Ben Sira,*" *BZ* 25 (1981) 103-11.

11. Cf. D. Dimant and J. Strugnell, "The Merkabah Vision in *Second Ezekiel* (4Q385 4)," *RevQ* 14 (1991) 331-48; B. Z. Wacholder and M. G. Abegg, Jr., *A Preliminary Edition of the Unpublished Dead Sea Scrolls: The Hebrew and Aramaic Texts from Cave Four, Fascicle 3* (Washington, D.C.: Biblical Archaeology Society, 1995) 230-31. According to Dimant and Strugnell (ibid., 348), 4Q385 4 represents "the oldest witness at our disposal to postbiblical exegesis of the biblical *Merkabah* vision." In Jewish literature of the Second Temple period, vision reports of the divine throne-chariot typically combine the basic elements of Merkabah mysticism from various parts of the Hebrew Bible. For example, *1 Enoch* 14:18-23, an Aramaic fragment of which was found among the Dead Sea Scrolls, clearly combines elements from Isaiah 6, Dan 7:9-10, and Ezekiel 1 and 10. See also *1 Enoch* 60:2; 71; 90:20; I. Gruenwald, *Apocalyptic and Merkavah Mysticism* (AGJU 14; Leiden: Brill, 1980) 29-72.

12. Cf. Schiffman, *Reclaiming the Dead Sea Scrolls,* 351-66.

13. Cf. C. Newsom, *Songs of the Sabbath Sacrifice: A Critical Edition* (HSS 27; Atlanta: Scholars Press, 1985) 17-18, 19, 53, 64-65, 71-72. See further Newsom, "Merkabah Exegesis in the Qumran Sabbath Shirot," *JJS* 38 (1987) 11-30.

14. Cf. Newsom, *Songs of the Sabbath Sacrifice,* 1: "The text is preserved in fragmentary form in eight manuscripts (4Q400, 401, 402, 403, 404, 405, 406, 407) that can be dated paleographically to the late Hasmonean and early Herodian periods. The end of another scroll of the Sabbath Shirot in Herodian script was found in Qumran Cave 11. In addition a single large fragment, written in fully developed Herodian script, was discovered by Y. Yadin in the excavations of Masada. There is no internal evidence by which one might establish a date for the composition. Paleographically, the hand of the oldest manuscript, 4Q400, may be dated to ca. 75-50 B.C., according to the script charts published by F. M. Cross."

sections, one for each of thirteen Sabbaths. The songs invoke angelic praise, describe the angelic priesthood and the heavenly Temple, and give an account of the worship performed on the Sabbath in the heavenly sanctuary. The twelfth Sabbath song begins with a lengthy description of the appearance and movement of the divine throne-chariot. Whereas the seventh and eleventh Sabbath songs refer to a plurality of מרכבות, the twelfth song describes *the* divine Merkabah, the throne of glory, borrowing heavily on terms from Ezekiel 1 and 10 (4Q405).[15] The appearance of the Merkabah is greeted with praise and blessing from the assembled ranks of angels: "They bless the image of the throne-chariot [which is] above the vault of the cherubim, and they sing [the splen]dor of the shining vault (which is) beneath the seat of his glory" (4Q405 20-22 ii 8-9). The worshipper who hears the songs has the sense of being in the heavenly sanctuary and in the presence of the angelic priests. The large number of manuscripts of the *Angelic Liturgy* found at Qumran (4Q400–407) makes it probable that the recitation of these songs was a major vehicle for the experience of communion with the angels as it is alluded to in the *Thanksgiving Hymns* (1QH 3:21-23; 11:13) and in the *Rule of the Community* (1QS 11:7-8). Carol Newsom suggests that the purpose of these Sabbath Songs may have been communal mysticism.[16] During the course of the thirteen-week cycle, the community that recites the compositions is brought through a lengthy preparation and is gradually led through the spiritually animate heavenly Temple until the worshippers experience the holiness of the Merkabah and the Sabbath sacrifice as it is conducted by the high priests of the angels.

Later Jewish Literature

Later Jewish tradition also has much to say about the divine throne-chariot. In fact, there is a whole body of Jewish literature called the Hekhalot (or "Palaces") literature that features contemplation of the divine throne-chariot in a special way.[17] God's throne stands in the innermost of seven concentric palaces, the way to which is barred by fierce guardian angels at the gate of each palace. In making the extremely hazardous ascent to the highest heaven and the innermost sanctum, the Merkabah mystic seeks, among other things, to ascend to the

15. Cf. Newsom, *Songs of the Sabbath Sacrifice,* 303-21. For a translation of the text, see F. García Martínez, *The Dead Sea Scrolls Translated: The Qumran Texts in English* (Leiden: Brill, 1994) 428-29.

16. Newsom, *Songs of the Sabbath Sacrifice,* 19.

17. Cf. P. Schäfer, "The Aim and Purpose of Early Jewish Mysticism," in *Hekhalot-Studien,* by Peter Schäfer (TSAJ 19; Tübingen: Mohr-Siebeck, 1988) 276-95; I. Chernus, "Visions of God in Merkabah Mysticism," *JSJ* 13 (1982) 123-46.

Merkabah itself in order to learn the Torah completely and permanently. It is fascinating to note the many similarities between the Hekhalot literature and the earlier Qumran texts.[18]

Interestingly enough, Rabbinic texts seem very wary of Merkabah mysticism and restrict its contemplation to the Torah scholar who understands the matter on his own (cf. *m. Ḥagiga* 2:1). As David Halperin has shown, the reason for this Rabbinic reaction against contemplation of the Merkabah is the idolatry that resulted from it at Sinai; calf worship is a routine hazard of contemplating the Merkabah, especially as practiced by the masses.[19] This comes out most explicitly in a midrash focusing on the golden calf incident (Exod 32:1-35) that refers to the chariot of God as a "four-mule chariot." The earliest version of the midrash (*Exod. Rab.* 43:8) accuses Israel of idolatrously contemplating the Merkabah when God descended to Sinai to deliver the Law to Moses. Here, we have evidence of a synagogue tradition which, in connection with Ps 68:19, held that God descended on Sinai with the Merkabah that Ezekiel saw, and that the very contemplation of the four living creatures/beasts harnessed to it caused the Israelites to "unhitch" one of them — the ox with the "calf's foot" (cf. Ezek 1:7, 10) — and thus to fall into the grievous sin of worshipping the golden calf. This midrash, together with other texts, shows that in Jewish tradition the Merkabah was commonly conceived as a quadriga drawn by the four living creatures/beasts.[20]

Expounding the Merkabah was evidently a common activity in the ancient Jewish synagogue. According to *t. Megilla* 3(4).28, "Many expounded the Merkabah and never saw it." The murals in the synagogue at Dura Europos include a picture of the Merkabah.[21] However, the Mishnah rules that "the Account of Creation (Gen 1:1–2:3) may not be expounded before two or more persons, nor the Merkabah (Ezekiel 1) before even one, unless he is a scholar

18. Cf. Dimant and Strugnell, "Second Ezekiel," 332; Schiffman, *Reclaiming the Dead Sea Scrolls*, 358-59; idem, "Merkabah Speculation at Qumran: The 4QSerekh Shirot 'Olat ha-Shabbat," in *Mystics, Philosophers, and Politicians: Essays in Jewish Intellectual History in Honor of Alexander Altmann*, ed. J. Reinharz et al. (Durham, NC: Duke University Press, 1982) 15-47; J. M. Baumgarten, "The Qumran Shirot and Rabbinic Merkabah Traditions," *RevQ* 13 (1988) 199-213.

19. D. J. Halperin, *The Faces of the Chariot: Early Jewish Responses to Ezekiel's Vision* (TSAJ 16; Tübingen: Mohr [Siebeck], 1988) 157-93; cf. P. Schäfer, ed., *Synopse zur Hekhalot-Literatur* (TSAJ 2; Tübingen: Mohr-Siebeck, 1981) §955.

20. Cf. Hab 3:8, where Yahweh is said to drive a horse-drawn *merkabah;* 1 Chron 28:18 ("his plan for the golden chariot of the cherubim"); the Gnostic *Hypostasis of the Archons* (NHC 2/4, 95:13-14), which describes the "great four-faced chariot of cherubim"; *3 Enoch* 22:11; 24:1; *Apoc. Moses* 33:2; *Apoc. Abraham* 18:11-12. See further M. Haran, "The Ark and the Cherubim," *IEJ* 9 (1959) 30-38 (esp. 37), 89-94; H. P. L'Orange, *Studies on the Iconography of Cosmic Kingship in the Ancient World* (Instituttet for Sammenlignende Kulturforskning A.23; Oslo: Aschehough-Nygaard, 1953) 37-79, 124-33.

21. Cf. J. A. Goldstein, "The Judaism of the Synagogues (Focusing on the Synagogue of Dura-Europos)," in *Judaism in Late Antiquity*, ed. Neusner, 109-57.

who understands of his own knowledge" (*m. Ḥagiga* 2:1). Those who ignored these injunctions did so at their own peril. The story is told in the Talmud of a certain Galilean who announced that he would publicly lecture on the Merkabah, but who was stung by a wasp and died (*b. Šabbat* 80b). A distinguished student who dabbled prematurely in chariot lore was said to have been smitten with leprosy (*y. Ḥagiga* 2:1, 77a). A child contemplated *hashmal* (Ezek 1:4) and was consumed by fire (*b. Ḥagiga* 13a). If we can thus trace a more or less continuous stream of tradition from the pre-Christian Qumran scrolls, through the synagogue, to the time of the later Hekhalot literature, we have the setting for the rabbinic reaction against the popular contemplation of the Merkabah.

Throne-Chariot Mysticism in Paul

Having briefly surveyed throne-chariot mysticism in Jewish tradition, we turn our attention next to the apostle Paul. He was a Jew who proudly characterized himself as such even after years of missionary work in the name of the resurrected Christ (cf. 2 Cor 11:22; Rom 11:1; Phil 3:5).[22] Furthermore, Paul was a Jew who even as an apostle of Jesus Christ continued to participate in the synagogue.[23] If, as we have seen, Merkabah mysticism was evidently practiced in the synagogue, was Paul acquainted with it as well?

Previous Research on the Question

Gershom Scholem, one of the pioneers of modern work on Jewish mysticism, maintained that Paul was indeed familiar with Merkabah mysticism. In 1960, Scholem published a famous essay in which he argued that in 2 Cor 12:2-4, Paul's rapture into Paradise or the third heaven should be understood against the background of the Rabbinic story of the "Four Who Entered *Pardes*,"

22. Cf. K.-W. Niebuhr, *Heidenapostel aus Israel: Die jüdische Identität des Paulus nach ihrer Darstellung in seinen Briefen* (WUNT 62; Tübingen: Mohr-Siebeck, 1992).

23. The forty lashes minus one that, according to 2 Cor 11:24, Paul received from the Jews refers to a form of corporal punishment administered in the synagogue; cf. S. Gallas, "'Fünfmal vierzig weniger einen . . .' Die an Paulus vollzogenen Synagogalstrafen nach 2Kor 11,24," *ZNW* 81 (1990) 178-91. According to Acts 22:19, Paul used to flog believers in the synagogues. Later, as a believer himself, the persecutor becomes the persecuted. Whenever he entered a new city, Paul used the synagogue as a basis for evangelism (cf. Acts 9:20; 13:5, 14; 14:1; 17:1-2, 10, 17; 18:4, 19, 26; 19:8). The fact that the apostle received a synagogal punishment not only tends to corroborate the testimony of Acts at this point, but also shows that he was taken seriously as a Jew who operated within the parameters of Judaism. Hence, in a backhanded way, the "forty lashes minus one" further underscores Paul's claim to being an Israelite in 2 Cor 11:22.

which is found in collections of traditions associated with Merkabah mysticism and in two Hekhalot texts.[24] This interpretation of 2 Cor 12:2-4 has often been questioned, most recently and powerfully by Peter Schäfer,[25] the editor of the Hekhalot literature.[26] Now, however, Schäfer's objections have been answered by C. R. A. Morray-Jones.[27] Hence, although the debate continues,[28] it now seems more probable than ever that in 2 Cor 12:2-4 Paul was indeed talking about a Merkabah experience he had had fourteen years previously.[29] This is in any case how the Gnostic *Apocalypse of Paul* understands the passage.[30]

Recently, there has been considerable interest in the Jewish mysticism of Paul, and particularly his Merkabah mysticism. For example, Alan F. Segal attempts to understand Paul as a visionary who underwent a mystical conversion akin to the experiences found in the Jewish mystical tradition exemplified in

24. Cf. G. Scholem, "The Four Who Entered Paradise and Paul's Ascension to Paradise," in *Jewish Gnosticism, Merkabah Mysticism, and Talmudic Tradition,* by Gershom Scholem (2d ed.; New York: Jewish Theological Seminary, 1965) 14-19.

25. Cf. P. Schäfer, "New Testament and Hekhalot Literature: The Journey into Heaven in Paul and in Merkabah Mysticism," *JJS* 35 (1984) 19-35.

26. In addition, Schäfer has translated the Hekhalot corpus into German and has written extensively on the issue. In the following, the Hekhalot literature will be cited according to P. Schäfer, ed., *Synopse zur Hekhalot-Literatur* (TSAJ 2; Tübingen: Mohr-Siebeck, 1981) with the section number (§).

27. Cf. C. R. A. Morray-Jones, "Paradise Revisited (2 Cor 12:1-12): The Jewish Mystical Background of Paul's Apostolate. Part 1: The Jewish Sources," *HTR* 86 (1993) 177-217; idem, "Paradise Revisited (2 Cor 12:1-12): The Jewish Mystical Background of Paul's Apostolate. Part 2: Paul's Heavenly Ascent and Its Significance," *HTR* 86 (1993) 265-92. On the connection of 2 Cor 12:2-4 to Jewish mysticism, see also Alan F. Segal, "Paul and the Beginning of Jewish Mysticism," in *Death, Ecstasy, and Other Worldly Journeys,* ed. J. J. Collins and M. Fishbane (Albany, NY: SUNY Press, 1995) 95-122 (esp. 108-9).

28. For a rebuttal of Morray-Jones's position, see now A. Goshen-Gottstein, "Four Entered Paradise Revisited," *HTR* 88 (1995) 69-133. I am grateful to James R. Davila for supplying me with a copy of his 1995 SBL paper on "The Hodayot Hymnist and the Four Who Entered Paradise," which responds to Goshen-Gottstein and strongly supports the contention of Morray-Jones, that his reconstructed earliest stratum of the story had its life-setting in the Hellenistic period. According to Davila, both the story of the Four and 1QH^a 16:4-26 tell of a sage who enters the celestial holy of holies in the Garden of Eden. The Garden is damaged by interlopers and guarded by dangerous angels. The sage, protected by God, is unmolested by the angels and moves about freely in the Garden.

29. According to C. Rowland, "Paul's Trance-vision in the Temple (Acts 22.17) is similar enough [to the 'Great Seance' of Hekhalot Rabbati] to suggest the [*merkabah*] tradition is this old," that is, as old as the first century CE. C. Rowland, "The Parting of the Ways: The Evidence of Jewish and Christian Apocalyptic and Mystical Material," in *Jews and Christians: The Parting of the Ways A.D. 70 to 135,* ed. J. D. G. Dunn (WUNT 66; Tübingen: Mohr-Siebeck, 1992) 213-37 (here p. 226).

30. Cf. D. M. Parrott, "The Apocalypse of Paul (V,2)," in *The Nag Hammadi Library in English,* ed. J. M. Robinson (3d ed.; San Francisco: Harper & Row, 1988) 256-59; see also H.-J. Klauck, "Die Himmelfahrt des Paulus (2 Kor 12,2-4) in der koptischen Paulusapokalypse aus Nag Hammadi (NHC V/2)," *SNTU* 10 (1985) 151-90.

the Qumran *Angelic Liturgy, 1 Enoch,* and later Merkabah mysticism.[31] Martin Hengel has also focused on the Merkabah experience of Paul, arguing that the apostle bears witness to an early Christian tradition based on Ps 110:1, that the crucified Messiah, Jesus of Nazareth, was raised and seated "at the right hand" of God, that is, enthroned as a co-occupant of God's own "throne of glory" (cf. Jer 17:12), located in the highest heaven.[32] Hengel suggests that Paul presupposes the Merkabah throne-chariot at many points in his extant writings. For if the resurrected and exalted Christ receives "the name which is above every name" (Phil 2:9), namely, the Tetragrammaton (יהוה; LXX: κύριος), the same unique name as God himself, then he also shares in the unique throne of God, the "throne of glory."[33] As a result of this heavenly communion between the Father and the Son on the throne, effected by the resurrection, the Father and the Son carry out activities either together or interchangeably.[34] This "unity of activity" elucidates Paul's assertion in 2 Cor 5:19 ("God was in Christ reconciling the world to himself"),[35] and it explains why in 2 Cor 5:10 he can state that "we must all appear before the judgment seat of *Christ* (τὸ βῆμα τοῦ Χριστοῦ)," whereas in Rom 14:10, written just a few months later, he can say that "we shall all stand before the judgment seat of *God* (τὸ βῆμα τοῦ θεοῦ)."[36] Moreover, Paul seems to recall a Merkabah vision in 2 Cor 12:2-4, one of many such visions of the Lord that he had received (cf. vv. 1, 7).[37]

If Scholem, Morray-Jones, Segal, and Hengel, among others, are correct that Merkabah visions profoundly influenced Paul's thinking and writing, not least in 2 Corinthians, we may be encouraged to consider whether 2 Cor 2:14

31. A. F. Segal, *Paul the Convert: The Apostolate and Apostasy of Saul the Pharisee* (New Haven: Yale, 1990); idem, "Paul and the Beginning of Jewish Mysticism," 93-122. Cf. also J. M. Vincent, "Some Reflections on ὤφθη (1 Cor 15:5) on the Background of Ezek 1," in *Festschrift Günter Wagner* (International Theological Studies: Contributions of Baptist Scholars 1; Bern: Lang, 1994) 191-202.

32. M. Hengel, " 'Setze dich zu meiner Rechten!' Die Inthronisation Christi zur Rechten Gottes und Psalm 110,1," in *Le Trône de Dieu,* ed. M. Philonenko (WUNT 69; Tübingen: Mohr-Siebeck, 1993) 108-94; see now idem, " 'Sit at My Right Hand!' The Enthronement of Christ at the Right Hand of God and Psalm 110:1," in *Studies in Early Christology,* by Martin Hengel (Edinburgh: Clark, 1995) 119-225. Cf. Eusebius, *Demonstratio evangelica* 4.15.33, 42; Schäfer, *Synopse zur Hekhalot-Literatur,* §233.

33. Cf. Schäfer, *Synopse zur Hekhalot-Literatur,* §137-38. Cf. Segal, *Paul the Convert,* 58.

34. Hengel, "Setze dich," 142.

35. Ibid., 142.

36. Ibid., 164. The main point is that God and Christ share the same throne, whether it is termed a "throne-chariot" or a "judgment seat." In light of Hengel's argument, it is interesting to note that, according to Josephus (*Jewish Antiquities* 13.84), Alexander Balas compelled his ally, the high priest Jonathan, when he came to Ptolemais, to take off his own garment and to put on a purple one, "making him sit with him on the judgment seat (ἐπὶ τοῦ βήματος)." Josephus describes the grand and glorious throne of Solomon as being "in the form of a tribunal (βῆμα), with six steps leading up to it" (*Jewish Antiquities* 8.140; cf. 17.201).

37. Ibid., 136, 167.

provides yet another reference to the apostle's encounter with the divine throne-chariot. In the following, I would like to explore the possibility that Paul's metaphorical use of θριαμβεύειν ("lead in triumphal procession") in 2 Cor 2:14 conjures up an image of God on his throne-chariot.

Paul's Use of Θριαμβεύειν *in 2 Cor 2:14*

As generally recognized, 2 Cor 2:14–7:4 constitutes a defense of Paul's apostleship that interrupts Paul's travel narrative in 2:12-13 and 7:5-16. The defense begins with an unusual thanksgiving: "But thanks be to God, who in Christ always leads us [i.e., Paul][38] in triumphal procession (τῷ πάντοτε θριαμβεύοντι ἡμᾶς ἐν τῷ Χριστῷ), and through us reveals in every place the fragrance of the knowledge of him" (2:14). As a search of the Thesaurus Linguae Graecae databank of Greek authors and works reveals, the term θριαμβεύειν unequivocally denotes "lead in triumphal procession."[39] For some interpreters, however, this usage of the term conjures up an image of the apostle that seems quite unlikely, coming as it does as part of a thanksgiving at the very beginning of his defense for the legitimacy for his apostolic ministry. For Paul would seem to be portraying himself as a complete disgrace, a prisoner of war who is led by the conquering general (God!) in a triumphal procession which culminates in the apostle's death. Many scholars have sought to avoid this interpretation either by positing an idiosyncratic usage of the θριαμβεύειν[40] or by assuming the use of a rhetorical strategy whereby the meaning of verse 14 is ultimately positive.[41] More recently, however, the trend has been to recognize the unequivocal usage of θριαμβεύειν, with its negative impli-

38. Here, as often in 2 Corinthians, Paul uses the first-person plural (the so-called "apostolic or literary plural") to refer to himself. Cf. M. E. Thrall, *A Critical and Exegetical Commentary on the Second Epistle to the Corinthians* (2 vols.; ICC; Edinburgh: Clark, 1994) 1.105-7.

39. Cf. C. Breytenbach, "Paul's Proclamation and God's 'Thriambos': Notes on 2 Corinthians 2:14-16b," *Neot* 24 (1990) 257-71 (esp. 262); S. J. Hafemann, *Suffering and the Spirit: An Exegetical Study of II Cor. 2:14–3:3 within the Context of the Corinthian Correspondence* (WUNT 2.19; Tübingen: Mohr-Siebeck, 1986) 33; J. Lambrecht, "The Defeated Paul, Aroma of Christ: An Exegetical Study of 2 Corinthians 2:14-16b," *LS* 20 (1995) 170-86; Thrall, *Second Corinthians,* 1.191-95; R. Yates, "Colossians 2.15: Christ Triumphant," *NTS* 37 (1991) 573-91 (esp. pp. 574-80). See further B. Kinman, *Jesus' Entry into Jerusalem in the Context of Lukan Theology and the Politics of His Day* (AGJU 28; Leiden: Brill, 1995) esp. 39-45.

40. Cf., e.g., V. P. Furnish, *II Corinthians* (AB 32A; New York: Doubleday, 1984) 187; G. Dautzenberg, "θριαμβεύω," *EDNT* 2 (1991) 155-56; idem, "Motive der Selbstdarstellung des Paulus in 2 Kor 2,14–7,4," in *Apôtre Paul: Personnalité, Style et Conception du Ministre,* ed. A. Vanhoye (BETL 73; Leuven: Leuven University Press, 1986) 150-62 (here 154).

41. Cf., e.g., P. B. Duff, "Metaphor, Motif, and Meaning: The Rhetorical Strategy behind the Image 'Led in Triumph' in 2 Corinthians 2:14," *CBQ* 53 (1991) 79-92 (here 87); C. J. Roetzel, "'As Dying, and Behold We Live': Death and Resurrection in Paul's Theology," *Int* 46 (1992) 5-18 (here 11-12).

cations for Paul, and then to correlate the passage with Paul's apostolic self-conception as expressed elsewhere, particularly in his admissions of personal weakness and suffering in the Corinthian correspondence (cf. 1 Cor 4:9; 2 Cor 4:10-11).[42] Certainly, triumphal procession imagery was sometimes used as a metaphor of social shame, as a contemporary Stoic text now documents.[43]

Whereas most interpretations of 2 Cor 2:14 consider the metaphor of triumphal procession only with respect to Paul, no interpretation so far has considered the metaphor with respect to God as the acting subject. What image or set of associations does this metaphor conjure up? What do we "see" when we think of God as leading his apostle in triumph? In order to consider this, we must recall a basic motif of the Roman triumphal procession, with its focus on the conqueror and his chariot.

The Roman triumphal procession was originally an epiphany procession, with the triumphant general appearing as the living image of Jupiter Optimus Maximus (Jupiter is frequently portrayed on Roman coins as driving a speeding horse quadriga).[44] By the time of the empire, however, the triumph was cele-

42. Cf., e.g., J. Murphy-O'Connor, *The Theology of the Second Letter to the Corinthians* (New Testament Theology; Cambridge: Cambridge University, 1991) 29-30. G. D. Fee argues that the imagery of Paul's being a captive in Christ's triumphal procession (2 Cor 2:14) "deliberately echoes 1 Cor 4.9 and thereby pushes back to the crucified Messiah in 1.18-25." G. D. Fee, " 'Another Gospel Which You Did Not Embrace': 2 Corinthians 11.4 and the Theology of 1 and 2 Corinthians," in *Gospel in Paul: Studies on Corinthians, Galatians, and Romans for Richard N. Longenecker*, ed. L. Jervis and P. Richardson (JSNTSup 108; Sheffield: JSOT Press, 1994) 111-33 (here 129). However, this suggestion is unlikely for several reasons. First, the alleged deliberate echo is muted by the "painful visit" and the "tearful letter" which came between the writing of 1 and 2 Corinthians. Second, there are substantial differences between the two passages in question. For example, in 1 Cor 4:9 Paul disparages being exhibited by God before the world in contrast to the Corinthians' self-commendation, whereas in 2 Cor 2:14 he actually exults in being led in triumphal procession and in its positive revelatory benefit for the world.

43. Cf. Seneca, *De vita beata* 25.4: "This is what Socrates will say to you: 'Make me victor over the nations of the world, let the voluptuous car of Bacchus convey me in triumph *(triumphantem)* from the rising of the sun all the way to Thebes, let the kings of the nations seek laws from me; when from every side I shall be greeted as a god, I shall then most of all remember that I am a man. Then with such a lofty height connect straightway a headlong fall to altered fortune; let me be placed upon a foreign barrow to grace the procession of a proud and brutal victor; no whit more humble shall I be than when I am driven in front of the chariot of another than when I stood erect upon my own.' " Without referring to this text, P. Marshall argues on the basis of Seneca, *De beneficiis* 2.11.1, that "the triumphal motif 'led captive in triumph' is simply a metaphor of social shame." P. Marshall, "A Metaphor of Social Shame: ΘΡΙΑΜΒΕΥΕΙΝ in 2 Cor. 2:14," *NovT* 25 (1983) 302-17 (here 313). On the triumphal procession of Bacchus/Dionysus, see C. Kondoleon, *Domestic and Divine: Roman Mosaics in the House of Dionysos* (Ithaca: Cornell University Press, 1995) 191-229.

44. Cf. H. S. Versnel, *Triumphus: An Inquiry into the Origin, Development and Meaning of the Roman Triumph* (Leiden: Brill, 1970) 1; E. Künzl, *Der römische Triumph. Siegesfeiern im antiken Rom* (Munich: Beck, 1988) 85-108. For the numismatic evidence of Jupiter in a quadriga, see S. W. Stevenson et al., eds., *Dictionary of Roman Coins, Republican and Imperial* (London: Bell, 1889; reprint, London: Seaby, 1982) 94, 187, 285, 286, 483, 672, 843.

brated as an offering procession held to honor the gods in thanksgiving for the victory. The procession consisted of the entrance into the city of the Roman magistrates, the Senate, people carrying booty from the campaign, the priests leading the bulls for sacrifice, and enemy captives (who were executed at the end of the ceremony), followed by the victorious general on a chariot leading his army.[45]

The chariot in which the triumphant general rode (the *currus triumphalis*) was a standard feature in all triumphal processions from the earliest period of Roman history (cf. Plutarch, *Romulus* 16.6, 8; *Publicola* 9.9; *Camillus* 30.2; *Marius* 22.1-5), and one which also distinguished a "major triumph" from a "minor triumph" or "ovation."[46] Normally, this chariot was a quadriga, a two-wheeled chariot drawn by four horses harnessed abreast, although four elephants were sometimes used instead (cf. Plutarch, *Pompeius* 14.4; Pliny, *Naturalis Historia* 8.4). Since Roman imperial coins frequently included images of the emperor in a triumphal chariot, the concept of triumphal procession was familiar throughout the Roman Empire.[47]

What do these findings imply for our text? If by using θριαμβεύειν, Paul portrays himself as being led by God in a Roman triumphal procession, then *the image is one of God riding in a quadriga.* Perhaps this image was regarded as particularly appropriate not only because the Romans closely associated Jupiter with the triumphator and his quadriga, but also because the Romans themselves identified Jupiter with the God of the Jews, evidently because they both were considered the supreme God.[48] Yet we may probe even more deeply into the background of Paul's image.

45. For a brief description of the *pompa triumphalis,* see Versnel, *Triumphus,* 95.

46. Cf. Versnel, *Triumphus,* 166. See further Plutarch, *Marius* 22.1-5.

47. Cf. Marshall, "A Metaphor of Social Shame," 304: ". . . the triumphal procession must have been a familiar institution to Greeks and Romans of all levels of society. Approximately 350 triumphs are recorded in their literature and they were most sought after and frequent in the Republican Period. Traditional processional themes or triumphal motifs were portrayed on arches, reliefs, statues, columns, coins, cups, cameos, medallions, and in paintings and the theatre." We may add that the triumphal procession was also a common theme in home mosaics and on sarcophagi; cf. Kondoleon, *Domestic and Divine,* 191-229. See further F. S. Kleiner, *The Arch of Nero in Rome: A Study of the Roman Honorary Arch before and under Nero* (Archaeologica 52; Rome: Bretschneider, 1985) 24, pl. I-XXXIV; H. Mattingly, *Coins of the Roman Empire in the British Museum, Vol. I: Augustus to Vitellius* (London: Trustees of the British Museum, 1965) pl. 1.20; 2.1, 10; 3.20; 8.16, 17, 18, 19, 20; 9.2, 3; 13.3, 4, 5; 14.10, 11; 15.6, 7; 22.1, 2, 3; 24.9, 10, 13; 25.2, 3; 30.9, 10). Note also that by ca. 150 CE at the latest, the monumental entrance to the Corinthian forum contained a triumphal arch crowned with chariots driven by Helios and his son Phaethon, respectively (cf. Pausanias 2.3.2). Furthermore, a Roman house in Corinth, dated to ca. 200 CE, contains a mosaic in which Dionysos stands in a tiger chariot (cf. Kondoleon, *Domestic and Divine,* 214-15).

48. Cf. M. Stern, *Greek and Latin Authors on Jews and Judaism* (3 vols.; Jerusalem: Israel Academy of Sciences and Humanities, 1974-84) 1.207, 210-11. In Valerius Maximus, *Iupiter Sabazius* is probably meant to be the Jewish God (ibid., 1.358-59).

The Jewish Background of Paul's Metaphor

2 Cor 2:14 presents us with a metaphor. When we use a metaphor, we have two thoughts of different things — tenor and vehicle — active together and supported by a single word or phrase, whose meaning is a result of their interaction ("two ideas for one").[49] The "tenor" is the underlying subject of the metaphor, and the "vehicle" is the means by which the tenor is presented. In our passage, the vehicle is the idea of a Roman triumphal procession in which a conquering general rides a quadriga. However, the underlying subject is different. Paul merely uses the idea of the Roman triumphal procession in order to convey another set of associations — the thought that God on his throne-chariot leads the apostle captive. By using the metaphor of triumphal procession, Paul is able to conjure up the image of God on his throne of glory, with Christ seated at his right hand.

To picture the scene that Paul has in mind here, we may adduce two pieces of evidence. First, we may compare the reverse of an *aureus* and a *denarius* minted in Rome during the reign of Nero (55 CE), showing an elephant quadriga surmounted by two thrones, with "divine" *(divus)* Claudius sitting at the right hand of Augustus.[50] Second, we may cite the words attributed to R. Hoshaya in *Genesis Rabbah* 8:10 on Gen 1:27, referring to the creation of man in the image of God:

> When the Holy One, blessed be he, came to create the first man, the ministering angels mistook him [for God] and wanted to say before him, "Holy" [the *Trisagion* in Isa 6:3]. To what may the matter be compared? To the case of a king and a governor (אפרכוס, ἔπαρχος) who sat in a chariot (קרוכין, *carruca*), and his subjects wanted to acclaim the king, "*Domine!* (Sovereign!)," but they did not know which one of them was which. What did the king do? He pushed the governor out and put him away from the chariot, so that the people would know who was king.[51]

49. On this "interactive" theory of metaphor vis-à-vis other current theories, see J. Soskice, *Metaphor and Religious Language* (Oxford: Oxford University Press, 1985) 24-53. Recently, the question of metaphor in 2 Corinthians has been the matter of considerable debate, especially with respect to establishing a method for approaching Pauline theology. Cf. S. J. Kraftchick, "Death in Us, Life in You: The Apostolic Medium," in *Pauline Theology. Volume II: 1 & 2 Corinthians,* ed. D. M. Hay (Minneapolis: Fortress, 1993) 156-81, and the response by B. R. Gaventa, "Apostle and Church in 2 Corinthians: A Response to David M. Hay and Stephen J. Kraftchick," in ibid., 182-99 (esp. 187-93).

50. Cf. C. H. V. Sutherland, *The Roman Imperial Coinage. Volume 1: From 31 BC to AD 69* (rev. ed.; London: Spink, 1984) 150 and pl. 17.6. On the elephant quadriga as a symbol of emperor deification, see Pfanner, *Der Titusbogen* (Mainz am Rhein: Zabern, 1983) 99.

51. Note the Greek and Latin loanwords, including *Domine,* which is a title of Caesar. This midrash well illustrates the scandal of Jesus' answer to the high priest in Mark 14:62: "I am [the Messiah, the Son of the Blessed One]; and 'you will see the Son of Man seated at the right hand

These texts provide evidence of a tradition of the Roman triumphal procession in which the emperor sits enthroned with a co-occupant riding on a chariot.[52] In fact, *Genesis Rabbah* 8:9 might be interpreting the "image of God" in Gen 1:27 in light of the Merkabah vision in Ezek 1:26, where Ezekiel sees on the divine throne an anthropomorphic image ("a form like the appearance of a man"), which is identified as "the appearance of the likeness of the glory of the Lord" (v. 28; cf. 2 Cor 3:18; 4:6).

We should not be surprised that Paul would use Roman imagery to evoke a biblical idea. For as Yigael Yadin has shown, the Qumran *War Scroll* (1QM) uses a Roman model to portray the weaponry, army divisions, and maneuvers of the final battle.[53] Furthermore, in later Hekhalot texts, there is a carefully

---

of the Power' (Ps 110:1), and 'coming with the clouds of heaven' (Dan 7:13)." As Hengel has rightly emphasized, the idea of a mortal sitting with God on the divine throne-chariot would have been an *Ungeheuerlichkeit* to contemporary Jewish sensibilities ("Setze dich," 174, 177). For, as *b. Sanhedrin* 38b (also *b. Ḥagiga* 14a; *Midraš Tanḥuma* B *Qedošin* §1) shows, R. Yose ha-Gelili rejected R. Aqiba's interpretation of Dan 7:9 as referring to two thrones, one for God and another for David, because it makes "profane" (חול) the divine presence; cf. Hengel, "Setze dich," 169; see further C. A. Evans, "Was Simon ben Kosiba Recognized as Messiah?" in *Jesus and His Contemporaries: Comparative Studies,* by Craig A. Evans (AGJU 25; Leiden: Brill, 1995) 183-211 (here 204-8); B. Ego, "Gottes Thron im Talmud und Midrash. Kosmologische und eschatologische Aspekte eines aggadischen Motivs," in *Le Thrône de Dieu,* ed. M. Philonenko, 318-33 (here 327-28). Note also that the seemingly disparate concept in Mark 14:62 of sitting on a throne *and* coming in the clouds is also found in *b. Ḥagiga* 12b, which explains Yahweh's sitting on "the throne of glory" with a citation of Ps 68:5 ("the one who rides [רכב] upon the clouds").

52. According to Diodorus Siculus, Phillip II displayed himself as "co-occupant of the throne (σύνθρονον) with the twelve gods" (cf. Diodorus Siculus 16.92.5; 95.1). In Pseudo-Callisthenes (*Historia Alexandri Magni* 1.36.2; cf. 1.38.2 [ed. W. Kroll]), the Persian king is said to be "king of kings, relative of the gods, co-occupant of the throne with the god Mithras" (σύνθρονος θεῷ Μίθρᾳ). This tradition, including the idea of the throne-chariot, was carried over into Roman imperial ideology and beyond; cf. E. H. Kantorowicz, "Oriens Augusti-Lever du Roi," *Dumbarton Oaks Papers* 17 (1963) 118-77 + plates. See also M. de Jonge, "Thrones," in *Dictionary of Deities and Demons in the Bible,* ed. K. van der Toorn et al. (Leiden: Brill, 1995) 1628-31. In Patristic literature, Jesus Christ is often called the σύνθρονος of God; cf., e.g., Eusebius, *Demonstratio evangelica* 4.15.33; 5.3.9, both citing Ps 110:1; see further C. Markschies, " 'Sessio ad Dexteram': Bemerkungen zu einem altchristlichen Bekenntnismotiv in der christologischen Diskussion der altkirchlichen Theologen," in *Le Trône de Dieu,* ed. Philonenko, 252-317. This is not the place to enter into a discussion of the name Metatron and its possible relationship to σύνθρονος; cf. Gruenwald, *Apocalyptic and Merkavah Mysticism,* 235-41 (an appendix by S. Lieberman); A. F. Segal, *Two Powers in Heaven: Early Rabbinic Reports about Christianity and Gnosticism* (SJLA 25; Leiden: Brill, 1977). According to Philo, the Logos is seated with God in the divine chariot (*De fuga et inventione* 101). The concept of a throne-chariot in which someone is seated at the right hand of the deity is very ancient. Cf. J. Jeremias, "Thron oder Wagen? Eine ausergewöhnliche Terrakotte aus der späten Eisenzeit in Juda," in *Biblische Welten: Festschrift für Martin Metzger zu seinem 65. Geburtstag,* ed. Wolfgang Zwickel (OBO 123; Freiburg: Universitätsverlag; Göttingen: Vandenhoeck & Ruprecht, 1993) 41-59 + pl. VI-VIII; Kantorowicz, "Oriens Augusti-Lever du Roi," 118-77.

53. Y. Yadin, *The Scroll of the War of the Sons of Light against the Sons of Darkness* (Oxford: Oxford University Press, 1962) 114-97.

worked-out parallelism between the court of the Roman emperor and the court of the celestial Emperor.[54] Paul, who does not like to discuss his visions and does so only under compulsion (cf. 2 Cor 12:1-4), uses a metaphor in order make his point without being overly explicit about ineffable matters (v. 4).[55]

The Tradition of Psalm 68:18-19

We have suggested in the foregoing that the first half of 2 Cor 2:14 should be interpreted in light of Paul's Merkabah mysticism: The apostle renders thanks to God for leading him in triumphal procession before the divine throne-chariot. But how does this imagery relate to the idea of revelation in the second half of the verse, where Paul continues his thanksgiving with the words: ". . . and through us [Paul himself] reveals the fragrance of the knowledge of him in every place"? In other words, what is the relationship between Paul's encounter with the Merkabah (v. 14a) and his role as revelatory mediator (v. 14b)? Can we more precisely define the Jewish Merkabah tradition that Paul seems to have in mind here? I would like to explore the possibility that Paul alludes to Ps 68:18-19 (Ps 67:18-19 in the LXX).

The text and interpretation of Psalm 68 are notoriously problematical, and this may have contributed to the complex reception of Ps 68:18-19 in subsequent tradition. According to the Septuagint version of the passage, when God in his chariot (τὸ ἅρμα τοῦ θεοῦ) ascended from Sinai into his holy sanctuary on high,[56] he led captivity captive and received (ἔλαβες) gifts among humanity. However, Eph 4:8 applies Ps 68:19 to the ascension of Christ[57] and

54. Cf. P. S. Alexander, "The Family of Caesar and the Family of God: The Image of the Emperor in the Hekhalot Literature," in *Images of Empire,* ed. L. Alexander (JSOTSup 122; Sheffield: JSOT Press, 1991) 276-97. Cf. *Genesis Rabbah* 8:9 (cited above); *b. Berakot* 58a.

55. This accords with the general reluctance in Jewish mystical and apocalyptic literature to describe certain aspects of the heavenly journey. According to *Hekhalot Zutarti,* the Merkabah mystic is to keep quiet about the mysteries he contemplates (Schäfer, *Synopse zur Hekhalot-Literatur,* §335). In Rabbinic Judaism, all study and discussion of the divine throne-chariot in public was prohibited, unless the person was a scholar (*m. Ḥagiga* 2:1). Those who ignored these injunctions did so at their own peril. On the reluctance of Jewish mystics to recount certain aspects of their heavenly journeys, see Morray-Jones, "Paradise Revisited. Part 2," 271-72, 281, 283; Segal, *Paul the Convert,* 58; M. N. A. Bockmuehl, *Revelation and Mystery in Ancient Judaism and Pauline Christianity* (WUNT 2.36; Tübingen: Mohr-Siebeck, 1990; Grand Rapids: Eerdmans, 1997) 175. Cf. Dan 12:4; *Apocalypse of Zephaniah* 5:6; *4 Ezra* 14:4-6, 44-46.

56. Cf. Ps 68:5(4), where רכב בערבות can be rendered "rider upon the clouds," as in *b. Ḥagiga* 12b. See W. Herrmann, "Rider Upon the Clouds," in *Dictionary of Deities and Demons in the Bible,* 1330-34.

57. Compare Paul's citation of Ps 68(67):19 (ἀναβὰς εἰς ὕψος) with 4Q458 2 ii 5, which likewise seems to interpret Ps 68:19 messianically: ". . . and he will ascend to the height" (והלך על הרום). Line 6 explicitly refers to "one anointed (משיח) with the oil of the kingdom of [. . .]."

the spiritual gifts, including apostles (v. 11), which he gave (ἔδωκεν) to the church. The strong verbal parallels between this citation and the Aramaic Targum make it probable that Eph 4:8 is following a variant text-form of Ps 68:19.[58] Furthermore, the intriguing connection here between Psalm 68 and apostleship deserves closer attention, especially in view of Paul's defense of his apostolic office in 2 Cor 2:14–7:4. As we shall see, the alternate text-form of the psalm gave rise to a Jewish tradition that Paul may well have appropriated in his defense.

As David Halperin has documented in detail, a synagogue tradition for the Feast of Weeks linked the Torah reading (Exodus 19–20: the theophany at Sinai) with the prophetic lection (Ezekiel 1: the throne-chariot vision) by means of Psalm 68.[59] According to Carol Newsom, "The Sabbath Shirot [of Qumran] perhaps provide evidence for the earliest exegetical association of the merkabah visions of Ezekiel with Psalm 68."[60] Quite commonly, the "chariotry/chariot of God" (רכב אלהים/τὸ ἅρμα τοῦ θεοῦ)[61] in Ps 68:18 is taken to refer to the Merkabah in which God descended to Mt. Sinai.[62]

However, the very next verse, Ps 68:19, is taken in some Jewish literature to refer not to God's ascent on high, corresponding to his Merkabah descent to Mt. Sinai in verse 18, but to the ascent of Moses, who took captive the Torah

58. As R. Rubinkiewicz observes, the citation in Eph 4:8 agrees with readings in the Targum to Ps 68:19 at two crucial points: Whereas the MT and the LXX have לקחת and ἔλαβες, respectively, Eph 4:8 and the Targum have ἔδωκεν and והבתא להין. Likewise, whereas the MT and the LXX have באדם and ἐν ἀνθρώπῳ, Eph 4:8 and the Targum have the plural τοῖς ἀνθρώποις and לבני נשא. See R. Rubinkiewicz, "Ps LXVIII 19 [= Eph IV 8]: Another Textual Tradition or Targum?" *NovT* 17 (1975) 219-24. On Eph 4:8, see further Max Wilcox, "The Aramaic Targum to Psalms," in *Proceedings of the Ninth World Congress of Jewish Studies, Division A: The Period of the Bible,* ed. M. Goshen-Gottstein (Jerusalem: World Union of Jewish Studies, 1986) 143-50 (here 144-45); idem, "The Aramaic Background of the New Testament," in *The Aramaic Bible: Targums in Their Historical Context,* ed. D. R. G. Beattie and M. J. McNamara (JSOTSup 166; Sheffield: JSOT Press, 1994) 362-78 (here 377); G. B. Caird, "The Descent of Christ in Ephesians 4,7-11," in *Studia Evangelica II* (TU 87; Berlin: Akademie-Verlag, 1964) 535-45; R. Schnackenburg, *Der Brief an die Epheser* (EKKNT 10; Zurich: Benziger Verlag; Neukirchen-Vluyn: Neukirchener Verlag, 1982) 179-80; R. A. Taylor, "The Use of Psalm 68:18 in Ephesians 4:8 in Light of the Ancient Versions," *BSac* 148 (1991) 319-36.

59. Cf. Halperin, *The Faces of the Chariot,* 141-56, 262-358. W. Zimmerli, however, argues that Ezekiel 1 itself alludes to the theophany at Sinai; W. Zimmerli, *Ezechiel 1–24* (2d ed.; BKAT 13.1; Neukirchen-Vluyn: Neukirchener Verlag, 1979) 83. For the use of Ps 68:19 in Sabbath discourses, see *Pesiqta de Rab Kahana* 12.22.

60. Newsom, *Songs of the Sabbath Sacrifice,* 319 (on 4Q405 20-21-22 ii 12-13); idem, "Merkabah Exegesis in the Qumran Sabbath Shirot," 28-29. Halperin argues that Ezek 43:2 LXX, which he attributes to pre-Christian Alexandria, understood the connection between God's chariotry at Sinai and Ezekiel's chariot vision (*The Faces of the Chariot,* 57-59).

61. The underlying Hebrew רכב, "chariotry," derives from the same root as מרכבה. A fragment of the Hebrew text of Ps 68:18, preserved in Cave 11 of Qumran (11QPs^{d}), contains the same reading as the MT.

62. Cf. Halperin, *The Faces of the Chariot,* 141-49.

from the angels and gave the gift of Torah to humanity.[63] For example, the Targum interprets Ps 68:19 as a reference to Moses, who ascended into heaven, received the Torah there, and brought the Torah to the sons of men. According to *Midr. Ps.* 68:19, Moses ascended to the divine beings and there received "free" the Torah as a "gift" for Israel. Finally, we may cite *Deuteronomy Rabbah* 11:10:

> . . . and I [Moses] ascended heaven and trod out a path there, and engaged in battle with angels, and received the law of fire, and sojourned under [God's] throne of fire, and took shelter under the pillar of fire, and spoke with God face to face; and I prevailed over the heavenly *familia,* and revealed unto the sons of man their secrets, and received the law from the right hand of God, and taught it to Israel.[64]

Hence, Ps 68:18-19 often refers in the Jewish tradition to Moses' Merkabah encounter with God on Sinai and to the revelation which he mediated to humanity.

Paul apparently makes a similar connection between his own Merkabah encounter and revelation in 2 Cor 2:14, for there the apostle states not only that God leads him in triumphal procession, but also that through him God "reveals (φανεροῦντι) the fragrance of the knowledge of him."[65] So Paul is presenting himself here as a mediator of divine revelation on a par with Moses himself.

The whole basis of Paul's apostleship is summarized in this one verse. By speaking of a Roman triumphal procession in connection with divine revelation, Paul evidently suggests the throne-chariot of God and the powerfully complex tradition of Ps 68:18-19. According to this tradition, God descended to Sinai in his Merkabah and revealed himself to Moses and all Israel. Moses, in turn, ascended on high, took the Torah captive, and gave it as a gift to humanity. Although Paul's image turns this tradition on its head by making the apostle a captive rather than the triumphator,[66] it nevertheless preserves the idea that an

63. Cf. ibid., 289-91 (here 303); P. Schäfer, *Rivalität zwischen Engeln und Menschen: Untersuchungen zur rabbinischen Engelvorstellung* (Berlin/New York: de Gruyter, 1975) 127-30, 136-40; H. L. Strack and P. Billerbeck, *Kommentar zum Neuen Testament aus Talmud und Midrasch* (4 vols.; Munich: Beck, 1922-61) 3.596-98. A. Kuyt suggests that the text in Schäfer, *Synopse zur Hekhalot-Literatur,* §336 ("in the hour that Moses ascended to the height, to God . . .") may be interpreted in light of the rabbinic interpretation of Ps 68:19; A. Kuyt, *The "Descent" to the Chariot: Towards a Description of the Terminology, Place, Function, and Nature of the Yeridah in Hekhalot Literature* (TSAJ 45; Tübingen: Mohr-Siebeck, 1994) 210-11.

64. Cf. also *Exodus Rabbah* 28.1 (on Exod 19:3); *Midraš Tanḥuma* B *Ha'azinu* §3; *Midraš Ha-Gadol* Exod. 395; *Pirqe Rabbi Eliezer* 46, 110b.

65. Here, the verb φανεροῦν is often incorrectly translated as "spread" (cf., e.g., the NIV and the NRSV), which obscures the idea of revelation in the text. In Pauline usage, φανεροῦν is synonymous with ἀποκαλύπτειν (cf., e.g., Rom 1:17 and 3:21).

66. See, however, 2 Cor 10:4-5, where Paul presents himself as a victor who destroys strongholds and takes captive. Here he alludes to Prov 21:22, which is often connected with Ps

encounter with the Merkabah effects a revelation to humanity through a mediator. Paul's claim is especially crucial in the situation at Corinth, where his opponents, who evidently claim to have numerous visions and revelations (cf. 2 Cor 12:1), have not only succeeded in turning the affections of the church at Corinth away from her founding apostle, but have also brought the legitimacy of Paul's apostleship into question. Therefore, Paul's opening salvo in the defense of his apostleship asserts his Merkabah experience and his role as revelatory mediator like Moses. In the Hekhalot literature, Moses is the Merkabah mystic par excellence.[67]

All of this fits well with the further development of Paul's argument in 2 Cor 2:14–4:6, where he contrasts his own ministry of the new covenant to Moses' less glorious ministry of the Sinaitic covenant. Although the revelation that Moses received was glorious, the revelation Paul has received is even more glorious. Hence, Paul defends himself here first and foremost on the basis of his position as the new revelatory mediator par excellence. As John J. Collins observes in another connection, prophetic visions of the divine throne typically serve two functions: They establish the credentials of the visionary, thereby legitimating him as an intermediary between heaven and earth, and they provide revealed information.[68] Likewise, at the beginning of his apology for his apostleship, 2 Cor 2:14 refers to Paul's encounter with the Merkabah and thereby underscores his legitimacy as a revelatory mediator.

Conclusion

We have suggested that at the very beginning of the defense of his apostleship in 2 Cor 2:14–7:4, Paul gives thanks for his encounter with the Merkabah and

---

68:19 and Moses' conquest of the angelic stronghold when he brought the Torah down to earth; cf. *Leviticus Rabbah* 31:5; *Pirqe Rabbi Eliezer* 46, 110b; *Midraš Psalms* 68:19; see further Schäfer, *Rivalität,* 126-27, 138, 235-36.

67. Cf. Schäfer, *Synopse zur Hekhalot-Literatur,* §§336, 340, 341, 342, 357, 388, 396, 397, 492, 498, 508, 514, 544, 564, 578, 606, 676, 694, 960, 961. According to *Hekhalot Rabbati,* the Merkabah mystic announces the witness that he receives before the throne of glory (cf. Schäfer, *Synopse zur Hekhalot-Literatur,* §§111, 169, 218). In fact, the Merkabah mystic is under compulsion to do so or else face divine punishment (Schäfer, *Synopse zur Hekhalot-Literatur,* §169). On the Merkabah mystic as a revelatory mediator, see further Schäfer, *Synopse zur Hekhalot-Literatur,* §§676, 686. Philo claims that his heavenly ascent gave him insights into the Law of Moses that enabled him to reveal unknown things to the multitude (*De specialibus legibus* 3.1-6); cf. Peder Borgen, "Heavenly Ascent in Philo: An Examination of Selected Passages," in *The Pseudepigrapha and Early Biblical Interpretation,* ed. J. H. Charlesworth and C. A. Evans (JSPSup 14; Sheffield: JSOT Press, 1993) 246-68. *T. Levi* 2:10 sees a heavenly dimension to Levi's priestly role: "For you will stand near the Lord and will be his minister and will declare his mysteries to men. . . ."

68. J. J. Collins, *The Scepter and the Star: The Messiahs of the Dead Sea Scrolls and Other Ancient Literature* (ABRL 10; New York: Doubleday, 1995) 140.

his resulting role as revelatory mediator like Moses (2:14). If this interpretation is correct, the metaphorical reference to the divine throne-chariot in θριαμβεύειν ("lead in triumphal procession") serves to establish Paul's credentials as an apostle, thereby legitimating him as an intermediary between heaven and earth.

This typological interpretation makes sense in light of the subsequent context of the apology, where the apostle compares himself to Moses both implicitly (2 Cor 2:16b, 17) and explicitly (2 Cor 3:7, 13, 15). Thus, when 2 Cor 2:17 refers to Paul's speaking "in the presence of God" (κατέναντι θεοῦ),[69] this is tantamount to saying that the apostle speaks to God face to face, just as Moses did. In the Hebrew Bible, Moses' mediatory role (Exod 19:9; 20:19; 24:1-2; cf. *T. Moses* 1:14) is indicated by the fact that the Lord used to speak to him "face to face (ἐνώπιος ἐνωπίῳ), as someone might speak to his own friend" (Exod 33:11; cf. Num 12:7-8; Deut 34:10; Sir 45:5). According to Exod 32:11, while Moses was on Sinai (enjoying the Merkabah experience!) and the people back in the camp had made the golden calf, God wanted to destroy the people and begin anew with Moses, but "Moses pleaded for mercy in the presence of the Lord God (καὶ ἐδεήθη Μωυσῆς κατέναντι κυρίου τοῦ θεοῦ)."[70] There is thus a unique, heavenly dimension to Paul's apostolic role that sets him apart from his opponents who peddle the word of God. Paul's revelatory ministry, like that of Moses and the prophets, derived from his own encounter with the glory of God. The difference is, as 2 Cor 4:4, 6 goes on to make clear, Paul experiences the glory of God as revealed "on the face of Christ" (v. 6), who is "the image of God" (v. 4).

As the revelatory mediator of a Merkabah experience, Paul mediates the glory of God in the midst of the Corinthians. Whereas Moses used to put a covering over his glorified face so that the Israelites might not see it, Paul acts with "complete openness" (2 Cor 3:12). In fact, as verse 18 goes on to state, through Paul's ministry, believers, with unveiled faces, see the glory of the Lord as in a mirror.[71] This probably alludes to Ezekiel 1, where Ezekiel's encounter with the glory of God is also portrayed in terms of seeing the "image" or "likeness" of God in human form in a mirror (cf. Ezek 1:1, 4, 5, 10, 16, and esp. 26-27). Like Ezekiel, who saw the Merkabah vision — "the appearance of the likeness of the glory of the Lord" — as in a mirror,[72]

69. The literal use of κατέναντι is by far the most common in the LXX and in the NT. Cf. D. A. Renwick, *Paul, the Temple, and the Presence of God* (BJS 224; Atlanta: Scholars Press, 1991) 61-94.

70. Cf. J. W. Wevers, *Notes on the Greek Text of Exodus* (SBLSCS 30; Atlanta: Scholars Press, 1990) 523-24.

71. The difficult *hapax legomenon* κατοπτρίζεσθαι probably denotes "to behold as in a mirror" (cf. Diogenes Laertius 2.33; 3.39) rather than merely "to see." See Thrall, *Second Corinthians,* 1.290-94.

72. On Ezekiel 1 as the background of 2 Cor 3:18, see, e.g., Segal, *Paul the Convert,* 60 with n. 94; Halperin, *The Faces of the Chariot,* 212 with n. 22, 230, 231-38, 265.

believers see the glory of God in the face of Christ, who is the "image of God" (4:4, 6).[73]

Without the Qumran Scrolls, our considerations in this paper would have been greatly hampered, because much of the evidence for Jewish Merkabah mysticism is otherwise relatively late. However, the Dead Sea Scrolls help us see that contemplation of the divine throne-chariot was already practiced in pre-Christian times. We have argued that the apostle Paul, who characterized himself as an Israelite from the tribe of Benjamin, as a Hebrew of Hebrews, and as a former Pharisee, is part of the stream of Jewish Merkabah tradition which extends from the Hebrew Bible, through the Dead Sea Scrolls, and on to the later Hekhalot literature.

73. On the christological interpretation of Ezek 1:26-28, see E. Dassmann, "Trinitarische und christologische Auslegung der Thronvision Ezechiels in der patristischen Theologie," in *Im Gespräch mit dem dreieinen Gott: Elemente einer trinitarischen Theologie: Festschrift zum 65. Geburtstag vom Wilhelm Breuning,* ed. M. Bohnke (Düsseldorf: Patmos, 1985) 159-74; J. Engemann, "Auf die Parusie Christi hinweisende Darstellungen in der frühchristlichen Kunst," *JAC* 19 (1976) 139-56, which discusses a connection with Roman triumphal arches.

"And When That One Comes": Aspects of Johannine Messianism

DIETMAR NEUFELD

Introduction

The Fourth Gospel represents the completion of a long developing tradition about the person and work of Jesus within the Johannine community. This is demonstrated by the author's incredibly rich use of almost every important christological appellation found in the New Testament (Lord, Son of God, Savior of the World, Holy One of God, Elect of God, King of Israel, Lamb of God, the Christ, and its transliteration twice as Μεσσίας). While these christological titles are thoroughly embedded in the narrative flow of the Gospel and reflect the belief that Jesus is the heavenly redeemer figure, they are nevertheless connected with the public world of Jewish messianic expectations that gave them operative currency.

The task of correlating Johannine messianism with what we know about messianism in the first century CE is complex. Contrary to traditional assumptions of a ubiquitous and consistent messianism in early Judaism, numerous recent studies have pointed out that messianism was a fluid and diverse phenomenon.[1] The expectation of a royal figure, a Davidic Messiah who would

1. Two recent collections of essays on this theme are J. Neusner, W. S. Green, and E. Frerichs, eds., *Judaisms and Their Messiahs at the Turn of the Christian Era* (Cambridge: Cambridge University Press, 1987) and J. H. Charlesworth, ed., *The Messiah: Developments in Earliest Judaism and Christianity* (Minneapolis: Fortress, 1992). The most important treatment to be published since the release of all the unpublished texts from Qumran Cave 4 is J. J. Collins, *The Scepter and the Star: The Messiahs of the Dead Sea Scrolls and Other Ancient Literature* (ABRL 10; New York: Doubleday, 1995). E. P. Sanders (*Judaism, Practice and Belief: 63 BCE–66 CE* [Philadelphia: Trinity, 1992] 295) emphasizes that the expectation of a Messiah was not common in Judaism. J. D. G. Dunn (*The Parting of the Ways between Judaism and Christianity and Their Significance for the*

restore the fortunes of Israel, was certainly current at the turn of the common era. Yet, a number of other messianic expectations conceived of a priestly Messiah, or an anointed prophet, or a heavenly figure. Christian messianism drew heavily upon all of these conceptions to give definition to Jesus as the Messiah.[2]

The Dead Sea Scrolls reflect this fluidity and diversity in messianic expectation. The *Community Rule* speaks of the expectation of at least two Messiahs, one priestly and one royal (1QS 9:2). Some Qumran texts refer to an eschatological prophet, possibly a messianic figure, someone similar to Elijah (1QS 9:11; 4Q175; 4Q521; cf. Deut 18:15-20; Mal 3:1; 4:5; Sir 48:10; 1 Macc 14:41). The text known as the *Aramaic Apocalypse* (4Q246) refers to one who will be called "Son of God," and some scholars have argued that the title designates a messianic figure.[3] While later Christian understandings of Jesus as the "Son of God" depart significantly from the Jewish "Son of God," the roots of the expectation are nevertheless to be found in Judaism.

The task of understanding Johannine messianism is also complicated by the fact that, while Christianity took certain aspects of Jewish messianism as a point of departure, it nonetheless advanced messianic notions that had no precedent in Judaism. Scriptural warrants for the idea that the Messiah should suffer and die were taken from Pss 89:52, 22:31, 69, and Psalm 22, but these originally nonmessianic passages had to be reinterpreted to fit the idea of a suffering and dying Messiah. Such a figure evidently had no precedent in pre-Christian Judaism, despite recent claims surrounding the so-called "Pierced Messiah" text from Qumran (4Q285).[4]

Also without a clear precedent in early Jewish sources is the notion of a man becoming Messiah by resurrection and elevation to heaven.[5] Some scholars maintain that the recently released Dead Sea Scrolls mention a messianic figure who will die for the sins of the world and one who will resurrect the dead

---

Character of Christianity [Philadelphia: Trinity, 1991] 18-36) argues that the four pillars of Second Temple Judaism are covenant, election, monotheism, and land and that messianism does not rank as one of them.

2. See Collins, *The Scepter and the Star.*

3. For the messianic interpretation of 4Q246, see J. J. Collins, "The *Son of God* Text from Qumran," in *From Jesus to John: Essays on Jesus and New Testament Christology in Honour of Marinus de Jonge,* ed. M. C. de Boer (JSNTSup 8; Sheffield: JSOT Press, 1993) 65-82; idem, *The Scepter and the Star,* 154-72. Other scholars, however, give the text a nonmessianic interpretation; proposed identifications include the following: Alexander Balas, son of Antiochus IV Epiphanes (J. T. Milik); the Antichrist (D. Flusser); Melchizedek/Michael/the Prince of Light (García Martínez); the Jewish people (M. Hengel). For details, see the studies of Collins. On the eschatological prophet at Qumran, see Collins, *The Scepter and the Star,* 116-23.

4. See Collins, *The Scepter and the Star,* 58-60, 70 nn. 36-40 and the literature cited there.

5. See M. Hengel, "Jesus, der Messias Israels," in *Messiah and Christos: Studies in the Jewish Origins of Christianity,* ed. I. Gruenwald et al. (TSAJ 32; Tübingen: Mohr-Siebeck, 1992) 155-76.

(4Q521; 4Q285). These identifications, however, have been hotly contested. It has also been noted that the notion of resurrection is rare in the Qumran corpus. Resurrection in the Scrolls is evidently not effected by a Messiah but accomplished by God without the mediation of a Messiah.[6]

Another formidable difficulty in tracking the transition from first-century messianism to Johannine christology is that Jesus did not conform to any fixed script of what a Messiah should do. There was no checklist of the identity and works of the Messiah in early Judaism. Without a fixed set of Jewish messianic expectations, we have no point of comparison by which to distinguish what is in basic agreement with Judaism from what deviates from it. The manner in which the Messiah was envisaged by varieties of Jewish groups changed over time in response to historical exigencies. Likewise, early Christian understanding of the terms *Christ* and *Messiah* also evolved over time.[7]

An additional complicating factor is the complex redactional history of the Fourth Gospel. The Gospel is generally regarded as a composite text made up of several sources.[8] Whether it is possible to trace Johannine messianism back to an early source, with either Mark or some other independent source (e.g., a "Signs Source") as its antecedent, has not yet been resolved. Moreover, the Gospel is thought to have been written on two levels. J. Louis Martyn has propounded the view that the Gospel's narrative operates on two levels, that of Jesus and his disciples and that of the early Johannine community in its conflict with the Jewish synagogue.[9] Chapter 9 is thought to provide a particularly clear example of this two-stage drama. It is generally agreed that the titular use of ὁ χριστός in the discussion with the Jews (οἱ Ἰουδαῖοι, John 1:19) among themselves and with Jesus belongs to the later layers of the Gospel's complex compositional history.[10] Yet we should not assume that messianic passages in the Gospel reflect monolithic expectations in Judaism. Further, the portrayal of "the Jews" in the Fourth Gospel cannot be taken as a reliable source for the views held by actual Jews of the period. In the Gospel "the Jews" are, to a great extent, literary characters that function to give expression to the christology of the author.

6. See in particular Lawrence Schiffman, *Reclaiming the Dead Sea Scrolls: The History of Judaism, the Background of Christianity, the Lost Library of Qumran* (Philadelphia and Jerusalem: Jewish Publication Society, 1994) 341-50.

7. See N. Dahl, "The Messiah and Messianic Ideas," in *The Messiah*, ed. Charlesworth, 383-89; Collins, *The Scepter and the Star*, 11-14.

8. See R. T. Fortna, *The Fourth Gospel and Its Predecessor: From Narrative Source to Present Gospel* (Philadelphia: Fortress, 1988).

9. J. L. Martyn, *The Gospel of John in Christian History: Essays for Interpreters* (New York: Paulist Press, 1978); idem, *History and Theology in the Fourth Gospel* (rev. ed.; Nashville: Abingdon, 1979).

10. J. Painter, *The Quest for the Messiah: The History, Literature and Theology of the Johannine Community* (Nashville: Abingdon, 1993); John 7:27, 31, 41b, 42.

The question of Jesus' self-understanding poses yet another difficulty. H. J. de Jonge has argued that Jesus probably thought of himself as a prophet and therefore expected to be rejected and to meet a violent death. On this view Jesus saw himself fulfilling the role of a suffering righteous man and therefore reckoned with the idea of suffering a violent death, later to be vindicated by God by being exalted to heaven. Jesus likely expected to be resurrected shortly after his death.[11] In addition, de Jonge claims that Jesus applied the term "anointed" to himself because he realized that he was a prophetic son of David. However, the designation "the anointed" as a title of an expected eschatological figure appears nowhere in the Hebrew Bible and only infrequently in Jewish sources from the beginning of the common era. "Messiah" was not a title or office entailing a fixed role to be played out by an eschatological figure. For this reason, it is not readily apparent what the writer of the Fourth Gospel had in mind in attributing to Jesus the title of "the Messiah."

The Fourth Gospel portrays the crowds, the Jews, followers, and others both claiming that Jesus is "the Christ" and questioning the validity of such a claim. Jesus, though, never directly applies the term to himself. With conflict swirling about him, Jesus is pictured as giving indirect assent to the implications of the title. He is also portrayed as clarifying misunderstanding and redefining the title by using other christological designations. Thus while the assertion that Jesus is "the Christ" is ubiquitous in the Fourth Gospel, the writer gives no indication of why or how the title became a cognomen of Jesus soon after his death and resurrection.

In this paper we will consider what, if anything, early Jewish messianic expectations have to do with the Fourth Gospel's view of Jesus. In particular, we will examine the questions raised in the narrative about the identity of John the Baptist and Jesus. The essay will also explore the question of which aspects of Johannine messianism correlate with the messianism expressed by the eschatological community of the Dead Sea Scrolls. Most scholars eschew a direct literary dependence of the Fourth Gospel on the thought world of the Dead Sea Scrolls but admit the possibility of an indirect interrelationship between the two.[12] By exploring this issue, we will seek to clarify the transition from Jewish messianism to Johannine christology.

11. H. J. de Jonge, "The Historical Jesus' View of Himself and of His Mission," in *From Jesus to John,* ed. de Boer, 21-37, here 21-22.

12. R. E. Brown, "The Qumran Scrolls and the Johannine Gospel and Epistles," in *The Scrolls and the New Testament,* ed. K. Stendahl (New York: Harper, 1957) 183-207; J. H. Charlesworth, ed., *John and the Dead Sea Scrolls* (New York: Crossroad, 1991). C. K. Barrett acknowledges the importance of the Qumran discoveries but then avers that when we count up what the Scrolls illuminate in terms of exegesis, "the result is extremely meagre . . . and the discoveries have not revolutionized the study of John" (*The Gospel according to St. John: An Introduction with Commentary and Notes on the Greek Text* [2d ed.; London: SPCK, 1978] 34).

Aspects of Johannine Messianism: ὁ χριστός in the Gospel of John

The term ὁ χριστός occurs with astonishing frequency in the Fourth Gospel, fifteen times compared to five occurrences in Mark.[13] Most of the statements are thought to reflect certain aspects of Johannine christology. Nevertheless, the author takes his point of departure from the complex of diffuse and diverse messianic expectations of the period. Johannine christology should not be read back into these expectations, nor should it be read out of these expectations. It is quite likely that some of Jesus' contemporaries attached to him certain messianic hopes. These messianic perceptions of Jesus survived his death and were transformed into christology, not least because of the belief in his resurrection.[14]

The Witness of John the Baptist: John 1:19-34

The first occurrence of ὁ χριστός is found in the context of the witness of John the Baptist (1:19-34). The Jewish authorities have sent out a deputation of priests and Levites from Jerusalem to investigate John's intentions and personal claims. Presumably at the heart of the inquiry was a curiosity about precisely how John thought of himself. The question put to John the Baptist is direct and to the point, "Who are you?" While the reader is not informed of the Baptist's answer to the first question about who he is, the deputation must subsequently have wondered whether he thought of himself as the Messiah. John, however, refuses all attempts to identify his person with the Messiah, confessing, "I am not the Messiah" (ὁ χριστός). Indeed, the Baptist's denial is recorded as a negative confession that he is not the Christ (καὶ ὡμολόγησεν καὶ οὐκ ἠρνήσατο, καὶ ὡμολόγησεν ὅτι Ἐγὼ οὐκ εἰμὶ ὁ Χριστός, 1:20).

The sending of the messengers and the form of this negative assertion suggest the possibility that those who had heard John preach considered him to be behaving in the manner of a messianic figure. Rudolf Schnackenburg argues that the Baptist refused to accept these potentially messianic titles so that the expectations centered in these individuals might converge upon the one person whom they had yet to recognize but who truly was the Christ. The writer

13. John 1:20, 25; 3:28; 4:25, 29; 7:26, 27, 31, 41, 42; 9:22; 10:24; 11:27; 12:34; 20:31. Compare Mark 8:29; 12:35; 13:21; 14:61; 15:32. See here the excellent study of M. de Jonge, "Jewish Expectations about the 'Messiah' according to the Fourth Gospel," *NTS* 19 (1972-73) 246-70.

14. M. Hengel has emphasized that in less than twenty years between the death of Jesus and the earliest Pauline epistle, the early Christian community was actively and creatively giving shape to christology. See M. Hengel, "Christologie und neutestamentliche Chronologie," in *Neues Testament und Geschichte*, ed. H. Baltensweiler (Tübingen: Mohr-Siebeck, 1972) 43-67.

of the Fourth Gospel wished to lead the readers to a deeper understanding about this Jesus whom they were about to meet through the Baptist's denials.[15] Other commentators suggest that the denial owes something to a polemic against those who rated John the Baptist too highly and that, therefore, the author is refuting Baptist sectarians.[16] Still others propose that the writer of the Gospel has the Baptist deny that he is the Messiah, or Elijah, or the Prophet as a dramatic contrast, a prelude if you will, before granting the titles to Jesus.[17] Nils Dahl observes that the "number and functions of 'eschatological persons' were open to considerable variation"[18] but that Mal 4:5-6; 3:1-4; Sir 48:10 and some later texts provided the basis for the hope that the Messiah might return as an Elijah-type figure. Raymond Brown argues that rather than just being a part of the Fourth Gospel's apologetic against the inflated claims of Baptist sectarians who thought him to be the Messiah, the denial reflects an accurate historical reminiscence. John did not think of himself as fulfilling the messianic role of an Elijah-like figure.[19] Some of the followers and rivals of the Baptist may have thought of him as a potential Messiah and questioned him even though he denied being the Messiah, Elijah, and the Prophet.

The deputation persists in its interrogation of the Baptist by asking him directly whether he is Elijah (John 1:21). The Baptist responds with an emphatic "No." The Baptist's pointed assertion that he is not Elijah clearly suggests to some commentators that the Messiah would be an Elijah-like figure. Because John does not think of himself as playing the role of Elijah, some commentators hold that the post-Easter community considered Jesus to be Elijah *redivivus,* while others point out that there is no evidence for the view of Jesus as Elijah *redivivus* in the post-Easter community.[20]

The Synoptic tradition preserves six specific references to Elijah absent from the Fourth Gospel. This fact supports the idea that some of Jesus' contemporaries regarded him as Elijah. The references are as follows:[21] (1) The

15. R. Schnackenburg, *Das Johannesevangelium* (Freiburg: Herder, 1965) 321-28.

16. The Pseudo-Clementine *Recognitions* provide some evidence that Baptist sectarians claimed that John the Baptist, and not Jesus, was the Messiah. See G. Richter, "Bist du Elias? (Joh 1,21)," *BZ* 6 (1962) 79-92.

17. Martyn, *The Gospel of John in Christian History,* 12-28; M. de Jonge, "Jewish Expectations about the 'Messiah' according to the Fourth Gospel," 252-56. See Pseudo-Clementine *Recognitions* 1.60.

18. N. Dahl, "Messianic Ideas and the Crucifixion of Jesus," in *The Messiah,* ed. Charlesworth, 386.

19. R. E. Brown, *The Gospel according to John I–XII* (AB 29; Garden City: Doubleday, 1966) 46.

20. F. Hahn, *The Titles of Jesus in Christology* (London: Lutterworth; New York: World, 1969) 352-406.

21. Martyn, *The Gospel of John in Christian History,* 12-13; R. L. Webb, *John the Baptizer and Prophet: A Socio-Historical Study* (JSNTSup 62; Sheffield: JSOT Press, 1991).

common folk's opinion of Jesus' identity admits the suggestion that Jesus is Elijah (Mark 6:14-16; Luke 9:7-9). (2) When Jesus inquires of his disciples who he is popularly held to be, they remark that some think him to be John the Baptist, others Elijah, and still others, one of the prophets (Mark 8:27-30; Matt 16:13-20; Luke 9:18-21). (3) Jesus' disciples, curious about why the scribes say it is necessary for Elijah to come first, ask him about it. Jesus affirms the saying and implicitly applies it to the Baptist (Mark 9:11-13; Matt 17:10-13; no Lukan parallel). (4) Jesus converses with Elijah and Moses during the transfiguration (Mark 9:2-10; Matt 17:1-9; Luke 9:28-36). (5) While speaking to the crowds about the Baptist, Jesus explicitly identifies John as Elijah (Matt 11:14; no Lukan parallel). (6) After hearing Jesus' cry from the cross, some of the bystanders wonder whether he is calling on Elijah and plan to wait and see whether the Tishbite will come to his aid (Mark 15:33-36; Matt 27:45-49; no Lukan parallel). From this evidence, we may conclude that some of Jesus' contemporaries envisaged him to be Elijah (Mark, Matthew, and Luke). In Matthew, Jesus himself holds the Baptist to be Elijah.

Elijah is mentioned only twice in the Fourth Gospel, and in each instance the mention is the result of questions raised about the identity of John the Baptist (John 1:21, 25). But neither the explicit references to Jesus being Elijah nor those having Jesus identify the Baptist as Elijah are to be found in the Fourth Gospel. So, while the author of the Fourth Gospel has very little interest in presenting John the Baptist or Jesus as Elijah *redivivus*, he nevertheless betrays an awareness of a messianic expectation centered in the figure of Elijah. He uses this expectation to delineate the roles of John the Baptist and Jesus.

In his study of messianism in the Dead Sea Scrolls and related literature, John Collins states that there were four distinct messianic paradigms in Judaism around the turn of the era: king, priest, prophet, and heavenly figure (Michael; Melchizedek; Son of Man).[22] He shows that these paradigms were not always distinct but would often flow into one other. That there were influential scriptural paradigms is attested by the appearance of a number of prophetic figures in the first century CE. Josephus reports on the activity of royal pretenders such as Judas, Simon, and Athronges in 4 BCE, the activity of the Samaritan prophet in 26-36 CE, and the activity of Theudas in 44-46 CE. All of these figures incited rebellion and managed to persuade the common folk to follow them.[23] Some of these figures either regarded themselves as Moses *redivivus* in accordance with Deuteronomy 18, or were perceived as such.

22. Collins, *The Scepter and the Star,* 195.

23. The following figures are mentioned in the works of Josephus: Athronges (*Antiquities* 17.278-85); Judas, son of Hezekiah (*Antiquities* 17.271-72; *Jewish War* 2.56); Simon (*Antiquities* 17.273-76); Judas, the Galilean (*Antiquities* 18.3-9, 23-25; *Jewish War* 2.118); Menahem, son of Judas the Galilean (*Jewish War* 2.433-34); Simon bar Giora (*Jewish War* 4.503).

On the basis of his activity, attire (hairy mantle), and teaching, it is quite likely that John the Baptist was regarded as a prophetic figure in the style of Elijah or perhaps as a prophet like Moses. There seems little doubt that Elijah played an important role in the religious imagination of the Jewish people; many thought that the resurrection of the dead would come through him. The basis of this expectation was that Elijah was credited with raising the dead during his historical career.[24]

In one notable Dead Sea Scroll (4Q521), there is evidence of the expectation of Elijah's return.[25] Whether this new Elijah is associated with a royal Messiah is a debated issue. It is often noted that the role of Elijah as the forerunner of the Messiah is not attested in Jewish texts before the rise of Christianity. In some Jewish literature Elijah is expected to act as an eschatological prophet. Scholars have inferred the idea that Elijah was expected to return prior to the appearance of the Messiah from the New Testament and then read it back into early Judaism.[26] It may well be that the idea of Elijah returning as the precursor of the Messiah was a Christian development. This assessment, however, may now have to be reevaluated in light of 4Q521.

Apparently not satisfied with the responses from the Baptist, the deputation from Jerusalem continues to interrogate John about his identity by asking him, "Are you the prophet?" (1:21). Once again John emphatically denies that he is the Prophet. That John the Baptist disclaimed traditional roles is clear, but what kind of prophetic figure his interlocutors had in mind and how this fits into Johannine messianic expectations remain unclear. The notion of a prophet-like figure such as Moses plays an important role in the Fourth Gospel's christology.[27] M.-É. Boismard argues that even though the text from Deut 18:18-19 is nowhere explicitly cited in the Fourth Gospel with regard either to Jesus or John the Baptist, the author subtly plays upon the theme of the Mosaic prophet and the images it evoked. The Baptist apparently refused the title, fully aware that it summoned forth expectations of Moses *redivivus* more properly reserved for one yet to come. Boismard reasons that the author of the Gospel quite self-consciously borrows from Samaritan traditions to present Jesus as

24. J. J. Collins, "The Works of the Messiah," *DSD* 1 (1994) 98-112. Cf. *Pesiqta de Rab Kahana* 76a: "Everything that the Holy One will do, he has already anticipated by the hands of the righteous in this world, the resurrection of the dead by Elijah and Ezekiel, the drying of the Red Sea by Moses. . . ."

25. So Collins, "The Works of the Messiah," 99-106; the identification is contested by M. G. Abegg, Jr., "The Messiah at Qumran: Are We Still Seeing Double?" *DSD* 2 (1995) 125-43.

26. See M. M. Faierstein, "Why Do the Scribes Say That Elijah Must Come First?" *JBL* 100 (1981) 75-86; D. C. Allison, "Elijah Must Come First," *JBL* 103 (1984) 256-58; J. A. Fitzmyer, "More about Elijah Coming First," *JBL* 104 (1985) 295-96; J. Marcus, *The Way of the Lord: Christological Exegesis of the Old Testament in the Gospel of Mark* (Louisville: Westminster, 1992).

27. W. A. Meeks, *The Prophet-King: Moses Traditions and the Johannine Christology* (NovTSup 14; Leiden: Brill, 1967).

"the Prophet," not just any prophet, who must come into the world. This prophet, continues Boismard, "can only be the one of whom Moses has written in the law (1:45; 5:46), that is, the prophet like Moses whom God has promised to send in Deut 18:18-19."[28] The author of the Fourth Gospel presents Jesus as the new Moses who speaks as if Moses himself were speaking. Thus, at one level, the eschatological hopes and aspirations of the Samaritans are realized in Jesus the Prophet, while, at another level, the superiority of Jesus over Moses is reinforced. Thus the Baptist's response to the question reflects a messianic expectation centered in a prophetic figure that was common enough to provoke curiosity about John and Jesus.[29]

In John 1:25 the same scene is repeated, although this time the delegation is made up of a group sent by the Pharisees. Evidently they have been informed by the previous delegation that John did not regard himself as the Messiah, Elijah, or the Prophet but as an Isaian voice sent to prepare the way. Having disclaimed the traditional eschatological roles, John, in his baptizing activity, has caught the attention of the emissaries. They therefore seek justification for his baptizing. The delegation asks him why he performs baptisms when he explicitly denies being the Messiah, Elijah, or the Prophet. They want to know why he is performing an eschatological activity when he does not claim a recognizable eschatological role. John responds by saying that he baptizes with water but that there is one among them whom they do not know. This is followed by the frequently repeated statement about the coming of one whose sandals he is not worthy to untie (1:27). The question put to the Baptist implies that the Messiah, Elijah, and the Prophet were expected to baptize.[30] The Baptist, however, continues to insist that he is not any of these anticipated figures but the Isaian voice preparing the way for the coming one.

In John 1:29 John the Baptist encounters Jesus the next day and says, "Behold the Lamb of God, who takes away the sin of the world," and then confirms his own secondary status (1:30). Indeed, says John, "I do not know him, but for this reason I came to baptize with water that he might be revealed to Israel" (1:31). The section climaxes with the Baptist's declaration that this is the Son of God (1:34).

28. M.-É. Boismard, *Moïse ou Jésus: Essai de christologie johannique* (BETL 84; Leuven: Leuven University Press, 1988); English translation, *Moses or Jesus: An Essay in Johannine Christology* (Minneapolis: Fortress, 1993) 66-67.

29. Some commentators think the import of the question is, "Why do you perform what appears to be an official act if you have no official status?" See R. A. Horsley, "Popular Prophetic Movements at the Time of Jesus: Their Principal Features and Social Origins," *JSNT* 26 (1986) 3-27; R. A. Horsley and J. S. Hanson, *Bandits, Prophets, and Messiahs: Popular Movements at the Time of Jesus* (Minneapolis: Winston, 1985).

30. Barrett, *The Gospel according to St. John*, 174.

John the Baptist's Witness in the Presence of the Two Disciples: John 1:35-52

In the presence of his two disciples, John the Baptist repeats and amplifies his witness to Jesus. John 1:41 records the first use of ὁ Μεσσίας along with a reminder to the reader that it means "Christ" or "Anointed." The statement is made in the context of John's confession that Jesus is the "Lamb of God" which, when overheard by two disciples, impels them to follow Jesus.[31] Jesus turns to ask the followers what or whom they are looking for, and in reply, they say, "Rabbi, where are you staying?" (1:38). Jesus takes them to where he is staying. The reader is then informed about the identity of the two unnamed disciples. Andrew, Simon Peter's brother, leaves to find his brother Simon, and greets him with the statement, "We have found the Messiah," followed by the statement, "which is translated Anointed" (1:41). Upon seeing Simon, Jesus exercises his power of insight and identifies Peter as Simon son of John — who is to be called Peter (1:42). When Philip finds Nathanael (perhaps a symbolic name) he informs him, "We have found him of whom Moses in the Law and also the prophets wrote, Jesus of Nazareth, the son of Joseph" (1:45). Nathanael, at first somewhat skeptical of Jesus' credentials, reacts by asking whether anything good can come out of Nazareth (1:46). Philip then invites Nathanael to come and see, and when he encounters Jesus he is so impressed that Jesus knows him that he replies, "Rabbi, you are the Son of God! You are the King of Israel" (1:49).

What is interesting about this section is not only the statement about seeking and finding the Messiah, a common theme in the Fourth Gospel, but the remarkable mixture of titles ascribed to Jesus and the varying opinions ventured about him.[32] He is referred to as "Rabbi" (1:38), "Messiah" (1:41), "the one about whom Moses and also the prophets wrote" (1:45), "Jesus son of Joseph from Nazareth" (1:45), "Son of God" (1:49), and "King of Israel" (1:49). Finally, Jesus refers to himself as "Son of Man" (1:51). Why Andrew concludes that he has found the Messiah is unclear, as is what type of Messiah he thinks Jesus to be, whether priest, prophet, or king. The rich variety of titles ascribed to Jesus might indicate that the Johannine community passed through several distinct stages in the development of messianic thinking, beginning with what the author considered to be wrongheaded notions about the person and work

31. It is often noted that because "Lamb of God" is not a messianic designation it is possible that the Baptist's disciples did not make such a declaration. Even if they did, how they would have understood it remains problematic. Most commentators deny that the title was uttered by the disciples and so explain with little consensus what the author may have had in mind. For the standard interpretative options, see L. Morris, *The Gospel according to John* (Grand Rapids: Eerdmans, 1971) 144-47.

32. Martyn takes the phrase "We have found the Messiah" as the message of the first speakers in the synagogue.

of Jesus and eventually ending with proper confession and belief. That there were different perceptions and expectations of the Messiah in the Johannine community is supported by John Painter, but rather than seeing these perceptions as indicating clear-cut transitions from one notion to another it is better to think of one perception being laid over another.[33] C. H. Dodd argued that the Baptist's declaration of Jesus as "Lamb of God" is equivalent to the title Messiah.[34] The disciples refer to him as Rabbi and then end up going to where Jesus resides, perhaps to be enlightened on his nature and exact identity, eventually to recognize him as the Son of God and King of Israel.

The Gospel writer suggestively overlays the concept of the Messiah with mention of Moses and what has been written about him in the Law and the Prophets and with the King of Israel. While it is possible that the concept of a Davidic Messiah involving political deliverance was prominent in the Johannine community for a time, the Johannine Jesus resists the role of a political redeemer. The royal notion is overshadowed by the prophetic. Jesus is portrayed as a prophet like Moses. Wayne Meeks has proposed that the eschatological Mosaic prophet was merged with the coming messianic king to highlight the prophetic mission of Jesus. Collins discusses the relationship of Jesus and the Davidic Messiah, noting the portrayal of Jesus in the Gospels as a nonmilitant figure.[35] In light of this discussion, scholars have argued that the term "Messiah" was originally applied to Jesus as prophet rather than king.

A passage in 4Q521 has aroused considerable interest because it refers to a Messiah that resonates with a Baptist passage from the Synoptic sayings source.[36]

> . . . heaven and earth will obey his Messiah, (2) [and all th]at is in them will not turn away from the commandments of the holy ones. (3) You who seek the Lord, strengthen yourselves in his service. (4) Is not in this that you will find the Lord, all who hope in their hearts? (5) For the Lord will seek out the pious and call the righteous by name, (6) and his spirit will hover over the poor, and he will renew the faithful by his might. (7) for he will glorify the pious on the throne of an eternal kingdom (8) releasing captives, giving sight to the blind and raising up those who are bo[wed down], (9) Forever I will cleave to [those who] hope, and in his kindness . . . (10) and the glorious things that have taken place the Lord will do as he s[aid], (12) for he will heal the wounded, give life to the dead and preach good news to the poor. (13) and

33. Painter, *The Quest for the Messiah,* 19.

34. C. H. Dodd, *Historical Tradition in the Fourth Gospel* (Cambridge: Cambridge University Press, 1963) 290.

35. Collins, *The Scepter and the Star,* 204-9.

36. Collins, "The Works of the Messiah," 98-112; idem, *The Scepter and the Star,* 117-22.

> he will sat[]isfy the [weak] ones and lead those who have been cast out and enrich the hungry . . . (14) . . . and all of them. . . .[37]

After John the Baptist hears about the deeds of Jesus while languishing in prison, he sends emissaries to ask Jesus, "Are you the one who is to come, or shall we to look for another?" (Matt 11:2-3). In response, Jesus answers, "Go and tell John what you hear and see: the blind receive their sight and the lame walk, lepers are cleansed and the deaf hear, and the dead are raised up, and the poor have good news preached to them" (Matt 11:3-5//Luke 7:22). While the signs or deeds mentioned in the passage could be taken to suggest that Jesus is Elijah *redivivus,* the statement in Matt 11:5 and Luke 7:22 is so placed as to undo this impression and to affirm that Jesus is greater than John. The lack of royal messianic vocabulary in reference to the Messiah in 4Q521 suggests to Collins that the Messiah in this text is to be understood as an anointed eschatological prophet, either Elijah or a prophet like Elijah, not a royal Messiah.[38]

On the whole, 4Q521 strengthens the case for a prophetic Jesus. Jesus in the Gospel of John, as the Anointed, is linked with Moses and referred to as the King of Israel. He is given both prophetic as well as royal attributes, which is not that strange given that both royal and prophetic attributes were sometimes attached to the same person. Philo of Alexandria portrays Moses as prophet, priest, and king, and the figure of Moses helps explain the association of prophet and king in the Gospel of John.[39]

The Witness of John Resumes: John 3:22-36

The evangelist continues developing the relationship between the Baptist and Jesus by portraying both of them pursuing their work simultaneously. Both are pictured as baptizing side by side, which precipitates a dispute between their respective disciples. John's baptism lies within the boundaries of the Jewish system of purification. A discussion arises between John's disciples and a certain Jew about purification with no details given about the nature of the dispute, but with the implication that Jesus is superior to this system. While the passage doubtless contains a historical reminiscence, the dispute also becomes a pretext of the author to clarify the relationship between the Baptist and Jesus.[40]

The conflict revolves around the question of purification but then quickly moves to the number of people going to Jesus to be baptized. When John's

37. Translation by Collins, *The Scepter and the Star,* 99.

38. Contrary to É. Puech, "Une Apocalypse Messianique (4Q521)," *RevQ* 15 (1992) 475-519, who identifies the Messiah in this text as a royal Messiah.

39. Collins, *The Scepter and the Star,* 205-7.

40. E. Haenchen, *John,* vol. 1 (Hermeneia; Philadelphia: Fortress, 1984) 209.

followers complain to him that Jesus has more people coming to him to be baptized, John once more reminds them that he is not the Messiah but has been sent ahead of him (3:28). The imagery of the bride and bridegroom and the friend of the bridegroom drives home the point that John must decrease while Jesus increases. Jesus is he who comes from above and is therefore above all. It is the Son of God whom God has sent who speaks the words of God — whoever believes in the Son has eternal life. Thus, with this juxtaposition of "Messiah" and "Son of God," the author appears to be trying to correct a faulty understanding of the Messiah that pays insufficient attention to Jesus as Son of God. "Son of God" is linked to the Logos that was in the beginning, the Word become flesh, and John's witness to that Word (1:1-14).

The Samaritan Woman: John 4:1-42

The encounter of the Samaritan woman with Jesus provides yet another fascinating example of the use of ὁ χριστός (4:25). The continuing conflict about baptism forces Jesus to travel through Samaria to Sychar and Jacob's well. At the well he encounters the Samaritan woman, and this meeting precipitates the living water discourse. Jesus' knowledge about the woman's past and her numerous husbands leads her to recognize him as a prophet who advocates worship at Jerusalem and not Mount Gerizim. Jesus proclaims that the hour is coming when worship will not take place on a mountain or in Jerusalem in spirit and in truth. The woman responds with a confession, "I know that Messiah is coming (who is called Anointed). When that one comes, he will proclaim all things to us" (4:25). Here one of the attributes of the Messiah is clearly that of a teacher. The woman then returns to her village to announce that she has found a man "who told me everything I have ever done. He cannot be the Messiah, can he?" (4:28-30). Thus, another attribute of the Messiah is that he is able to discern the secrets people hold. C. K. Barrett speaks of this as a messianic secret, not of the kind in Mark, but a secret progressively being revealed even to the outsider.[41] Many of the Samaritans believe on account of the woman's testimony and are convinced that Jesus is truly the savior of the world (4:42).

Commentators often point out, however, that the Samaritan woman does not expect a Messiah in the sense of an anointed king from the house of David. Samaritans, at least as far as can be determined, did envisage a figure who would have an integral part in bringing about a future age. They longed for the coming of the *Taheb,* apparently their term for the Messiah. The term itself means "restorer" and points toward not a new David but a new Moses — Moses

41. Barrett, *The Gospel according to John,* 812.

redivivus. The woman's statement, "When that one comes he will proclaim all things to us," fits the image of the *Taheb* as a teacher.[42]

The Bread from Heaven Discourse: John 6:22-65

The bread from heaven discourse follows the feeding miracle. The feeding of the five thousand leads to an attempt by the crowd to crown Jesus king and precipitates the question from the crowd about what sign Jesus is going to give them (John 6:22-58). In reply, Jesus links his feeding miracle with Moses and the manna miracle which, however, did not come from Moses but God. It is the bread from heaven that gives life to the world. In response to the crowd's request for some of the bread, Jesus answers, "I am the bread of life" (6:35). Unhappiness with this reply leads to the complaint that Jesus is only the son of Joseph. The Jews complain, "Is not this Jesus, the son of Joseph, whose father and mother we know? How can he now say, 'I have come down from heaven'?" (6:42). When the disciples hear Jesus' teaching, many of them comment that his teaching is difficult to accept (6:60). It is difficult not because it is obscure but because it is offensive, deriving from one who is merely the son of Joseph. He is not recognized for who he truly is. He remains, in a sense, hidden from them.

The theme of a hidden Messiah who is not recognized at first and who must be sought, discovered, and found, is common in the Fourth Gospel. The failure to recognize the Messiah as the Messiah may well relate to the notion of the hidden Messiah who is to come incognito, mentioned in 4 Ezra.[43] This Messiah is to appear at his appointed time and remain hidden from mortal eyes. Another notion held that the Messiah would be on earth but unaware that he himself was the Messiah.[44] The point in John may be that when the Messiah appears he will not remain incognito. Even though he is not recognized at first, he will be revealed as the Son of God at one with the Father.

Jerusalem and Controversy: John 7:1-13, 14-52

In John 7 the resistance to Jesus has heated up to such an extent in Judea that he journeys to Galilee. The narrator informs the reader that the Jews were

42. See discussion in M. de Jonge, "Jewish Expectations about the 'Messiah' according to the Fourth Gospel," 268-70; J. Macdonald, *The Theology of the Samaritans* (London: SCM, 1964). Brown, *The Gospel according to John,* vol. 1, 172.

43. See M. E. Stone, "The Messiah in 4 Ezra," in *Judaisms and Their Messiahs,* ed. Neusner et al., 209-24.

44. See *1 Enoch* 48:6; 62:7; *2 Baruch* 29:3; 39:7; 73:1; 4 Ezra 7:28; 12:32; 13:26, 32, 52; 14:9.

seeking an opportunity to kill Jesus and that the Jewish festival of Booths was near. His brothers, however, urge him to leave Galilee and travel to Judea so that the disciples may see the works that he is doing, "for no one keeps his actions hidden and still expects to be in the public eye" (7:4).[45] Jesus then shortly ventures into the public again but is incognito (7:10). The Jews continue to seek him while the crowds mutter and grumble about him, some saying, "He is a good man" but others objecting, "No, he is deceiving the crowd" (7:12). About the middle of the festival Jesus begins to teach, but his teaching does not elicit a good response from the crowd, who accuse him of being demon possessed (7:20). It finally dawns upon some of the people of Jerusalem that this is the man whom the authorities have been trying to kill, yet here he is in public, openly teaching without recrimination. The crowds then wonder whether the authorities are keeping something to themselves, saying, "Can it possibly be that the authorities really know that this is the Christ?" (7:26). In other words, they ask whether the authorities have changed their minds about the identity of Jesus, recognized he truly is the Messiah, but for whatever reason have chosen not to inform them.

This explanation is deemed improbable, though, for the Jerusalemites raise the objection that they know whence this one comes; therefore, he cannot possibly be the Messiah. It appears that Jesus was known to have hailed from Nazareth. Hence, the people of Jerusalem opine, "When the Messiah comes, no one will know where he is from" (7:27). This opinion is probably grounded in the popular notion of the hidden Messiah who will become known because he will be a descendant of David and make his appearance in Bethlehem.[46] Again, the fourth evangelist betrays an awareness of popular messianic beliefs and adapts them to lead up to the next pronouncements.

The confusion and the debate about the true identity of Jesus that follow the discourse on rivers of living water corroborate the notion of a hidden Messiah. Jesus offers to quench the thirst of people by inviting them to drink from the living water, that is, believe in him. The response of some is, "Surely this one is a prophet," while others remark, "This is the Messiah" (7:41). Still others question Jesus' legitimate claim to messianic status: "Surely the Messiah isn't to come from Galilee? Doesn't the Scripture say that the Messiah, being of David's family, is to come from Bethlehem, the village where David lived?"[47]

In the discussion between the Temple police, chief priests, Pharisees, and

45. Translation from Brown, *The Gospel according to John,* vol. 1, 305.

46. Cf. Justin Martyr, *Dialogue with Trypho* 8.4; 110.1. The Jew Trypho states: "Messiah, even if he be born and actually exist somewhere, must wait until Elijah comes to anoint him and make him known."

47. This reference to Bethlehem is problematic and is adduced from such passages as *Tg. Micah* 5:1; Matt 2:6; Mic 5:1, 3; Matt 2:5, 6. See E. D. Freed, *Old Testament Quotations in the Gospel of John* (NovTSup 11; Leiden: Brill, 1965).

Nicodemus, the chief priests and Pharisees query Nicodemus about whether Jesus is from Galilee. They then urge him, "Search and you will see that no prophet is to rise from Galilee" (7:52). In his attempt to convince his audience that Jesus is the supernatural heavenly redeemer, even though he springs from Galilee, the evangelist uses well-known Jewish beliefs but adapts them to his own ends.[48] M. de Jonge is convinced that this passage reflects a critical attitude toward those insisting that the Messiah have a proper pedigree — that he must be a royal figure from the house of David.[49] The author uses the objection of this verse to introduce the pronouncement that though they know whence he comes, those are not his real origins because he comes from the Father who has sent him.

Again, the pronouncement does not ingratiate Jesus with the crowd. Some of them try to lay hands upon him to arrest him, while others speculate, "When the Messiah comes, will he do more signs than this man has done?" (7:31). Martyn has argued that a miracle-working Messiah was not a standard Jewish expectation but then offers the suggestion that the fourth evangelist has equated the wonder-working prophet with the Messiah.[50] C. K. Barrett, however, proposes that even though the Jewish people might not have expected a miracle-working Messiah, if confronted by miracles, they might have wondered whether the miracle worker was not a Messiah.[51]

The signs of the Messiah are part of what has become known as the Signs Source. This is not the place to discuss this complex issue, but the messianism presupposed in the Signs Source deserves comment. Georg Richter argues that the Signs Source portrays Jesus as the eschatological Mosaic prophet based on Deut 18:15-20.[52] Robert Fortna asserts that the messianism presupposed by the Signs Source is not "the political, Davidic liberator expected by so many. He is not military victor but healer, a worker of miracles," one who does works (τὰ ἔργα ἃ ποιεῖς) like Elijah and Moses. Both Moses and Elijah had a reputation for performing miracles.[53] The paucity of evidence about a returning Elijah or Moses working miracles weakens his case. H.-J. Kuhn notes the absence of a miracle-working Messiah in Jewish tradition and so postulates a *theios anēr* christology for the Signs Source by relating it to the "Son of God" appellation found in the source. The "Son of God" designation was more appropriate to

48. Barrett, *The Gospel according to John,* 322.

49. M. de Jonge, "Jewish Expectations about the 'Messiah' according to the Fourth Gospel," 260.

50. Martyn, *The Gospel of John in Christian History,* 16-28.

51. Barrett, *The Gospel according to John,* 323.

52. G. Richter, "Die Fleischwerdung des Logos im Johannesevangelium," *NovT* 14 (1972) 256-58.

53. Fortna, *The Fourth Gospel and Its Predecessor,* 38, 225-34; Painter, *The Quest for the Messiah,* 11.

the Jewish and early Christian contexts. The christology of the Signs Source, then, is the result of the merging of Jewish and non-Jewish Hellenistic elements.[54] Other solutions have been offered, none of which, however, seems satisfactory.

At this point, we may return to 4Q521, which has an extraordinary parallel to Jesus' answer to the Baptist recorded in Q (Matt 11:2-6 = Luke 7:18-23). As we have seen, 4Q521 refers to a Messiah, a figure probably to be associated with the anointed prophet of Isaiah 61, an anointed one who is an agent of the works of YHWH. He is to bring good news to the oppressed, to bind up the brokenhearted, proclaim liberty to the captives, and release prisoners. Collins avers that if the understanding of this text is correct, then the works of this agent were seen to be both the works of the Messiah and of God before the Gospel tradition. Since Jesus is characteristically portrayed as engaged in the specific works mentioned, "the epithet 'anointed' or 'messiah' may have become attached to him because of his words and deeds."[55]

Although such a direct parallel is not to be found in the Fourth Gospel, we may wonder whether the notion of an anointed figure engaged in the works of God might not have had an influence on the Johannine portrayal of the Messiah as one who does works and signs. In John 10:24 the Jews ask Jesus, "How long will you keep us in suspense? If you are the Messiah, tell us plainly." Jesus replies, "I have told you, and you do not believe. The works that I do in my Father's name testify to me; but you do not believe, because you do not belong to my sheep" (10:25-26). In 6:30, shortly after the feeding miracle and the bread of heaven discourse, the crowd asks Jesus what they must do to perform the works of God. Jesus responds, "This is the work of God, that you believe in me." Not satisfied with the response, the crowd asks Jesus, "What sign are you going to give us then, so that we may see it and believe you? What work are you performing?"

The Man Born Blind: John 9:1-41

A man blind from birth is healed in order to display the works of God (John 9:3) and to provide the occasion for the saying, "I am the light of the world" (9:5). The healing takes place on the Sabbath. It confuses those who have known the man; some think it is he, but others that it is only someone like him. When they inquire how his eyes were opened, the man describes how Jesus healed him. When they ask him where Jesus is, he says, "I do not know" (9:11-12). The

54. H.-J. Kuhn, *Christologie und Wunder: Untersuchungen zu Joh. 1:35-51* (Regensburg: Pustet, 1988).

55. Collins, "The Works of the Messiah," 110; idem, *The Scepter and the Star,* 205.

man is eventually brought before the Pharisees and the Jews, who interrogate him and his parents for confirmation that he was blind from birth. The Jews conclude, "This man (Jesus) is not from God, for he does not keep the Sabbath" (9:16-19). When the man is pushed to reveal the identity of the one who has healed him, he replies, "He is a prophet" (9:17). In John 9:22 the narrator informs the reader that the Jews had already agreed that anyone who confessed Jesus to be the Messiah would be put out of the synagogue. It is for this reason that the parents refuse to answer the questions put to them about the restored vision of their son (9:18-23).

In the discussions that ensue between the Jews and the man whose eyesight has been restored, the origin of Jesus remains at issue. When the Jews maintain that Jesus is a sinner, the man insists, "I do not know whether he is a sinner. One thing I do know, that though I was blind, now I see" (9:25). The Jews scoff at him, claiming, "You are his disciple, but we are disciples of Moses. We know that God has spoken to Moses, but as for this man, we do not know where he comes from" (9:28-29). The man then retorts that Jesus cannot be a sinner since God does not listen to sinners and that if Jesus were not from God, he could do nothing. The Jews respond by driving the man out of the synagogue. When Jesus finds out that the Jews have driven the man out, he approaches the man and puts the question to him, "Do you believe in the Son of Man?" (9:35). When questioned about who the Son of Man was, Jesus says, "You have seen him, and it is he who speaks to you" (9:37). This knowledge elicits the confession, "*Kyrios,* I believe" (9:38).

The confession of Jesus as the Christ leads to the expulsion of the blind man from the synagogue. Martyn and others have noted how the man's christological confession becomes progressively "higher" the more he is pressed in conflict with the Jews (the man called Jesus; a prophet; man from God; Son of Man; Lord). As a two-level drama, the story has been thought to model in a stylized way the development of christological thinking in the Johannine community. After an extensive investigation of the term, M. de Jonge observes that ὁ χριστός is perhaps not the most important title in the Fourth Gospel and that the Gospel writer uses the other titles and the conflict that swirls about them to correct inadequate confessions and insufficient perceptions about Jesus resident within the Johannine community.[56]

Lazarus: John 11:1-44

The narrative about the raising of Lazarus is filled with intricate narrative detail: a lengthy illness; Jesus delaying his trip to Bethany for two days before respond-

56. M. de Jonge, "Jewish Expectations about the 'Messiah' according to the Fourth Gospel."

ing to the appeal to heal Lazarus; Lazarus dying; Jesus not appearing at the tomb of Lazarus until four days after his death; an odorous, decaying body; the onlookers observing that he who opened the eyes of a blind man could have kept this man from dying (John 11:37). The extravagant detail of the narrative serves to heighten the extraordinary character of the miracle and the power of Jesus over death. The miracle of the raising of Lazarus also permits the writer of the Fourth Gospel to begin developing the theme of the resurrection of Jesus and its relationship to the Messiah. Jesus says to Martha, "I am the resurrection and the life, do you believe this?" (11:25). She does not answer the question directly but replies with the words, "Yes, *Kyrios,* I believe that you are the Messiah, the Son of God, the one coming into the world" (11:27). It seems that the many remarks made by various characters in the Fourth Gospel about the Messiah who is to come (4:25; 7:27; 7:31) finally receive their resolution in this confession.

The coalescence of a number of christological titles and the term "the Messiah" is significant and points to what appears to be the agenda of the writer, namely, to reveal to the world that the one who is coming into the world, though unknown to the world (1:10), is himself the resurrection and the life, the Son of God who has power over life and death. For the fourth evangelist, the title "the Messiah" does not fully or adequately capture Jesus' identity and status; he therefore corrects faulty or incomplete messianic perceptions by applying to Jesus the title "Son of God." Here, the fourth evangelist appears to invest the title "Son of God" with notions of divinity. Preparations for such a move appear to have been available in early Jewish messianic thinking.

The title "Son of God" is an important one in the Fourth Gospel as well as in the Synoptic Gospels. John Collins has studied the occurrence of the term in a number of passages from the Hebrew Bible and the Dead Sea Scrolls (2 Samuel 7; Psalm 2; Isaiah 7, 9, 11; Zechariah 9; and Dan 9:26; 4Q174, the *Florilegium;* 1QSa, the *Messianic Rule;* 4Q369; and 4Q246, the *Son of God* text). With 4Q246 in view, he maintains that "Son of God" in an early Jewish context is a functional title, used of a warrior figure who will subdue the nations, restore Israel, and establish peace. It is not a metaphysical title, yet the human being given this title "stands in a special relationship" to God; "he is not an ordinary mortal." His conclusion bears quoting at length:

> The notion of a messiah who was in some sense divine had its roots in Judaism, in the interpretation of such passages as Psalm 2 and Daniel 7 in an apocalyptic context. This is not to deny the great difference between a text like 4Q246 and the later Christian understanding of the divinity of Christ. But the notion that the messiah was Son of God in a special sense was rooted in Judaism, and so there was continuity between Judaism and Christianity in

> this respect, even though Christian belief eventually diverged quite radically from its Jewish sources.[57]

Given the evidence, it seems safe to conclude that the writer of the Fourth Gospel drew on certain messianic expectations of a Son of God figure current in some quarters of Judaism and then extended their import and applied them to Jesus who, in his thought, was the supernatural heavenly redeemer.

The Anointing: John 11:55–12:11

The days before the Passover set the stage for the narrative of John 12. Mary anoints the feet of Jesus, surely an act suggestive of his anointed status, but as one who is on his way to his death and burial. During his trip into Jerusalem, the crowds hail him as "King of Israel" (John 12:13). Jesus finds and sits upon a young donkey. The disciples find these events incomprehensible and are unable to decipher their deeper significance. The Greeks at the festival express the desire to see Jesus. Jesus predicts that the hour has arrived for the "Son of Man" to be glorified and clearly recognizes that his hour is close — he will be lifted up from the earth — with the narrator interjecting that this was said to indicate the kind of death he was to die. The crowd raises an objection, "We have heard from the Law that the Messiah remains forever. How can you say that the Son of Man must be lifted up? Who is this Son of Man?" (John 12:34).

It is clear that the crowd is aware that Jesus is referring to himself when he speaks of the Son of Man (5:23; 3:14; 7:28; 12:31-33). Even though the Son of Man imagery is not explicitly equated with the title Messiah, the crowds make a virtual identification. Once more, the author of the Fourth Gospel seems to be dipping into a pool of commonly held, though not necessarily widespread, assumptions concerning the Messiah. For the evangelist, the Messiah is a supernatural heavenly redeemer who has become incarnate in the person of Jesus. Jesus is also the Son of Man, who in some early Jewish sources is pictured as a preexistent, transcendent figure of heavenly origin.[58] Yet the Johannine Son of Man must suffer and die, whereas the Son of Man of the *Similitudes of Enoch* and 4 Ezra does not undergo suffering or death.

57. Collins, *The Scepter and the Star,* 168-69.

58. Collins, *The Scepter and the Star,* 173-94. See J. D. G. Dunn, *Christology in the Making: A New Testament Inquiry into the Origins of the Doctrine of the Incarnation* (Philadelphia: Westminster, 1980) 65-97; G. Vermes, "The Son of Man Debate," *JSNT* 1 (1978) 19-32.

Conclusions

The diverse titles applied to Jesus in the Fourth Gospel are reflective of the variegated, often overlapping configuration of terms applied to several eschatological figures in the literature of early Judaism. The Gospel of John's own social setting and theology in large measure determine how the Jews, the crowds, the Pharisees, the disciples, and the common people come to express beliefs and objections about the identity of Jesus. Some acknowledge the truth about the Johannine Jesus by their confession of belief in him, while others raise objections and questions designed to highlight in relief the Johannine view of Jesus. Misconceptions about the Messiah abound in the Gospel and become opportunities for the author to correct them. Jesus is presented as the preexistent Logos to whom the Baptist gives witness, the Prophet-King, the ascending-descending Man from Heaven, the Son of God, the Holy One of God, the Son of Man who is to be raised up on high, and the crucified but exalted Messiah. Some of these images have their origins in the popular messianic expectations of the day. The fourth evangelist apparently had to wrestle with diverse Jewish traditions that did not provide a clear and uniform set of messianic expectation for Jesus to fulfill.

Labels such as "Son of God" and "Son of Man" cannot be removed from Jewish messianism and relegated to later, Hellenistic Christianity. The title "Son of God" is not the product of a church that arbitrarily changed "Son of God" from designating a messianic king to denoting a figure of heavenly origin. While the fourth evangelist diverges quite radically from his immediate Jewish context in his recontextualization of the title Messiah, we may discern a greater degree of continuity between the thought world of the evangelist's Jewish contemporaries and that of the Johannine community. Some of the Dead Sea fragments make this reassessment possible. A heavenly, transcendent Messiah was not a unique invention of the Christian community but the outgrowth of reflection that had its roots in Judaism.[59]

59. My thanks to Robert Cousland, friend and colleague, for reading earlier versions of the paper and making helpful comments throughout.

Discussion

From the audience: "Would a Greek-speaking audience understand Paul's usage of θριαμβεύειν ('to lead in a triumphal procession') as having anything to do with Merkabah mysticism?"

James Scott: "If a Greek-speaking audience was confronted with this concept without prior background information, I would have to say that it is very unlikely because admittedly this is a very vague reference. But given the context in which Paul is writing, there is a greater possibility that his audience would catch the reference. Remember, we have opponents in Corinth who are seeing things themselves. They have their own visions. In a certain sense, Paul is forced to talk about his own visions because of his critics and opponents. Beyond that we have to assume that there were Jews in the congregation in Corinth. We don't know how many; it may have been a minority. I talked to Margaret Thrall on this very issue, and she thinks there may even be more than most people assume. So, I'll leave that open for now — what the constitution of the church of Corinth is. But given the context, I think there is a possibility for seeing this use of the verb in light of Merkabah mysticism."

Gordon Fee: "Being an older New Testament scholar on this panel who didn't catch Qumran fever the first time it came around, I feel like a fox thrown into the chicken house, as it were. I'm concerned with some of the methodology. I have to admit that the Old Testament papers helped me more than did the New Testament papers. And the methodology, particularly in this instance, Jim, is what concerns me, because, certainly in 1 Cor 4:9, there is already an allusion to the triumph. For God has exhibited Paul as the one who at the end of the procession is going to die in the arena. The point is that in this very Roman city Paul has already used this imagery to refer to his own role in a triumphal procession. That ought to affect how we hear *this* text. Furthermore, there is not one shred of evidence of Jewishness in 1 Corinthians. Nor is there evidence for outside opponents. Here is where my problem starts. Here you have a community that is part of Roman culture. What do these people know of Jewish mystical traditions? Paul does not depend on Merkabah mysticism or draw from it at all. He is simply describing something that becomes illegitimate for him to speak about. And now you have some alleged opponents. Margaret Thrall does not think there were any. I happen not to agree with her, but you have some alleged opponents who bring in a Moses tradition, Merkabah mysticism, and all the rest. In my opinion, they could not possibly have understood Merkabah mysticism. And now we have Merkabah tradition as a way of understanding this Pauline passage. I have methodological problems with this approach."

Craig Evans: "Please respond to these objections, Professor Scott."

Scott: "I should defer to my older colleague, who has also written a commentary on 1 Corinthians, because of his expertise on that letter to the Corinthians. However, it is doubtful that 2 Cor 2:14 would have been understood by the Corinthians as a deliberate echo of 1 Cor 4:9, for the allusion is muted by the 'painful visit' and the 'tearful letter,' which came between the writing of 1 and 2 Corinthians. Furthermore, there are substantial differences between the two passages in question. For example, in 1 Cor 4:9 the apostle disparages being exhibited by God before the world in contrast to the Corinthians' self-commendation, whereas in 2 Cor 2:14 he actually exults in being led in triumphal procession and in its positive revelatory benefit to the world. We must be sensitive to the various contexts in which Paul writes."

Fee: "My point is that you are already reconstructing something in a mirror reading that, with reference to what the opponents may have said already, is somewhat dubious. I admit that you could make a good case of 2 Corinthians 3, as Margaret Thrall has done, though without opponents. So to reconstruct by mirror reading and now come back to something Paul has already used in its ordinary metaphorical sense, and to argue that he now uses it in a totally different way — I have my doubts; you can see my hesitance."

Scott: "My approach to the interpretation of 2 Cor 2:14 depends neither on mirror reading nor on a particular reconstruction of Paul's opponents in Corinth. I mention the opponents only to explain why Paul may have resorted to Merkabah tradition at this point. Actually, my interpretation derives from the context of 2 Cor 2:14–4:6 itself, which also otherwise employs Moses typology (e.g., 2 Cor 2:16b; 3:1-18), interacts with synagogue tradition (e.g., 2 Cor 3:14-15), and describes a theophany reminiscent of Ezekiel 1 (cf. 2 Cor 3:18).

Certainly Professor Fee will not want to deny the 'Jewishness' of *this* passage. My point is that in such a context, which so stresses Paul's role as a revelatory mediator like Moses, the apostle may well have resorted to Merkabah tradition in order to reinforce his claim to true apostleship."

Evans: "I hope you (the audience) appreciate this. This is the kind of thing that we do. This is a good example of the debate that takes place at a Society of Biblical Literature meeting, or the like. Scholars really get into it. We hammer out the interpretation of these texts. We debate what to do with these Scrolls and the various noncanonical writings that are frequently brought into the discussion. The debate can be lively, sometimes even heated, but it is always in the spirit of collegiality and respect."

From the audience: "When Paul says that God leads us in triumphant procession, couldn't that mean that he is following in the train of God and really he is just part of the army of God — that he is on God's side and not being led as a captive?"

Scott: "Well, that has been tried before by commentators, but unsuccessfully, unfortunately. We would all like to believe that Paul is on the side of God, which would make good sense. But the problem is that the verb θριαμβεύειν itself does not allow this interpretation. Paul is the object of that verb, and if you trace its usage in Greek texts, all the way through the literature, every time there is an object of that verb it is talking about those who are being led in triumph. They are the captives, not members of the victorious army."

From the audience: "First question, say more about the deity of the 'Son of God' individual in the 4Q246 'Son of God' text. Second question, was there at Qumran the belief that the Teacher of Righteousness, who possibly was the founder of the Essenes, atoned in any way through his suffering and martyrdom?"

Evans: "Would you care to answer these questions, Professor Collins?"

John Collins: "Actually this was addressed to you, Professor Evans! As to the deity of the Son of God in the 'Son of God' text, I agree with Professor Evans in that we both think this is a messianic figure — not everybody does. If so, I take it that this is an honorific title. It is not a matter of metaphysics, although I should not underestimate the force of a title. The main point I want to make here is that you do not have any conception here that is analogous to the Christian concept of the Trinity, for example. It comes out of the background of the royal psalms, which we heard about this morning. There was some sense that the king was more than an ordinary human being. But this certainly was not putting him on par with the Almighty. So when I say honorific title, I think it may have some implications that he is more than an ordinary human being, but by no means what we would mean by divinity in a Christian context. With respect to the second question of the atoning death of the Teacher of Righteousness, I don't think it happened. At various points in the history of Qumran scholarship people have speculated about this. I just don't see any evidence for it. There are figures in the Scrolls who are said to atone for the sin of the people, especially in a fragmentary Aramaic text, 4QAaron^{a}. But I assume that in that context one is talking about a priestly figure who atones for people by offering the proper sacrifices. I don't think there is any concept of atoning death anywhere else. Maybe somebody would like to respond to that?"

Evans: "I agree with that response. I might add that with respect to the first question, a reading in 1QSa, 'when God will have begotten the Messiah' (and there is some debate over this reading, because there are holes in the text in a couple of inconvenient places!), generated a great deal of controversy. Does this text, assuming that my reading represents the original, somehow foreshadow the virgin birth of the Messiah? I do not think so. That is to overinterpret the text. It is echoing the language of Psalm 2. A text using language such as being the 'Lord's anointed' and 'today I have begotten you' is poetic. For early Christians advancing the virgin birth, the divine birth, the divine conception of Jesus, a text like that is useful. But the text by itself, whether it is Psalm 2 or a Dead Sea Scroll like 4Q246 or 1QSa, does not require that interpetation."

From the audience: "I attended a conference where the Lubavitchers were present. You may remember that it was in the news a couple of years ago. At that time some believed that this aged rabbi might be the Messiah. During discussion time I asked what meaning the Dead Sea Scrolls and messianism had for the Lubavitchers. Surprisingly, they were not interested in the question. So let me ask the members of the panel: What have the Dead Sea Scrolls meant for Jews, that is, practicing religious Jews? Are there messianic implications of the Scrolls for Jews today?"

Collins: "I will give you one comment on it. Unfortunately, none of us here is Jewish, right? And to speak to your questions with any authority we would need to be. But I have Jewish colleagues, and I think what probably most Jews would say is that this stuff is a curiosity. This is not part of the tradition that was handed down to us. It may happen to confirm that tradition in part or not confirm it in part, but what is more authoritative for more traditional Jews, at least, is the teaching of the rabbis. And the rabbis rejected these people. That is why this stuff was left in the caves. So, what this tells us, I would say in large part, is that this is the kind of Judaism that was to a great degree disowned by the rabbinic tradition. Now you will meet an occasional Jewish scholar who would want to emphasize the continuity of this material with the rabbinic tradition, but even in doing so the attempt is to legitimate the Dead Sea Scrolls by appeal to the authority of the rabbis. But it is the rabbis who are authoritative, and there is no contest on that, I think."

PETER FLINT: "Following on from what Professor Collins has said, I don't think that all of us here realize that one form of Judaism has come down to us, namely, rabbinic Judaism, which was largely informed by the Pharisaic traditions. What the Dead Sea Scrolls have underscored is the fact that in antiquity there were many types of Judaism and there were many Jews who were intensely messianic. The bottom line is as follows: If a Jewish person looks at this material and decides to think messianically, it is not a betrayal of Judaism, because that form of Judaism was there. It is just that rabbinic Judaism survived and the other expressions of Judaism fell by the wayside. This helps us see that Judaism was much more diverse and variegated in antiquity; and, of course, the Qumran community had many similarities to the Christians, which itself was another messianic community."

EVANS: "Let me share with you a personal experience that bears out particularly what Professor Collins has said. Last May I and several students from Trinity and Fuller Seminary were in Israel. We visited the ruins at Qumran. After an exciting day of hiking up the cliffs and looking at the caves, we returned to our bus for the drive back to Jerusalem. Just a few minutes down the road we stopped to pick up a man waiting at a bus stop, because our tour guide had recognized him. We pulled over and picked him up. His name was Jacob, and it turned out he works at Qumran as part of the staff. So we took the opportunity to put some questions to him. This very question came up: What is the relevance of messianism and the Scrolls for Judaism? It was clear by his answer that they are not very important. What was so interesting was that he finally said, 'If you *really* want to know all about messianism, read the Talmud.' He also told us that the next time we see him he will have his Talmud with him and show us what is really important. I think this bears out what has been said."

FROM THE AUDIENCE: "Are there parallels and is there a relationship between the Dead Sea Scrolls and the Coptic, Gnostic books found in Nag Hammadi, Egypt, about the same time as the discovery of the first cave containing the Scrolls?"

FEE: "This is not an area of expertise for me, but the very word 'parallel' is what begins to raise the methodological question. We just had the suggestion, and I think this is where I would stand, that we are dealing with a milieu of many kinds of Judaism. Because it is Judaism, there will be a significant amount of overlap, but not in terms of direct borrowing, influence, and parallel — and by 'parallel' I mean in the sense that one is using the other — but it is a milieu in which these diverse expressions of Judaism emerged. It seems to me that the Nag Hammadi stuff is conceptually a million miles from this milieu, in every kind of way, especially its worldview. In fact, the milieu of Nag Hammadi is almost as nonapocalyptic as the Dead Sea Scrolls and Christianity are apocalyptic. Gnosticism constitutes a radically different worldview. The difference between Qumran and Nag Hammadi has to do with the overall fundamental worldview."

COLLINS: "Yes, I basically agree with that, but I think in the context of a complicated academic discussion you can trace connections between Qumran and Nag Hammadi. Now some people, like my colleague, Professor Robert Grant, argue that Gnosticism developed in some way out of a kind of transformation of Jewish apocalypticism. But you would have to say that it was transformed considerably. So, there are points of connection. People have argued that you could look at Qumran as a kind of gnosis. Well, it is, but it is a very different kind of gnosis. So, there are connections between Qumran and Nag Hammadi, but there are enormous transformations in the process."

EVANS: "Gnosis is the Greek word that means 'knowledge.' An adherent whose beliefs revolve around the quest for ultimate knowledge is called a 'gnostic.' These systems of knowledge are called 'Gnosticism.' There are some general parallels between Nag Hammadi and Qumran. There is dualism at Qumran, such as light and darkness, truth and falsehood. And dualism, of course, is a major ingredient in Gnosticism; hence the interest scholars have in making comparisons. But I agree with Professor Fee, these different kinds of literature share a common geographical world, the eastern Mediterranean basin. That is what they have in common, as well as some general language, common to that part of the world at that time."

FROM THE AUDIENCE: "How do we know that the Dead Sea Scrolls are actually significant and can contribute to the knowledge that we regard as important, such as early Christian origins, early Judaism, and so on? Or is Qumran something that is really off the beaten track, a sort of 'cult,' with the result that too much attention is being paid to it?"

MARTIN ABEGG: "This material (the Scrolls) obviously shares a different historical connection to Christianity and Judaism than something more recent, like Mormonism, or David Koresh, which one could say represent some of the more recent messianic movements. So in that regard it is more important because we share similar origins. The Christian 'experiment,' so to speak, originated at about the same time or a little later than the Qumran 'experiment.' We can learn from what was going on at that period of time and from the various things that were being said, the theologies, the texts that were being used, the way of interpreting Old Testament texts. We can learn quite a bit about that milieu and period of time — much more than we can learn from Mormonism, Jehovah's Witnesses, David Koresh, or something else of that nature. Some connections can be demonstrated. The difference obviously would be that this particular messianic experiment (the Qumran experiment) did not work. It was viable for several centuries, it attracted some attention, but it failed ultimately. In contrast to that experiment, the Christian messianic experiment did work. Christianity continues, whereas the Essenes are lost in the shadows of time. Again, we can learn much from their experiment, because they came before us and we are working with some of the same materials."

FEE: "So the analogy doesn't have to do with Christian origins and an offshoot Jewish, let's say, 'cult' — to allude to the question — because they belong to the same period. Therefore there is this milieu in which they fit. The real question when you come to something like the Book of Mormon is to compare the Book of Mormon with all of the stuff that was going on in New York State in the early 1800s and all the religious fervor and messianism that was everywhere about and then see how the Book of Mormon helps us understand American Christianity. And it will, even though for Christians it is off in another area. It would certainly help us understand the history of the Church at that period in American history."

EVANS: "That is a good way of putting it. The problem with the Book of Mormon is that there is no evidence that it, as well as the gold tablets, which supposedly it translates, existed earlier than Joseph Smith. Now, if someone found the Book of Mormon in Hebrew, or another Near Eastern language, in a cave, dating to the first century, that would change a lot of things!"

FROM THE AUDIENCE: "Who is the Teacher of Righteousness? My question concerns the last part of Professor Abegg's paper. Were you suggesting that he is the character to whom Paul refers in 2 Corinthians?"

ABEGG: "No, I think Paul is referring to himself. I did not make that clear. I assumed that we would all understand that. I think there is a possibility of a parallel here. This is where I leave off in my study and where I need to pick up the next time I address this question. It would seem to me very possible that Paul is speaking of himself as having also experienced this heavenly council, but that he is being a little more humble in his mention of it. In contrast, the Teacher of Righteousness, if we have related and interpreted these texts correctly, is obviously less reticent in claiming, boasting actually, of being part of this council. Who the Teacher of Righteousness actually is — I'm afraid those details are lost in the shadows of time. We do not know. Several different figures in history have been put forward. John Trever, one of the very first to see the Scrolls, has even suggested that the Teacher of Righteousness was the author of the book of Daniel. But all that we know from the Scrolls themselves is that he was called the 'Teacher of Righteousness.' That is all we know."

FEE: "I wanted to ask Martin a similar question. It has to do with the title, 'ascent.' Obviously we are dealing with somebody who considers himself to be in the heavenly court. But, when you start using the language of 'ascent,' I wonder if there is anything in the Dead Sea Scrolls, or anywhere else, that explains how a revelatory experience will get him up there? How does he appear in heaven, and is the language 'ascent' proper language to use for describing this phenomenon that, on the one hand, he is in heaven, and yet if he is the Teacher of Righteousness, he remains on earth below as the leader of the Qumran community?"

ABEGG: "From what I know of the Scrolls, there is nothing that explains *how* the Teacher of Righteousness or anyone can ascend into heaven."

COLLINS: "It is just that if he sat on a throne in heaven, one assumes he got up there somehow. The Qumran material stands in contrast to what we normally call ascent literature, which you also have in some of the apocalypses. In those cases they usually describe what they saw on the way up, so that there is a tour element. And at Qumran it is not that at all. You have 'mystical' experiences in the Qumran Scrolls. It is also of a very immediate kind. They talk about gazing on eternal light, or on the mystery, and so forth. But you do not, that I can think of, find 'tours of the heavens,' or the sightseeing of heaven and hell that you find in many of the apocalypses."

FEE: "Which is exactly why I rejected this in my writing on the passage with regard to Jim Tabor's work earlier. It seems to me that that is the real stuff of the ascent literature. What Paul describes is a revelatory experience. He does not even know if he is in spirit or in body. It is revelatory, and there is no concern for how he gets there. He's just there and can't say a word about it. So, this was my question, is it a revelatory experience, do you think, or does it belong to the ascent literature?"

ABEGG: "We can only speculate, quite frankly, because it isn't in the text. But given the Teacher or Righteousness's connection with these things, it seems to have begun by a giving of the spirit to him from God. I would think that it is revelatory rather than actual."

FEE: "I would think so, too."

COLLINS: "I would think that Paul is more like what you have in the Scrolls than what you have in the apocalypses."

PANELISTS: "Yes."

FROM THE AUDIENCE: "My question has to do with Qumran's two Messiahs, the political Messiah, presumably Davidic, and the priestly Messiah, and the notion that the political Messiah is subject to the priestly Messiah."

FROM THE AUDIENCE: "Perhaps we should refer to 1QSa, where the priestly Messiah presides and the Davidic Messiah is subject to him."

FROM THE AUDIENCE: "Are there really two Messiahs at Qumran?"

COLLINS: "It is always the case when you have one who is in subjection to another, you have to have two!"

EVANS: "That's right. It does seem that there are two anointed figures, even if some of the pertinent texts have not always been properly interpreted. It is always the priestly Messiah at Qumran who is superior."

FROM THE AUDIENCE: "Is it not a reflection of the priestly character of the Essenes? The priests take precedence in the council of the community."

EVANS: "Yes. The priestly Messiah is always superior and that undoubtedly reflects the priestly orientation of the Qumran community."

ABEGG: "I think it does bear saying, though, that this 1QSa text never mentions the fact that the priest there is a Messiah figure. That is a reconstruction, for example, in Vermes's translation."

FROM THE AUDIENCE: "Given the priestly orientation at Qumran and the Essenes' claim to have descended from the Zadokite line, and given what might have been an estrangement from the Temple in Jerusalem, what archaeological evidence is there at Qumran of a tabernacle, or an altar, or something like that, or other paraphernalia that would relate to sacrifice?"

COLLINS: "That is a much disputed question. There have been scholars who have argued that there were sacrifices at Qumran. The main evidence I can remember being cited for it was the burial of animal bones. But now whether the discovery of bones requires that they performed actual sacrifices, I think is maybe a bit of a stretch. And I do not recall that anybody found an altar, although I am not sure that somebody has not in fact claimed it. In fact, somebody has written an article in the last year arguing that they had, in effect, their own temple. But I really don't have the details of that fresh in my mind. Does anybody else, by any chance?"

EVANS: "At one time it was claimed that an altar had been found. But it is a small, square stone. Almost no one thinks it really was an altar. This is very dubious evidence. But there are a couple of texts among the Scrolls (e.g., 4QFlorilegium 1:6-7) that talk about offering up prayers as incense."

ABEGG: "But there is an exegetical problem there, too."

EVANS: "Yes, that is true."

ABEGG: "Apart from the sacrifice interpretation, these texts could be taken in a couple of different ways."

EVANS: "True again."

FEE: "Of course, the messianic movement called Christianity may throw light on Qumran. After all, the temple imagery is rich and full, especially in Paul, and the Spirit is the key to that. And there is certainly no sacrificial system of any kind, although he uses this language with great regularity. So it might be that Paul helps us to understand Qumran."

COLLINS: "I must say, I don't think they had sacrifices at Qumran. Their quarrel was with the way the Temple was being run. Their quarrel concerned the calendar and maybe the particular priest who was in power. But I think to set up shop apart from the Jerusalem Temple would be to go directly against Deuteronomy. Now there were Zadokite priests who did that kind of thing. We know of one who did it in Egypt, but for people who were strict constructionists of the laws, as the people of Qumran seem to have been, I find it hard to imagine that they would have done that."

ABEGG: "Actually there is one word that can be studied throughout the Scrolls. It is the word *ʿabôdah* ('service') which in the biblical text always refers to the service in the Temple, for example, *ʿabôdat bêt ʾAdōnai* ('service of the House of the Lord'; cf. 1 Chron 23:32). In the Qumran text it is always public service, or the giving of oneself, the work for one's brother. So they seem to have left the temple imagery behind, and as Professor Evans has suggested, rabbinic Judaism has replaced it with prayer to some degree."

FROM THE AUDIENCE: "How is Amos 9:11, which is cited in Acts 15, seen as fulfilled from a Qumran perspective?"

COLLINS: "It is quoted and interpreted in the *Damascus Document* (CD 7:15-17). It is a surprising exegesis, because the 'fallen booth of David' is understood to be the Law, which the 'Seeker of the Law,' presumably the Teacher of Righteousness, has 'set up,' that is, restored. Part of Amos 9:11 is also quoted in 4QFlorilegium 1:10-13, where it is understood in a more conventional sense. The 'Branch of David' will arise with the 'Seeker of the Law' and sit on the throne of Zion at the end of days, in fulfillment of the prophecy, 'I will raise up the booth of David which is fallen.'"

ABEGG: "As I understand the *Damascus Document,* they are incorporating it into how they are the fulfillment of this text, how it had been fulfilled in their own history."

COLLINS: "It is a highly allegorical usage of this prophetic text."

EVANS: "Yes, setting the fallen booth of David back up is what they are doing and studying the Torah correctly is part of their task. The interpretation found in the *Damascus Document* is different from the one in Acts 15."

SCOTT: "I agree."

EVANS: "Well, thank you very much, panel; and thank you to all of you; you have been an excellent audience."

Select Bibliography

Abegg, Martin G., Jr. "The Messiah at Qumran: Are We Still Seeing Double?" *DSD* 2 (1995) 125-44.

———. "Messianic Hope and 4Q285: A Reassessment." *JBL* 113 (1994) 81-91.

Allegro, John M. "Further Messianic References in Qumran Literature." *JBL* 75 (1956) 174-87.

Anderson, Hugh. "The Jewish Antecedents of the Christology of Hebrews." In *The Messiah: Developments in Earliest Judaism and Christianity,* edited by James H. Charlesworth, 512-35. Minneapolis: Fortress, 1992.

Bauckham, Richard. "The Messianic Interpretation of Isa. 10:34 in the Dead Sea Scrolls, 2 Baruch and the Preaching of John the Baptist." *DSD* 2 (1995) 202-16.

Berger, Klaus. "Die königlichen Messiastraditionen des Neuen Testaments." *NTS* 29 (1973-74) 1-44.

Betz, Otto. "Die Bedeutung der Qumranschriften für die Evangelien des Neuen Testaments." *BK* 40 (1985) 54-64. Reprinted in *Jesus: Der Messias Israels. Aufsätze zur biblischen Theologie,* by Otto Betz, 318-32. WUNT 42. Tübingen: Mohr-Siebeck, 1987.

Black, Matthew. "Messianic Doctrine in the Qumran Scrolls." In *Studia Patristica 1,* edited by K. Aland and F. L. Cross, 1.441-59. 2 vols. TU 63. Berlin: Akademie, 1957.

———. "The Messianism of the Parables of Enoch: Their Date and Contribution to Christological Origins." In *The Messiah: Developments in Earliest Judaism and Christianity,* edited by James H. Charlesworth, 145-68. Minneapolis: Fortress, 1992.

———. *The Scrolls and Christian Origins: Studies in the Jewish Background of the New Testament.* New York: Scribner's, 1961. Reprint, Chico: Scholars Press, 1983.

Bockmuehl, Markus N. A. "A 'Slain Messiah' in 4Q Serekh Milḥamah (4Q285)?" *TynBul* 43 (1992) 155-69.

Boer, P. A. H. de. "The Son of God in the Old Testament." *OTS* 18 (1973) 188-201.

Bokser, Baruch M. "Messianism, the Exodus Pattern, and Early Rabbinic Judaism." In *The Messiah: Developments in Earliest Judaism and Christianity,* edited by James H. Charlesworth, 239-60. Minneapolis: Fortress, 1992.

Borgen, Peder. "'There Shall Come Forth a Man': Reflections on Messianic Ideas in Philo." In *The Messiah: Developments in Earliest Judaism and Christianity,* edited by James H. Charlesworth, 341-61. Minneapolis: Fortress, 1992.

Braun, Herbert. *Qumran und das Neue Testament,* 2.75-84. 2 vols. Tübingen: Mohr-Siebeck, 1966.

Brooke, George J. "The Amos-Numbers Midrash (CD 7,13b–8) and Messianic Expectation." *ZAW* 92 (1980) 397-404.

———. "The Messiah of Aaron in the Damascus Document." *RevQ* 15 (1991) 215-30.

———. "4QTestament of Levi[d](?) and the Messianic Servant High Priest." In *From Jesus to John: Essays on Jesus and New Testament Christology in Honour of Marinus de Jonge,* edited by Martinus C. de Boer, 83-100. JSNTSup 84. Sheffield: JSOT Press, 1993.

Brown, Raymond E. "J. Starcky's Theory of Qumran Messianic Development." *CBQ* 28 (1966) 51-57.

———. "The Messianism of Qumrân." *CBQ* 19 (1957) 53-82.

———. "The Teacher of Righteousness and the Messiah(s)." In *The Scrolls and Christianity,* edited by Matthew Black, 37-44, 109-12. SPCK Theological Collections 11. London: SPCK, 1969.

Brownlee, W. H. "Messianic Motifs of Qumran and the New Testament." *NTS* 3 (1956-57) 12-30, 195-210.

Caquot, André. "Le messianisme Qumrânien." In *Qumrân: Sa piété, sa théologie et son milieu,* edited by M. Delcor, 231-47. BETL 46. Gembloux: Duculot, 1978.

Carmignac, Jean. "Le retour du Docteur de Justice à la fin des jours?" *RevQ* 1 (1958-59) 235-48.

Charlesworth, James H. "From Jewish Messianology to Christian Christology: Some Caveats and Perspectives." In *Judaisms and Their Messiahs at the Turn of the Christian Era,* edited by Jacob Neusner et al., 225-64. Cambridge: Cambridge University Press, 1987.

———. "The Messiah in the Pseudepigrapha." *ANRW* II.19.2 (1979) 188-218.

———, ed. *The Messiah: Developments in Earliest Judaism and Christianity.* Minneapolis: Fortress, 1992.

Chester, Andrew. "Jewish Messianic Expectations and Mediatorial Figures." In *Paulus und das antike Judentum*, edited by Martin Hengel and Ulrich Heckel, 17-89. WUNT 58. Tübingen: Mohr-Siebeck, 1991.

Collins, John J. "'He Shall Not Judge by What His Eyes See': Messianic Authority in the Dead Sea Scrolls." *DSD* 2 (1995) 145-64.

———. "Messiahs in Context: Method in the Study of Messianism in the Dead Sea Scrolls." In *Methods of Investigation of the Dead Sea Scrolls and the Khirbet Qumran Site: Present Realities and Future Prospects*, edited by Michael O. Wise et al., 213-29. Annals of the New York Academy of Sciences 722. New York: The New York Academy of Sciences, 1994.

———. "Messianism in the Maccabean Period." In *Judaisms and Their Messiahs at the Turn of the Christian Era*, edited by Jacob Neusner et al., 97-109. Cambridge: Cambridge University Press, 1987.

———. *The Scepter and the Star: The Messiahs of the Dead Sea Scrolls and Other Ancient Literature*. ABRL 10. New York: Doubleday, 1995.

———. "The *Son of God* Text from Qumran." In *From Jesus to John: Essays on Jesus and New Testament Christology in Honour of Marinus de Jonge*, edited by Martinus C. de Boer, 65-82. JSNTSup 84. Sheffield: JSOT Press, 1993.

———. "The Son of Man in First-Century Judaism." *NTS* 38 (1992) 448-66.

———. "Teacher and Messiah? The One Who Will Teach Righteousness at the End of Days." In *The Community of the Renewed Covenant: The Notre Dame Symposium on the Dead Sea Scrolls*, edited by Eugene Ulrich and James VanderKam, 193-210. Christianity and Judaism in Antiquity 10. Notre Dame: University of Notre Dame Press, 1994.

———. "A Throne in the Heavens: Apotheosis in Pre-Christian Judaism." In *Death, Ecstasy, and Other Worldly Journeys*, edited by John J. Collins and Michael Fishbane, 43-58. Albany: State University of New York Press, 1995.

———. "The Works of the Messiah." *DSD* 1 (1994) 98-112.

Colpe, Carsten. "Der Begriff 'Menschensohn' und die Methode der Erforschung messianischer Prototypen." *Kairos* 12 (1970) 81-112.

Cook, Edward M. "4Q246." *BBR* 5 (1995) 43-66.

Dahl, Nils A. "Messianic Ideas and the Crucifixion of Jesus." In *The Messiah: Developments in Earliest Judaism and Christianity*, edited by James H. Charlesworth, 382-403. Minneapolis: Fortress, 1992.

Davenport, Gene L. "The 'Anointed of the Lord' in Psalms of Solomon 17." In *Ideal Figures in Ancient Judaism: Profiles and Paradigms*, edited by John J. Collins and George W. E. Nickelsburg, 67-92. SBLSCS 12. Chico, CA: Scholars Press, 1980.

Davies, W. D. "The Jewish Sources of Matthew's Messianism." In *The Messiah: Developments in Earliest Judaism and Christianity*, edited by James H. Charlesworth, 494-511. Minneapolis: Fortress, 1992.

Deichgräber, R. "Zur Messiaserwartung der Damaskusschrift." *ZAW* 78 (1966) 333-43.

Dunn, James D. G. "Messianic Ideas and Their Influence on the Jesus of History." In *The Messiah: Developments in Earliest Judaism and Christianity,* edited by James H. Charlesworth, 365-81. Minneapolis: Fortress, 1992.

Evans, Craig A. *Jesus and His Contemporaries: Comparative Studies,* 53-181. AGJU 25. Leiden: Brill, 1995.

———. "Messiahs." In *Encyclopedia of the Dead Sea Scrolls,* edited by Lawrence H. Schiffman and James C. VanderKam. Oxford: Oxford University Press, forthcoming.

———. "Mishna and Messiah 'in Context': Some Comments on Jacob Neusner's Proposals." *JBL* 112 (1993) 267-89.

———. "A Note on the 'First-Born Son' of 4Q369." *DSD* 2 (1995) 185-201.

———. "Prince of the Congregation." In *Encyclopedia of the Dead Sea Scrolls,* edited by Lawrence H. Schiffman and James C. VanderKam. Oxford: Oxford University Press, forthcoming.

Fitzmyer, Joseph A. "The Aramaic 'Elect of God' Text from Qumran Cave 4." *CBQ* 27 (1965) 348-72. Reprinted in *Essays on the Semitic Background of the New Testament,* by Joseph A. Fitzmyer, 127-60. London: Chapman, 1971; Missoula: Scholars Press, 1974.

———. "4Q246: The 'Son of God' Document from Qumran." *Bib* 74 (1993) 153-74.

Flint, Peter. "4Qpseudo-Daniel ar^{c} (4Q245) and the Restoration of the Priesthood." In *Hommage à Józef T. Milik,* edited by F. García Martínez and Émile Puech = *RevQ* 65-68 (1996) 137-50.

——— and John J. Collins. "Pseudo-Daniel." In *Parabiblical Texts, Part 3,* edited by James C. VanderKam, 95-164 + pls. VII-X. DJD 22. Oxford: Oxford University Press, 1996.

Flusser, David. "The Hubris of the Antichrist in a Fragment from Qumran." *Immanuel* 10 (1980) 31-37. Reprinted in *Judaism and the Origins of Christianity,* by David Flusser, 207-13. Jerusalem: Magnes Press, 1988.

García Martínez, Florentino. "The Eschatological Figure of 4Q246." In *Qumran and Apocalyptic: Studies on the Aramaic Texts from Qumran,* by Florentino García Martínez, 162-79. STDJ 9. Leiden: Brill, 1992.

———. "Messianic Hopes in the Qumran Writings." In *The People of the Dead Sea Scrolls: Their Writings, Beliefs and Practices,* by Florentino García Martínez and Julio Trebolle Barrera, 159-89. Leiden: Brill, 1995.

———. "Messianische Erwartungen in den Qumranschriften." *JBT* 8 (1993) 171-208.

———. "Nuevos Textos Messiánicos de Qumran y el Messias del Nuevo Testamento." *Communio* 26 (1993) 3-31.

Goldstein, Jonathan A. "How the Authors of 1 and 2 Maccabees Treated the

'Messianic' Promises." In *Judaisms and Their Messiahs at the Turn of the Christian Era,* edited by Jacob Neusner et al., 69-96. Cambridge: Cambridge University Press, 1987.

Gordis, Robert. "The 'Begotten' Messiah in the Qumran Scrolls." *VT* 7 (1957) 191-94.

Green, William S. "Introduction: Messiah in Judaism: Rethinking the Question." In *Judaisms and Their Messiahs at the Turn of the Christian Era,* edited by Jacob Neusner et al., 1-13. Cambridge: Cambridge University Press, 1987.

Grelot, Pierre. "Le Messie dans les Apocryphes de l'Ancien Testament." In *La venue du Messie: Messianisme et eschatologie,* edited by E. Massaux et al., 19-50. RechBib 6. Paris: Gabalda, 1962.

Gruenwald, Ithamar. "From Priesthood to Messianism: The Anti-Priestly Polemic and the Messianic Factor." In *Messiah and Christos: Studies in the Jewish Origins of Christianity,* edited by Ithamar Gruenwald et al., 75-93. TSAJ 32. Tübingen: Mohr-Siebeck, 1992.

——— et al., eds. *Messiah and Christos: Studies in the Jewish Origins of Christianity.* TSAJ 32. Tübingen: Mohr-Siebeck, 1992.

Grundmann, W. "Die Frage nach der Gottessohnschaft des Messias im Lichte von Qumran." In *Bibel und Qumran: Beiträge zur Erforschung der Beziehungen zwischen Bibel- und Qumranwissenschaft,* edited by S. Wagner, 86-111. Berlin: Evangelische Haupt-Bibelgesellschaft, 1968.

Hanson, Paul D. "Messiahs and Messianic Figures in Proto-Apocalypticism." In *The Messiah: Developments in Earliest Judaism and Christianity,* edited by James H. Charlesworth, 67-78. Minneapolis: Fortress, 1992.

Hecht, Richard D. "Philo and Messiah." In *Judaisms and Their Messiahs at the Turn of the Christian Era,* edited by Jacob Neusner et al., 139-68. Cambridge: Cambridge University Press, 1987.

Hengel, Martin. "Jesus, der Messias Israels: Zum Streit über das 'messianische Sendungs-bewußtsein' Jesu." In *Messiah and Christos: Studies in the Jewish Origins of Christianity,* edited by Ithamar Gruenwald et al., 155-76. TSAJ 32. Tübingen: Mohr-Siebeck, 1992.

———. *The Son of God: The Origin of Christology and the History of Jewish-Hellenistic Religion.* Philadelphia: Fortress, 1976.

Higgins, A. J. B. "The Priestly Messiah." *NTS* 13 (1966-67) 211-39.

Horbury, William. "The Messianic Associations of 'The Son of Man.'" *JTS* 36 (1985) 34-55.

Horsley, Richard A. "'Messianic' Figures and Movements in First-Century Palestine." In *The Messiah: Developments in Earliest Judaism and Christianity,* edited by James H. Charlesworth, 276-95. Minneapolis: Fortress, 1992.

Horsley, Richard A. and John S. Hanson. *Bandits, Prophets, and Messiahs: Popular Movements at the Time of Jesus.* Minneapolis: Winston, 1985. Reprint, San Francisco: Harper & Row, 1988.

Jonge, Marinus de. "The Earliest Christian Use of *Christos:* Some Suggestions." *NTS* 32 (1986) 321-43.

———. "Josephus und die Zukunftserwartungen seines Volkes." In *Josephus-Studien,* edited by O. Betz et al., 205-19. Göttingen: Vandenhoeck & Ruprecht, 1974.

———. "Messiah." *ABD,* vol. 4, 777-88.

———. "The Role of Intermediaries in God's Final Intervention in the Future according to the Qumran Scrolls." In *Studies on the Jewish Background of the New Testament,* edited by O. Michel et al., 44-63. Assen: Van Gorcum, 1969.

———. "Two Messiahs in the Testaments of the Twelve Patriarchs?" In *Tradition and Reinterpretation in Jewish and Early Christian Literature,* edited by J. W. van Henten et al., 150-62. SPB 36. Leiden: Brill, 1986. Reprinted in *Jewish Eschatology, Early Christian Christology and the Testaments of the Twelve Patriarchs: Collected Essays,* by M. de Jonge, 191-203. NovTSup 63. Leiden: Brill, 1991.

———. "The Use of the Word 'Anointed' in the Time of Jesus." *NovT* 8 (1966) 132-48.

Knibb, Michael A. "The Interpretation of *Damascus Document* vii,9b–viii,2a and xix,5b-14." *RevQ* 15 (1991) 243-51.

———. "Messianism in the Pseudepigrapha in the Light of the Scrolls." *DSD* 2 (1995) 165-84.

———. "The Teacher of Righteousness — a Messianic Title?" In *A Tribute to Geza Vermes: Essays on Jewish and Christian Literature and History,* edited by P. R. Davies and R. T. White, 51-65. JSOTSup 100. Sheffield: JSOT Press, 1990.

Kuhn, G. "Röm 1,3f und der davidische Messias als Gottessohn in den Qumrantexten." In *Lese-Zeichen für Annelies Findreiß zum 65. Geburtstag am 15. März 1984,* edited by Christoph Burchard and Gerd Theissen, 103-13. Heidelberg: Carl Winter, 1984.

Kuhn, K. G. "The Two Messiahs of Aaron and Israel." *NTS* 1 (1954-55) 168-80. Reprinted in *The Scrolls and the New Testament,* edited by Krister Stendahl, 54-64, 256-59. New York: Harper, 1957. Reprint, New York: Crossroad, 1992.

Landman, Leo, ed. *Messianism in the Talmudic Era.* New York: KTAV, 1979.

LaSor, William S. "The Messiahs of Aaron and Israel." *VT* 6 (1956) 425-29.

———. "The Messianic Idea in Qumran." In *Studies and Essays in Honor of Abraham A. Neuman,* edited by M. Ben-Horin et al., 343-64. Leiden: Brill, 1962.

Laurin, R. B. "The Problem of Two Messiahs in the Qumran Scrolls." *RevQ* 4 (1963-64) 39-52.

Levey, S. H. *The Messiah: An Aramaic Interpretation. The Messianic Exegesis of the Targum.* MHUC 2. Cincinnati: Hebrew Union College/Jewish Institute of Religion, 1974.

Liver, J. "The Doctrine of the Two Messiahs in Sectarian Literature in the Time of the Second Commonwealth." *HTR* 52 (1959) 149-85. Reprinted in *Messianism in the Talmudic Era,* edited by Leo Landman, 354-90. New York: KTAV, 1979.

Lust, J. "Messianism and Septuagint." In *Congress Volume Salamanca (1983),* edited by J. A. Emerton, 174-91. VTSup 36. Leiden: Brill, 1985.

Mach, Michael. "Christus Mutans: Zur Bedeutung der 'Verklärung Jesu' im Wechsel von jüdischer Messianität zur neutestamentlichen Christologie." In *Messiah and Christos: Studies in the Jewish Origins of Christianity,* edited by Ithamar Gruenwald et al., 177-98. TSAJ 32. Tübingen: Mohr-Siebeck, 1992.

Massaux, E., et al., eds. *La venue du Messie: Messianisme et eschatologie.* RechBib 6. Paris: Gabalda, 1962.

Mendels, Doron. "Pseudo-Philo's *Biblical Antiquities,* the 'Fourth Philosophy,' and the Political Messianism of the First Century C.E." In *The Messiah: Developments in Earliest Judaism and Christianity,* edited by James H. Charlesworth, 261-75. Minneapolis: Fortress, 1992.

Neusner, Jacob. *Messiah in Context: Israel's History and Destiny in Formative Judaism.* Philadelphia: Fortress, 1984.

———. "Mishnah and Messiah." In *Judaisms and Their Messiahs at the Turn of the Christian Era,* edited by Jacob Neusner et al., 265-82. Cambridge: Cambridge University Press, 1987.

——— et al., eds. *Judaisms and Their Messiahs at the Turn of the Christian Era.* Cambridge: Cambridge University Press, 1987.

Nickelsburg, George W. E. "Salvation with and without a Messiah: Developing Beliefs in Writings Ascribed to Enoch." In *Judaisms and Their Messiahs at the Turn of the Christian Era,* edited by Jacob Neusner et al., 49-68. Cambridge: Cambridge University Press, 1987.

Nodet, E. "Miettes messianiques." In *Messiah and Christos: Studies in the Jewish Origins of Christianity,* edited by Ithamar Gruenwald et al., 119-41. TSAJ 32. Tübingen: Mohr-Siebeck, 1992.

Oegema, Gerbern S. *Der Gesalbte und sein Volk: Untersuchungen zum Konzeptualisierungsprozess der messianischen Erwartungen von den Makkabaern bis Bar Koziba.* Göttingen: Vandenhoeck & Ruprecht, 1994.

Pilhofer, P. "Wer salbt den Messias? Zum Streit um die Chronologie im ersten Jahrhundert des jüdisch-christlichen Dialogs." In *Begegnungen zwischen Christentum und Judentum in Antike und Mittelalter: Festschrift für Heinz Schreckenberg,* edited by Dietrich-Alex Koch and Hermann Lichtenberger, 335-45. Göttingen: Vandenhoeck & Ruprecht, 1993.

Priest, J. F. "The Messiah and the Meal in 1QSa." *JBL* 82 (1963) 95-100.

Puech, Émile. "Une Apocalypse Messianique (4Q521)." *RevQ* 15 (1992) 475-519.

———. "Fragment d'une apocalypse en araméen (4Q246 = pseudo-Dan) et le Royaume de Dieu." *RB* 99 (1992) 98-131.

———. "Fragments d'un apocryphe de Lévi et le personnage eschatologique. 4QTestLévi[a-d](?) et 4QAJ." In *The Madrid Qumran Congress: Proceedings of the International Congress on the Dead Sea Scrolls, Madrid, 18-21 March, 1991,* edited by Julio Trebolle Barrera and Luis Vegas Montaner, 2.449-501. 2 vols. STDJ 11. Leiden: Brill, 1992.

———. "Messianism, Resurrection, and Eschatology at Qumran and in the New Testament." In *The Community of the Renewed Covenant: The Notre Dame Symposium on the Dead Sea Scrolls,* edited by Eugene Ulrich and James VanderKam, 235-56. Christianity and Judaism in Antiquity 10. Notre Dame: University of Notre Dame Press, 1994.

Ringgren, Helmer. *The Faith of Qumran: Theology of the Dead Sea Scrolls.* Philadelphia: Fortress, 1963. Reprint, New York: Crossroad, 1995.

Roberts, J. J. M. "The Old Testament's Contribution to Messianic Expectations." In *The Messiah: Developments in Earliest Judaism and Christianity,* edited by James H. Charlesworth, 39-51. Minneapolis: Fortress, 1992.

Sacchi, Paolo. "Esquisse du développement du messianisme juif à la lumière du texte qumrânien 11Q Melch." *ZAW* 100 (1988) 202-14.

Schiffman, Lawrence H. "Messianic Figures and Ideas in the Qumran Scrolls." In *The Messiah: Developments in Earliest Judaism and Christianity,* edited by James H. Charlesworth, 116-29. Minneapolis: Fortress, 1992.

Scholem, Gershom. *The Messianic Idea in Judaism and Other Essays on Jewish Spirituality.* New York: Schocken, 1971.

Schweitzer, F. M. "The Teacher of Righteousness." In *Mogilany 1989: Papers on the Dead Sea Scrolls Offered in Memory of Jean Carmignac,* edited by Zdzislaw J. Kapera, 2.53-97. 2 vols. Qumranica Mogilanensia 2-3. Kracow: Enigma, 1991-93.

Segal, Alan F. "The Risen Christ and the Angelic Mediator Figures in Light of Qumran." In *Jesus and the Dead Sea Scrolls,* edited by James H. Charlesworth, 302-28. ABRL. New York: Doubleday, 1992.

Silberman, Lou H. "The Two 'Messiahs' of the Manual of Discipline." *VT* 5 (1955) 77-82.

Smith, Morton. "Ascent to the Heavens and Deification in 4QM[a]." In *Archaeology and History in the Dead Sea Scrolls: The New York University Conference in Memory of Yigael Yadin,* edited by Lawrence H. Schiffman, 181-88. JSPSup 8. JSOT/ASOR Monographs 2. Sheffield: JSOT Press, 1990.

———. "Two Ascended to Heaven — Jesus and the Author of 4Q491." In *Jesus and the Dead Sea Scrolls,* edited by James H. Charlesworth, 290-301. ABRL. New York: Doubleday, 1992.

———. "What Is Implied by the Variety of Messianic Figures?" *JBL* 78 (1959) 66-72.

Starcky, Jean. "Les quatres étapes du messianisme à Qumrân." *RB* 70 (1963) 481-505.

Stefaniak, L. "Messianische oder eschatologische Erwartungen in der Qumransekte?" In *Neutestamentliche Aufsätze: Festschrift für Prof. Josef Schmid zum 70. Geburtstag,* edited by J. Blinzler et al., 294-302. Regensburg: Pustet, 1963.

Stone, Michael E. "The Concept of the Messiah in IV Ezra." In *Religions in Antiquity: Essays in Memory of Erwin Ramsdell Goodenough,* edited by Jacob Neusner, 295-312. NumSup 14. Leiden: Brill, 1968.

———. "Excursus on the Redeemer Figure." In *Fourth Ezra: A Commentary on the Book of Fourth Ezra,* by Michael Edward Stone, 207-13. Hermeneia. Minneapolis: Fortress, 1990.

———. "The Question of the Messiah in 4 Ezra." In *Judaisms and Their Messiahs at the Turn of the Christian Era,* edited by Jacob Neusner et al., 209-24. Cambridge: Cambridge University Press, 1987. Reprinted in *Selected Studies in Pseudepigrapha and Apocrypha. With Special Reference to the Armenian Tradition,* by Michael E. Stone, 317-22. SVTP 9. Leiden: Brill, 1991.

Tabor, James D., and Michael O. Wise. "4Q521 'On Resurrection' and the Synoptic Gospel Tradition: A Preliminary Study." *JSP* 10 (1992) 149-62.

Talmon, Shemaryahu. "The Concept of *Māšîaḥ* and Messianism in Early Judaism." In *The Messiah: Developments in Earliest Judaism and Christianity,* edited by James H. Charlesworth, 79-115. Minneapolis: Fortress, 1992.

———. "Types of Messianic Expectation at the Turn of the Era." In *King, Cult and Calendar in Ancient Israel,* by Shemaryahu Talmon, 202-24. Jerusalem: Magnes, 1986.

———. "Waiting for the Messiah: The Spiritual Universe of the Qumran Covenanters." In *Judaisms and Their Messiahs at the Turn of the Christian Era,* edited by Jacob Neusner et al., 111-37. Cambridge: Cambridge University Press, 1987.

———. "Waiting for the Messiah at Qumran." In *The World of Qumran from Within,* by Shemaryahu Talmon, 273-300. Jerusalem: Magnes; Leiden: Brill, 1989.

Thoma, C. "Entwürfe für messianische Gestalten in frühjüdischer Zeit." In *Messiah and Christos: Studies in the Jewish Origins of Christianity,* edited by Ithamar Gruenwald et al., 15-30. TSAJ 32. Tübingen: Mohr-Siebeck, 1992.

VanderKam, James C. "Jubilees and the Priestly Messiah of Qumran." *RevQ* 13 (1988) 353-65.

———. "Messianism in the Scrolls." in *The Community of the Renewed*

Covenant: The Notre Dame Symposium on the Dead Sea Scrolls, edited by Eugene Ulrich and James VanderKam, 211-34. Christianity and Judaism in Antiquity 10. Notre Dame: University of Notre Dame Press, 1994.

———. "Righteous One, Messiah, Chosen One, and Son of Man in 1 Enoch 37–71." In *The Messiah: Developments in Earliest Judaism and Christianity,* edited by James H. Charlesworth, 169-91. Minneapolis: Fortress, 1992.

Vermes, Geza. *The Dead Sea Scrolls: Qumran in Perspective,* 182-88, 194-97. Philadelphia: Fortress, 1977.

———. "The Oxford Forum for Qumran Research Seminar on the Rule of the War from Cave 4 (4Q285)." *JJS* 43 (1992) 85-90.

Wcela, E. A. "The Messiah(s) of Qumran." *CBQ* 26 (1964) 340-49.

Weiss, K. "Messianismus in Qumran und im Neuen Testament." In *Qumran-Probleme,* edited by H. Bardtke, 353-68. Berlin: Akademie, 1963.

Wieder, N. "The Doctrine of the Two Messiahs among the Karaites." *JJS* 6 (1955) 14-23.

Wise, Michael O., and James D. Tabor. "The Messiah at Qumran." *BAR* 18/6 (1992) 60-65.

Woude, A. S. van der. *Die messianischen Vorstellungen der Gemeinde von Qumrân.* SSN 3. Assen: Van Gorcum, 1957.

———. "Le Maître de Justice et les deux messies de la communauté de Qumrân." In *La secte de Qumrân et les origines du Christianisme,* by J. van der Ploeg et al., 121-34. RechBib 4. Brussels: Desclée de Brouwer, 1959.

———. "Melchisedek als himmlischer Erlösergestalt in den neugefundenen eschatologischen Midraschim aus Qumran Höhle xi." *OTS* 14 (1963) 354-73 + 2 pls.

Index of Modern Authors

Index of Ancient Writings

INDEX OF ANCIENT WRITINGS

III. Dead Sea Scrolls

IV. New Testament